WOUNDS NOT HEALED BY TIME

WOUNDS NOT HEALED BY TIME

The Power of Repentance and Forgiveness

Solomon Schimmel

OXFORD
UNIVERSITY PRESS
2002

OXFORD
UNIVERSITY PRESS

Oxford   New York
Auckland   Bangkok   Buenos Aires   Cape Town   Chennai
Dar es Salaam   Delhi   Hong Kong   Istanbul   Karachi   Kolkata
Kuala Lumpur   Madrid   Melbourne   Mexico City   Mumbai   Nairobi
São Paulo   Shanghai   Singapore   Taipei   Tokyo   Toronto

and an associated company in Berlin

Published by Oxford University Press, Inc.
198 Madison Avenue, New York, New York 10016

www.oup.com

Oxford is a registered trademark of Oxford University Press

Library of Congress Cataloging-in-Publication Data
Schimmel, Solomon
Wounds not healed by time : the power of
repentance and forgiveness / Solomon Schimmel.
p.   cm.
Includes bibliographical references and index.
ISBN 0-19-512841-9
1. Forgiveness   2. Repentance   I. Title.
BJ1476 .S34   2002
179'9—dc21   2002022029

1 3 5 7 9 10 8 6 4 2

Printed in the United States of America
on acid-free paper

This book is dedicated to the memory of my father,
Murray Schimmel, of blessed memory, a compassionate man,
and one who did not bear grudges

CONTENTS

PERMISSIONS

The publishers have generously given permission to use extended quotations from the following copyrighted works. From *The Railway Man: A POW's Searing Account of War, Brutality, and Forgiveness,* by Eric Lomax. Copyright 1995 by Eric Lomax, reprinted by permission of W. W. Norton & Company, Inc. and the Random House Group, Ltd. From *The Faith and Doubt of Holocaust Survivors,* by Robert Reeve Brenner. Copyright 1997 by Robert Reeve Brenner, reprinted by permission of Robert Reeve Brenner and Jason Aronson Publishers. From *The Palm Tree of Deborah*, by Moses Cordovero, translated by Louis Jacobs. Copyright 1960 by Louis Jacobs, reprinted by permission of Louis Jacobs and Frank Cass Publishers. From "Marital Forgiveness: Theoretical Foundations and an Approach to Prevention," by Michael E. McCullough in *Marriage and Family: A Christian Journal.* Copyright 1997 by the American Association of Christian Counselors, reprinted by permission of Michael E. McCullough and the American Association of Christian Counselors. From *Promoting Forgiveness: An Empathy-Based Model for Psychoeducation,* by Michael E. McCullough (Unpublished Forgiveness Manual). Reprinted by permission of Michael E. McCullough. From *Repentance: A Comparative Perspective,* edited by Amitai Etzioni and David Carney. Copyright 1997 and reprinted by permission of Amitai Etzioni. From "Psychology and Repentance," by Allen E. Bergin in *BYU 1994–95 Devotional and Fireside Speeches.* Copyright 1995 and reprinted by permission of Brigham Young University. From "Interpersonal Forgiveness Within the Helping Professions: An Attempt to Resolve Differences of Opinion," by Robert Enright et al., in *Counseling and Values.* Copyright 1992 and reprinted by permission of the American Counseling Association. From "Pyramid of Forgiveness" or "The Forgiveness Teacher's Toughest Test" by Everett L. Worthington Jr, in *Spirituality and Health.* Copyright 1999 and reprinted by permission of Everett L. Worthington Jr.

Scripture quotations herein (except where otherwise noted) are from the *New Revised Standard Version of the Bible,* copyright 1989 by the Division of Christian Education of the National Council of the Churches of Christ in the USA. Used by permission. All rights reserved.

Writing this book *Wounds Not Healed by Time* has been a long and arduous journey. With the journey complete, it is not only a duty but a pleasure to thank those who have made it possible and assisted along the way. I ask forgiveness in advance of those whom I may have inadvertently forgotten to mention here.

First and foremost, I must thank Hebrew College and its students, academic leadership, and library staff. My students have not only learned from what I have taught them about the topics of this book, but have also taught me much about its themes in class discussions, in papers they wrote, and often in very moving testimonies of how they have personally grappled (as all of us must) with anger, resentment, forgiveness, and reconciliation.

Barry Mesch, colleague, Provost of Hebrew College, and, far more important, a dear friend, has consistently supported and encouraged me in my academic pursuits. He is an administrator who loves ideas.

David Gordis, President of Hebrew College, an institution devoted primarily to Jewish Studies, has, with his ecumenical vision, encouraged me to explore my interests in Christianity and other faiths and philosophies of life.

The dedicated staff of the Hebrew College library has always responded to requests for assistance with alacrity, professional expertise, and good cheer.

I am grateful to the Fulbright Foundation for awarding me a Senior Fulbright Fellowship that allowed me to spend six magnificent months in 1998 at Cambridge University in England, where a substantial amount of my research on forgiveness and repentance was conducted. In Cambridge I had the pleasure of affiliation with the Faculty of Divinity, where I was invited to be a Visiting Fellow, and the privilege of scholarly discourse with my sponsor, Dr. Fraser Watts, an eminent scholar of the psychology of religion, and with his coterie of colleagues and students who were interested in my work. While in Cambridge I was a Visiting Fellow at Clare Hall College. The depth and breadth of my interactions with members of Clare Hall, and with guests and visitors in Cambridge whom I met while there—such as John de Gruchy, Dean of Graduate Studies in the Humanities at the University of Capetown, and an important contributor to the South African Truth and Reconciliation Commission—provided a unique intellectual stimulus that I fondly cherish.

Arthur Schwartz of the Templeton Foundation arranged for a research grant to assist me on this project, and I am grateful to him and to the Foundation for its support of my and others' forgiveness research. Arthur and the Foundation have also shown a concrete interest in related work of mine on the interface of psychology and religion in the study and nurturance of character, which I greatly appreciate.

I had the good fortune of spending three weeks in Capetown, South Africa, as a Visiting Scholar at the Kaplan Centre for Jewish Studies and Research at the University of Capetown, where I researched and lectured on repentance, forgiveness, and reconciliation. The South African experience with its Truth and Reconciliation Commission has been a fruitful source of inspiration and insight into the complex questions of the balance between justice and forgiveness that I address in the book. Special thanks to Milton Shain, Director of the Centre and gracious host.

Early in my research I had the good luck to meet Heather Wilson, who generously provided me with copies of the large archive of journal articles on forgiveness she had accumulated in the course of her own doctoral research on the topic. Logos Research Systems made available to me, gratis, their digital library of religious texts, which facilitated my work.

In order to·thank everyone from whom I have learned—whether I agree or disagree with their points of view—I would have to reprint in this section most of the names that appear in the bibliography, which, understandably, I will not do. However I would like to mention Michael McCullough, through whose invitation to participate in and present a paper at a conference on virtues, I had the opportunity to meet him and other psychologists who have been devoting their talents and efforts to the study of forgiveness, and who have been applying their analyses and findings in clinical settings.

Last, and perhaps most, I am indebted to Cynthia Read, my editor at Oxford University Press. Cynthia enthusiastically supported and shepherded through the chain of command at OUP my proposal to write a book on forgiveness and repentance. Her editorial suggestions, ranging from "higher" to "lower" criticism—from grand themes to literary style—have immensely improved the final product over its first draft. Cynthia forced me to be more precise and concise in what I say and more rigorous in defending it. But what I found most impressive was that she respected my right to say things that some, including Cynthia herself, might find provocative or even offensive. The book that has emerged from the initial proposal she read differs significantly from my original expectations, because my views on justice, repentance, and forgiveness have been modified in the process of researching and writing about them.

WOUNDS NOT HEALED BY TIME

On September 11, 2001, terrorists hijacked four civilian airplanes and crashed them into the World Trade Center, the Pentagon, and a field in Pennsylvania, murdering several thousand innocent people. The attack was perpetrated almost entirely by Arabs, in the name of Islam, as part of a holy war conducted by Osama bin Laden and his supporters against the United States. Many, perhaps most, Muslim authorities condemned the attack as a violation of Islamic law and morality.[1]

How have Americans responded to this attack? Reactions have ranged from one extreme to the other. There was the college student leading an anti-war rally who argued against any use of force or violence in response to these deeds. She claimed that by responding to the terrorists with peace and love, her and her followers' "peace energies" would radiate out to those who hate the United States and Americans and would dispel their hatred. She preached compassion, forgiveness, and turning the other cheek. In a similar vein, the novelist Alice Walker declared that "the only punishment that works is love."

At the other end of the spectrum was the man who said that the United States should "nuke" Afghanistan and any other regime that "supports" Osama bin Laden. He felt it was unfortunate that hundreds of thousands of innocents would die but believed an attack such as this on the United States demanded revenge at all costs. Nuking Afghanistan would, he believed, also deter future terrorists. He advocated unbridled vengeance and retribution.

The more common response was that retribution and punishment are necessary, but civilian casualties should be minimized. The killers and their supporters need to be brought before the bar of justice, or brought to justice, in a just war. As President Bush said, "Whether we bring our enemies to justice or bring justice to our enemies, justice will be done." They acknowledge, though, that even in a just war, innocents may suffer.

Some called upon us and our government to understand why the terrorists hate us, why they attacked us, and why they were willing to commit suicide in the process. They might have legitimate grievances against our government or our culture. They are poor and we are rich, they lack resources and we live in luxury, they are oppressed and we are free. A few who argue thus imply that legitimate grievances justify the attack, and (it would seem to follow) that it is permissible to ignore all moral constraints and to deliberately target innocent people if one's objective is to rectify perceived injustices. This is a perspective often held by terrorists and those who support and condone them.

Others argued that by understanding why the terrorists and their supporters hate us, we can critically reflect on our behavior as a nation and society and become aware of wrongs we have committed. Although our national wrongs do not justify the terrorist attack, the introspection that it should stimulate might induce us to change our ways. We should repent of our arrogance.[2]

A particularly interesting view is that although we have a right to protect ourselves against any such future attack with the use of force, we should realize that many who hate really have no choice as to whether or not to hate. They are socialized from childhood to believe that the United States embodies evil, immorality, and arrogance, without ever having been exposed to another viewpoint. Many of the haters live in politically and religiously dictatorial or authoritarian countries and societies. They have been "brainwashed" by leaders and clerics, such as the Taliban, and cannot be expected to have any other attitude toward us than the one they have. So we cannot hold them morally responsible for their hatred, even though we have a moral right to protect ourselves, and to take their lives if necessary in order to do so. Yet we should pity them rather than be angry, even if we have no choice but to kill them. However, to the extent that we can protect ourselves without harming them, we must do that, and also try to open their closed societies so that they will no longer be brainwashed to hate us.

Others responded that we have to strengthen our efforts at dialogue with the Islamic world so that our real or perceived conflicts with it can move toward reconciliation rather than toward spirals of violence and counterviolence. This response does not justify the attack or argue against the right to eliminate the terrorists with force if necessary. Rather, it seeks to emphasize the importance of envisioning and actively working toward a future that will transcend hatred so that similar events will not occur.

As we reflect on responses to the terrorist attack, we see a constellation of emotions, attitudes, and values surface when we are deeply hurt—vengeance and justice, hatred and compassion, forgiveness and repentance, hostility and reconciliation. These feelings and values are the subject of this book.

· · ·

As I think back on my own initial, gut reactions to the World Trade Center massacre on the morning of September 11, which were a desire for revenge, retribution, and deterrence, I recall a horrific childhood fantasy. In it, I would become President of the United States in order to perform one specific action. As President, I would order the Strategic Air Command, armed with nuclear weapons, to totally annihilate Germany and the German people so that never again would Germans be able to do to the world and to the Jewish people what they had done in World War II and the Holocaust. Once this mission was accomplished, I would resign from the Presidency, satisfied that I had exacted just revenge and retribution on the Nazis and saved the world from future aggression, brutality, torture, and murder.

Fortunately, I was never able to execute my childhood plan. I have not forgotten nor have I forgiven (what right do I have to forgive evils that were perpetrated on others?) what the Nazis and their collaborators did during their years in power. And whenever I read accounts of Nazi crimes, my blood boils and the childhood rage and desire for vengeance and retribution against Germans is triggered. I know, however, that these feelings, directed against an entire nation, most of whose citizens, living in the year 2001 were not in any way involved with or sympathetic to the teachings and deeds of Nazism, are irrational and immoral. But even in the late 1940s, when I experienced these fantasies, it would have been morally wrong to take collective vengeance on all Germans, for several reasons. Although many, perhaps most, Germans supported Hitler and his policies, several million did not. German children could not be held responsible for what their Nazi fathers did. Moreover, not all who were sympathetic or collaborated were direct perpetrators of the crimes; killing them would have been an injustice, because the punishment would have been disproportionate to their crime. Furthermore, by taking the law into my own hands, I would have unleashed a dangerous precedent, that vengeance and retribution should be administered by vigilante justice rather than with due process through a recognized judicial system.

Had I been a Christian, I might have condemned my fantasy of revenge, on the grounds that Nazi and German sinners need to be forgiven, as some Christians have maintained. In certain formulations of this Christian value, not only vengeance, but even the desire for *just* retribution and for punishment of a perpetrator is a moral and spiritual weakness, whereas forgiveness is a virtue of the highest order.

What would I do today if I came across a Nazi who had committed horrible crimes but had and would continue to elude punishment? Would I punish him by taking the law into my own hands? I think that I might, but don't really know how I would act if faced with such a situation.

What would I feel toward a Nazi who had sincerely repented of his crimes and spent his life trying to make amends for them? Would I be able to defuse my anger and rage at what he had done to my relatives and my people, the Jews? I honestly don't know the answer to that either.

In the 56 years since the end of World War II, there have been numerous instances of fresh crimes against humanity, the World Trade Center bombing being among the most recent, though far from the most destructive of human life. The "killing fields" of the Khmer Rouge in Cambodia, the Hutu massacres of the Tutsi in Rwanda, the Serbian ethnic "cleansing" of the Muslims in the former Yugoslavia and of the Albanians in Kosovo, and the unbelievable brutalities of civil wars in Angola, Sierra Leone, and many other countries are among the many crimes against humanity that the twentieth century witnessed. The same questions of revenge, justice, forgiveness, and repentance, and the proper balance among them, arise repeatedly. Humanity's inhumanity makes us ask, from whence does this evil derive, and how shall we deal with the evil in others and the evil in ourselves? (I, who wanted to punish the evil in others, was willing, at least in my fantasies, to use evil means to respond to evil deeds.)

Evil desires and evil deeds are not exclusively borne of national or ethnic conflicts. They pervade everyday existence. Read your local daily paper. Rape, murder, robbery, fraud, marital infidelity, dishonesty, and sexual and domestic abuse abound. Of course, the media emphasize the evil that men do; the good is oft interred because it doesn't sell. There is much good in us as well: compassion, altruism, fairness, honesty, empathy, mercy, forgiveness, and love. Yet the persistence of evil requires response. How are we to respond to the evils that others perpetrate against us or against other innocent victims? How are we to respond to the evil that we ourselves perpetrate on others?

Religions have grappled with these questions for millennia, as have philosophers, legal thinkers, poets, and playwrights. In the last few centuries, modern disciplines have emerged and differentiated themselves from theology and

the book explores why, how, and whom to forgive, and how to repent, in the hope that by cultivating our capacity and our will to do both, we will reduce the resentments in our hearts and our evil behavior toward one another. To the extent that we can do so, we approach the biblical ideal "Love your neighbor as yourself" (Lev. 19:18; Mark 12:31) in our personal and societal relationships. I hope that this book can, in a small way, help us come closer to the biblical vision of love founded on justice, compassion, and self-transformation.

Revenge & Justice

Revenge is one of the most powerful of human emotions. Acts of revenge range from the trivial to the horrific. A waiter annoyed by a boorish customer might spit in the bowl of soup before delivering it with a feigned smile. The waiter takes pleasure in knowing what he has done even though the customer is unaware of the added ingredient. At the other extreme, men have committed bloody massacres to avenge their impugned honor. In some "honor" cultures, as of certain mountain people in Albania, it is considered shameful to allow an insult to go unanswered, and the answer is often to kill the offender or his kin, and not merely to return one insult with another.[1] Some proponents of capital punishment are motivated by a desire for revenge and many a murder is committed by a husband avenging the infidelity of his wife. Divorces are often characterized by irrational vengeance by one or both spouses who perceive themselves as innocent victims of the other, rather than by rational and compassionate concern for the welfare of the no-longer loved spouse and of the innocent children of the couple. Many acts of revenge are clandestine in nature or camouflaged by a veneer of innocence, such as the damaging slanderous comment made in pretended good faith by a resentful person in the hopes of thwarting an "enemy's" promotion in the workplace or receipt of a deserved honor or award. Vendettas are known to go on for years and even generations. One retaliatory act of revenge by a victim spurs a reciprocal response by the initial perpetrator, with the cycle of vengeance and retaliation spiraling out of control until it is no longer possible to distinguish between perpetrators and victims. Eventually all who are involved in the vendetta become both victims and perpetrators of evil.

Some psychologists think that revenge, and the pleasure it often provides, evolved, in part, because prior to the development of institutions of justice it served as a deterrent. If a person who planned to harm another in some way knew that the victim or his kin would avenge the offense, perhaps even seventy-seven fold, as the biblical Lamekh bragged to his wives he would do to anyone who dared injure him, he might think twice or more before perpetrating the harm. The emotion of revenge, which would spur a victim's retaliation, had survival value because the vengeful response would eventually deter threats to one's life and resources.[2]

Although deterrence may be a biological reason for the evolution of revenge, people often seek revenge even when deterrence is irrelevant, such as when the offender is imprisoned and neither he nor his family has any way of further threatening the victim. Vengeance often provides pleasure at seeing its object suffer, and the greater that suffering, the greater the avenger's pleasure. This is one reason why acts of revenge usually exact greater pain and suffering on their victims than would be justified by strict justice—the avenger's pleasure trumps his morality.

However, many of us seem to have a need for revenge, or at least retribution by way of punishment, to satisfy a sense of fairness or justice. It just isn't right that an offender should be let off the hook. Perhaps this feeling is rooted in the notion of responsibility. If we believe that people are responsible for their actions, then they must be held accountable for them. Punishment supports and maintains the principle of accountability, for the perpetrator and for society as a whole. Whether the need for satisfying a sense of justice is innate or learned is difficult to assess. The philosopher Mackie suggests that the survival value of retaliatory behavior as a deterrent led to the development of revenge that in turn developed into the moral sense that the group has a social responsibility to punish wrongdoers.[3]

More probably, the desire for justice is a product of how we are socialized. From early childhood we are told to be fair and to give everyone a turn, and that violators of the rules of fairness will be penalized. These values are embedded in our biblical moral heritage, in our democratic ethos, and in our belief in the rule of law. They are transmitted to our children at home and school, on the playground and the sports field. We eventually take it for granted that life *should* be fair and just, even if it often falls short of the mark. We consider it self-evident that these values should be enforced, whether by us or by others. (Too often, though, we expect and demand justice for ourselves while overlooking others' right to justice.) Thus is born the retributive component of "justice," which is grafted on to the more primitive, biologically based deterrent and pleasure motives of revenge.

Susan Jacoby, who has examined revenge from religious, literary, and legal perspectives, maintains that we do ourselves and others a disservice if we try to extirpate a victim's desire for retribution, and criticize those who have suffered from heinous crimes for wanting revenge. Jacoby does not advocate or justify uncontrolled vengeance, or vigilante justice. But she argues that a society is deeply flawed, ethically and psychologically, if it ignores the emotions of revenge and retribution by shirking its responsibility to uphold a judicial system that channels these emotions properly, for example, by punishing offenders at a level appropriate to their criminal behavior. Citizens will lose trust and confidence in the state's commitment to justice and will harbor more resentment and hate toward offenders than if the justice system assuages their legitimate need and desire for revenge and retribution with fair, rather than overly lenient sentencing and plea-bargaining arrangements. "Dismissing the legitimate aspects of the human need for retribution only makes us more vulnerable to the illegitimate, murderous, wild impulses that always lie beneath the surface of civilization—beneath, but never so deep that they can be safely ignored."[4]

The desire for revenge and retribution, properly controlled, serves the useful purpose of maintaining a level of justice in a society that hasn't figured out (as no society has) how to eliminate crime.

Do revenge and retribution actually make victims feel better? Does it give them peace of mind to see or know that the offender is being, or has been, punished? We have to distinguish between having peace of mind and "feeling better" on the one hand, and feeling of closure when justice has been done on the other. If someone embezzles my life savings and squanders the money, I suffer several kinds of pain. One derives from the fact that now I am poor, with all of the painful material consequences for me and my family. Another painful feeling is that the embezzler has demeaned my dignity and sense of self-worth by taking advantage of me. He might have made me feel like a fool and appear a fool to others. A third painful emotion I experience results because the embezzler has violated my sense of fairness and justice. If he is not caught and punished, he has unjustly benefited from my years of labor, and he has also flouted the principles of responsibility and justice to which I adhere (assuming I am law-abiding).

When society arrests, tries, convicts, and punishes the embezzler, *some* of these painful emotions will be allayed. If he doesn't give me my money back, the material pains of poverty will continue to trouble me. On the other hand, my shame may be somewhat alleviated, especially if I had a role in helping to apprehend him. True, he might have fooled me and made a fool of me, but I have rebounded by getting even with him, via the judicial system, thereby restoring my honor to some extent. The third painful emotion will be replaced with a new feeling that the principles of justice and accountability have been upheld. So, although revenge and retribution might not provide full "peace of mind" because it often can't restore that which was lost, it can provide some positive emotional gains.

It is probably the case that people desiring revenge overestimate the degree of *permanent* pleasure and peace of mind it will bring them. Perhaps this is because the desire for revenge is so powerful and unrelenting that we imagine that satisfying it will provide intense joy and relief. We forget that our pain and loss is deeper than whatever relief revenge can actually provide. Yet there are some who consider the satisfaction of their desire for revenge to be worth more than the years they spend in prison for their crimes of vengeance.

Some relatives of murder victims are left unsatisfied when a brutal murderer is executed by the state because they feel that the murderer should have suffered at least as much as his victim, but our methods of execution are not particularly painful or protracted. If the principle of retribution is morally just, why should someone who tortured and terrorized a child for days before finally killing him be allowed to "go to sleep" in a few minutes? A racist Klansman was sentenced to death for the vicious murder of a black man, whom he attached to the back of a truck and dragged for several miles, dismembering him before he finally died. This killer wrote to a fellow inmate that it was worth doing what he had done because the worst that could happen to him was to receive a long-lasting sleeping pill. Perhaps if the Klansman, while planning his crime, had known that if he were to be apprehended and convicted he would be slowly tortured to death, he might have been deterred from committing it.[5] The desire that sinners and criminals should be tortured underlies some religious conceptions of Hell. The punishments of Hell provide retributive justice proportional to the sin or crime, and deter those who believe in Hell from sinning.

The Hebrew Bible is a main source of the value of intrinsic and unique human worth, as most succinctly expressed when it describes humans as being created in the image and likeness of God.[6] It does not permit torture as a punishment for crimes. (It does mandate mutilation for one crime.[7] A woman who, coming to the defense of her husband in a quarrel, grabbed his antagonist by the testicles was to have her hand amputated as punishment.)[8]

One of the main arguments against retributive punishment is that there is no moral justification for inflicting suffering on a human being, if that suffering will not be educative, therapeutic, or a deterrent to him or to others. Punishment, according to this view, can only be justified on non-retributive, utilitarian grounds. This is why many people are opposed to capital punishment, especially if it is demonstrated that capital punishment does not deter other prospective criminals. It does of course prevent the murderer from committing further crimes, but life imprisonment would accomplish the same goal.[9]

In contrast to such utilitarian views, the philosopher Immanuel Kant maintains that retribution is the only moral justification for judicial punishment.[10] Kant presents the case of a murderer on an island who had been sentenced to death. All of the residents of the island were about to depart it, so that the murderer would remain alone on the island for the rest of his life. Should he be put to death by the others before they depart? Those who justify punishment only on the grounds of deterrence or reform would say that he should be allowed to live, since there is no need to deter or reform the murderer, given that he will live out his life in total isolation from humanity and so cannot be a threat to anyone's welfare. Kant, however, argues that justice requires the death of the murderer. Although Kant argues that retributive punishment is mandated by justice, he considers the *emotions* of revenge or hatred inappropriate, even when directed against those whom we are to punish justly.

On the other hand, the philosopher Jeffrie Murphy defends the moral legitimacy of "retributive hatred," not just retributive action. While acknowledging the great danger that inheres even in morally justifiable hatred and the desire for retribution, Murphy maintains that, in principle, they are defensible, although they must be rigorously controlled. These emotions

> might be felt, for example . . . by a man towards his wife and his best friend when he discovers that they have betrayed him and have been conducting an adulterous affair behind his back, or by a woman towards a rapist whose attack has left her forever terrified and sexually insecure. . . . It is sometimes both therapeutic for the victim and appropriately directed toward the wrongdoer. . . . Retributive hatred is a strategy designed to see (and to let the victim see) that people get their just desserts; as such it is neither irrational nor immoral.[11]

The basic premise justifying retribution against evildoers and sinners is that their harmful actions were freely chosen by them. They had the choice either to do or not do that which they finally did. In traditional philosophical and theological language, they had free will. Those who believe that humans do not have free will, however, and that our behavior is determined by biological, psychological, or social causes, argue against retributive punishment. Determinists hold that it is an illusion to believe that anyone could have chosen to have done other than what they actually did. We might justify punishing a wrongdoer because the punishment will induce fear, which will deter him from wrongdoing in the future, or because it might morally educate him so that in the future he will behave properly. The punishment becomes a new and added factor to the influences that will determine his future behavior. If we accept the determinist argument, then the justification for "getting even" with someone who has offended or injured me, or for putting to death Kant's murderer on the abandoned desert island, falls by the wayside. So too does the theological justification for torturing the wicked in Hell, based on concepts like "measure for measure" or "punishment to fit the crime," unless it serves some future desirable goal, such as purgation of the soul. The determinist cannot, on moral grounds, punish people strictly as retribution for past misdeeds. Moreover, from a determinist point of view, we should not harbor hatred, resentment, and grudges against those who hurt us, because they could not have done otherwise.[12]

. . .

The themes of vengeance, retribution, and justice appear frequently in the Bible. Sometimes it is individuals, tribes, or nations that punish wrongdoers or enemies, either on their own initiative or after being instructed to do so by God or a prophet. At other times, God is described as punishing or threatening to punish those who disobey him, whether by violating taboos, ignoring prescribed rituals, or unjustly oppressing or harming innocents. The Hebrew Bible and the New Testament, reflecting the views of many authors over a period of a millennium or more, contain varied approaches to revenge, retribution, and justice that are not always consistent with one another.[13] Let us examine some of the biblical texts that address these themes.

Perhaps the best known of these is this passage from Leviticus. "He who kills a man shall be put to death. . . . When a man causes a disfigurement in his neighbor, as he has done it shall be done to him, fracture for fracture, eye for eye, tooth for tooth" (Lev. 24:17, 19–20).

Similarly, in Genesis, God instructs Noah and his sons, "Whoever sheds the blood of man shall his blood be shed; for God made man in his own image" (Gen. 9:6).

It may have been the case, early in Israelite history, that this principle of *lex talionis* (the law of retaliation) was interpreted literally, not only with respect to capital punishment, but with respect to bodily injuries as well. Later it was understood to be a metaphorical way of expressing the idea of just and proportionate monetary restitution for injuries caused by one person to another, intentionally or otherwise. When viewed in the context of other ancient Near Eastern law codes, the biblical "eye for an eye" is emphasizing the principle of "only an eye for an eye, but not two eyes or a life as retribution for having blinded someone in one eye." The *lex talionis* says that we can reasonably, but not disproportionately, punish or demand restitution from someone who harms us. It includes the principle of justice along with strict limits on vengeance.

The Bible, however, considers premeditated murder to be such a heinous crime that, unlike the Koran, for example, it prohibits monetary compensation in lieu of capital punishment.[14]

What is the connection between the biblical view that man is created "in the image of God" and the divine command to put a murderer to death? Several interpretations have been suggested. Being created in the "image of God" endows man with the ability to know right from wrong and to control his behavior. He is therefore to be held responsible for killing an innocent human being. Or, because the human victim was made in "the image of God," to kill him is much worse than to kill an animal who was not made in the "image of God." Killing an innocent human being is a sacrilegious act—it is, so to speak, an attack on God himself, since man reflects God's "image." Another interpretation is that the verse in Genesis is explaining why God empowers humans, through their courts and judges, to put a murderer to death. One of the roles God plays in biblical theology is that of guarantor of ultimate justice. Duly appointed judges, applying the divine law, receive their authority by virtue of their having been created (along with everyone else) in the "image of God." In justly judging and punishing a murderer, they are acting as God's agents for the administration of justice. People endowed with the "image of God" have the responsibility, and the moral and rational capacity, to administer capital punishment to the murderer.

Another passage in Leviticus (19:17–18) attempts to control the lust for vengeance:

> You shall not hate your brother in your heart, but you shall reason with your neighbor, lest you bear sin because of him. You shall not take vengeance or bear any grudge against the sons of your own people, but you shall love your neighbor as yourself; I am the Lord. (The *Holy Bible,* RSV)

This admonition explicitly forbids taking revenge. It suggests that one way of dealing with our hostile emotions toward someone who has offended us is to call the offense to his attention and try to resolve our differences amicably. Perhaps he will explain that he didn't intend to hurt us, or apologize for having done so and offer some reparation, material or psychological, that can reestablish the bonds of brotherhood between us. Harboring hidden resentment and revenge are prohibited. Reconciliation is the proper path.

This passage refers to restraints on revenge in the context of "your people," "your brother," and "your neighbor." Groups often maintain a dual ethic, one for the internal governance of their own members and another for relating to outsiders, especially those perceived as threats to or enemies of the group.[15]

The prohibition in Leviticus against harboring grudges and exacting revenge applies to interpersonal conflicts within a cohesive group wherein one individual feels slighted or injured by another member of his community. It is in such a context that one should not let hostility fester and should strive for amicable resolution of conflict.

The story of Joseph and his brothers illustrates this value. Joseph was abducted by his brothers in Canaan, sold into slavery, and brought down to Egypt. Eventually he became the regent of Egypt with the power to exact revenge on his brothers who, at his behest, had moved to Egypt and depended on him for their survival. However, rather than avenge their crime against him or, for that matter, even punish them in due proportion to it, Joseph forgives them. Joseph's disavowal of vengeance models the Leviticus commandment, and he is held up as a paragon of virtue and righteousness in Jewish tradition because of his ability to control the 'normal' lust for revenge (as well as for his spurning the sexual advances of Potiphar's wife).[16]

Another biblical law that tries to control hatred and revenge is in Exodus 23:4-5. "When you come upon your enemy's ox or donkey going astray, you shall bring it back. When you see the donkey of one who hates you lying under its burden and you would hold back from setting it free, you must help to set it free."

Although the verse doesn't tell us who my enemy is or why he is my enemy, it probably refers to a fellow Israelite, as did the law in Leviticus.

Why should I help my enemy?

Jewish commentators offered several explanations.

One is that by helping my enemy I might reconcile with him. The objective of the law is peaceful and harmonious relationships.

A gesture of goodwill toward an enemy can go a long way toward making peace. In 1999 Turkey was hit by a severe earthquake causing thousands of deaths and injuries. Greece, its long-time enemy and rival, hastened to provide humanitarian assistance. One result was a warming of the relationship between the two countries.

Another talmudic interpretation is that the purpose of the law is to teach us how to overcome hatred, which is an undesirable emotion. The law is concerned with the inculcation of virtue, moral self-improvement.

In the Talmud it is further taught that if one is confronted with a friend who needs assistance in unloading his animal and an enemy who needs assistance in loading his animal, he is to first help his enemy in order thereby to "subdue his [evil] inclination." In other words, one must act contrary to one's feelings of animosity, to the extent not only of helping one's enemy, but even to give one's enemy precedence over one's friend, even in a situation where the general rule is that unloading takes precedence over loading.[17]

An even more demanding biblical passage teaches, "If your enemy is hungry, give him bread to eat; and if he is thirsty, give him water to drink; for you will heap live coals on his head, and the Lord will reward you"(Prov. 25: 21–22).

Why should I provide food and water to my hungry and thirsty enemy and in what sense does doing so "heap live coals on his head"?

In ancient Egypt, a penitent would place live coals on his head as a mark of contrition and remorse, and this is probably how the verse is using the image. As one biblical commentator explains,

> Kindness shown to an enemy, because it is undeserved, awakens feelings of remorse. . . . The food and drink which his enemy gave him not only put an end to his hunger and thirst; they also put an end to his enmity. . . . This is how to deal with an enemy and to punish him in the most constructive way. He is to have pain inflicted on him by his experience of the magnanimity and generous forgiveness of the one from whom he expected enmity. In this way he will be punished and, at the same time, reinstated as a brother.[18]

In this spirit, Abraham Lincoln, when criticized for the "unnaturalness" of his magnanimity toward his enemies, responded that he has destroyed his enemies by making them into his friends.

Paul instructs a small community of his followers in Rome, "Bless those who persecute you. . . . Do not repay anyone evil for evil. . . . Never avenge yourselves, but leave room for the wrath of God; for it is written 'Vengeance is mine, I will repay, says the Lord' " (Deut. 32:35).

He then quotes the above passage from Proverbs and concludes, "Do not be overcome by evil, but overcome evil with good" (Rom. 12).

Paul's admonitions were addressed to his beleaguered community, for whom internal harmonious, loving relationships were probably critical for survival in the face of external persecution. Paul also believed that God would soon appear to punish the wicked and save the righteous. Therefore it made sense to forego acts of vengeance and leave that work to God. It is unclear whether Paul meant his ethic to be universally applicable and appropriate at all times.[19]

Paul is also not opposed to the desire to see one's enemies punished, since he looks for the day when God will avenge. In fact, he might even understand the heaping of live coals on the head not as a sign of contrition, but of the pain, shame, and humiliation that the enemy will experience when God eventually punishes him.[20] However, his message, at least to the community of the faithful, is not to exact revenge against one another (they didn't have the power to exact revenge against their external persecutors in any case), and instead to bless their persecutors. The nature of the blessing is not specified. Perhaps the blessing is that the enemies should acquire the sense to repent of their evil ways. The blessing might also be a general one, a prayer to God that he benevolently care for the persecutors. It is doubtful that Paul is asking his followers to bless their persecutors with material or worldly success and domination.[21]

The Bible does not tell me how I can overcome my natural hatred for my enemy and come to his assistance. It simply commands me to do so. Perhaps the Bible believed that accepting the command as God's will would suffice to motivate the devout Israelite to follow it. It is possible that the law does not assume that I must *first* cultivate the emotion of compassion or forgiveness toward my enemy and *then* come to his assistance as a result. Rather I must force myself to *behave* compassionately or forgivingly toward my enemy, and this might eventually generate the *feelings* of compassion or forgiveness and, with practice, the *traits* of compassion and forgivingness. This is similar to Aristotle's view of how virtue is acquired. Compassionate or forgiving behavior produces compassion and forgiveness. We will discuss several specific strategies for overcoming hatred later in the book.[22]

In contrast to Joseph's magnanimity toward his brothers, when it came to outsiders who had offended their family's honor, Joseph's brothers, especially Simon and Levi, were ruthless. Their sister Dinah was abducted, raped, and kept under confinement by Shekhem, a Canaanite prince who had taken a fancy to her. While keeping Dinah under his control, he requested permission from Jacob to marry her. Jacob's two sons tricked Shekhem and his entire clan into undergoing circumcision on the pretext that this would make it possible for the clan of Jacob to give its daughters in marriage to the clan of Shekhem. While the Shekhemites were incapacitated by the pain of circumcision, Simon and Levi killed every Shekhemite male and took the women and belongings of the Shekhemites as booty. Jacob was aghast at his sons' violence, fearing that other Canaanite tribes would join in alliance against him. When he rebuked Simon and Levi, they responded bluntly and tersely, "Should he treat our sister as a harlot?" In their eyes, the sullying of the honor of their sister and, hence, the honor of their family, justified more than a mere "eye for an eye," but rather the annihilation of all of the males of the offending clan (who seem to have supported the actions of their prince).[23]

The biblical institution of the "blood avenger" and "cities of refuge" was an attempt to control revenge in the case of accidental homicide. A kinsman of the victim could avenge his relative's death before the killer reached a designated city of refuge, but not after he entered it. Once the killer is inside the city, the avenger has to bow to the decision of those who investigate the precise circumstances of the homicide. The law reflects a society in which there are no permanent, readily accessible courts. It is the right and even responsibility of close relatives to protect one another from harm. The law seeks a compromise between the passion and privileges of the "blood avenger" and the requirements of an objective assessment of the degree of guilt of the killer.

Some modern law codes acknowledge the emotional force of vengeful passion, under the guise of the exonerating concept of "irresistible impulse," which has been used as a temporary insanity defense in certain crimes. Even when an avenger is held criminally responsible for his vengeful retaliation, judges may take into consideration as a mitigating factor in sentencing the understandable and normal passion for revenge that is aroused by certain crimes against loved ones.

Before we morally judge avengers too harshly, we should imagine scenarios in which those dearest to us have been maimed, raped, murdered, or otherwise injured. Imagine that the one person who is most precious to you, whose relationship with you endows your life with its deepest meaning, hope, and satisfaction, is killed or brutalized by someone because of his lust, greed, jealousy, addiction, sadism, or psychopathic indifference to human life. Would you not want to retaliate? Would you be calm, dispassionate, and understanding in the face of the evil that was perpetrated, the agony that was produced, and the long-term suffering that will ensue? If someone were to murder my child (I cringe with pain at the very thought), I would want vengeance—passionately.

This is not to say that the desire for vengeance is always rational, just, or worthy of action. It is often irrational, unjust, and socially destructive when acted upon directly by the victim of a crime or injury, or by a family avenger of a victim. However, we should not condemn the emotion, per se, but instead try to understand, control, and channel it. Some people condemn the desire for vengeance or retribution as immoral, even when it is directed at remorseless sinners and acted upon through legal channels. Many Christians teach that victims should "turn the other cheek" and forgive instead. For them, to forgive in this context is an especially heroic spiritual act, requiring the most difficult emotional effort, but one which they are commanded to make. However, as we saw earlier, some people see this requirement to forgive as reflecting insufficient empathy for the suffering of the victim, and a violation of the requirements of justice. Others argue that the Christian command is so contrary to human nature that it is either impossible or psychologically unhealthy. The best way to cultivate forgiveness, reconciliation, and love, and the emotional healing that they can bring, is not, according to this view, by utopian demands to suppress all retributive emotions, but by according both justice and compassion their due.[24]

Although the desire for revenge is natural and at times moral, it is also very dangerous. If allowed to run its course without social control or judicial due process, it can result in injustice. The retribution exacted by an avenger will often be disproportionate to the original injury being avenged. Even if, in a given instance, an avenger's "taking the law into his own hands" would not result in disproportionate punishment of the offender, society cannot allow exceptions to the rule of law, lest it degenerate into anarchy. We have to forfeit our right to act out our justifiable vengeful impulses for the sake of the greater good—a society that in the long run will be more, rather than less, just. In giving up this right, we expect that society, and especially its legal system, will act on our behalf to pursue justice, so that we will be vindicated and criminals will be held accountable for their misdeeds and punished appropriately. Ideally, our moral culture and our legal system should also provide mechanisms for offenders to make reparations to their victims.

When our personal relationships have been morally violated, by betrayal of trust, infidelity, insensitivity, insult, or humiliation, we also feel a desire to get even. Here, where the legal system does not have jurisdiction over offenders, religious teachings are of particular value. As we shall see, they can teach us how to properly chastise the person who hurt us and encourage his or her repentance. They can likewise encourage our own repentance when we are the offender. They can also teach us how to control or dissipate our anger and forgive, when that is the desirable response.

Why does the impulse for revenge—rooted, at least in part, in a sense of fairness and justice—often result in unjust acts?

The psychologist Roy Baumeister offers several reasons that revenge so often degenerates into vicious cruelty and disproportionate punitiveness.[25] Perhaps the most important factor is the "magnitude gap." The perpetrator and the victim of a given injury tend to assess the degree of pain and harm inflicted differently. The victim considers the harm he has suffered to be greater than the perpetrator does. The victim might retaliate with an attack that he considers appropriate to the injury he suffered. The original perpetrator will feel that the retaliation was disproportionate and will want to even the score. This psychological process leads to spiraling attacks and counterattacks. This is why it is essential that parties to a conflict be willing (or even compelled) to leave the assessment of injury and the appropriate retribution, reparation, or punishment in the hands of more objective assessors. Depending upon the context of the conflict, these may be mutually trusted friends, marriage counselors, therapists, clergy, trained mediators, judges, or juries.

Furthermore, many acts of revenge are attempts to punish an offender for having damaged one's self-esteem, even when no physical or financial injury was caused. It is particularly difficult to assess loss of face, shame, or harm to one's reputation caused by slander. How can the victim or his surrogate avenger honestly determine the correct measure of his loss or the harm suffered? Although courts of law and juries do try to attach a monetary value to these injuries, doing so is a complex and imperfect process that is no better left in the hands of the injured person, given his emotional involvement. Moreover, the harm that a perpetrator caused by defaming his victim's character or by humiliating him can last forever. Does that mean that the perpetrator should receive a lifetime of punishment for actions that were committed over a brief period of time? Degree of guilt for wrongful actions is also a function of malicious intent. It is difficult for a victim to ascertain the thoughts and feelings that the offender had when he committed the injurious deed.

There are simply too many impediments to a victim's ability to objectively assess the degree of guilt and responsibility of the perpetrator, to allow him to exact revenge on his own.

The same considerations come up in our personal lives, as any psychotherapist can testify. Husbands and wives in painful marital distress because

of perceived wrongs of one against the other often have very different perceptions and interpretations of their spouse's actions and intentions. One
function of the therapist or counselor is to help each spouse see how the other
views their conflict. This does not mean that both spouses are equally guilty
for the conflict and suffering in the marriage, but only that it is often useful
and even necessary to have a more objective outsider assess the causes of the
conflict and educate the partners as to how one or both need to change.
Withholding sex in order to avenge your husband's belittling comments towards you, or having an affair in order to avenge your wife's emotional cool-
ness, is not the best way to resolve the conflict and bring about healing and
reconciliation.

Another danger of revenge comes from our tendency to generalize both
with respect to the perpetrator himself and the group to which he belongs.
When someone hurts us we focus on the evil side of their personality and
ignore the good. We do not see them in their human complexity, an admix-
ture of good and evil. We ignore the fact that as much as they might have
hurt us, they may have done many kind things on behalf of others. A thief,
or even a murderer, may also be a loving father. This does not exonerate the
thief or murderer from their sin against me. But it does broaden the perspective that should be taken into consideration in punishing the sinner. Victims, impelled by a desire for revenge, find it very difficult to see any aspect
of their enemy in a positive light. Judges and juries or, in the interpersonal
sphere, compassionate adjudicators of disputes, are more capable of seeing the
"whole picture" when they determine the degree to which an offender should
be punished for what he has done.

In addition to inappropriately generalizing from "he harmed me by a specific evil deed" to "he is an evil person," we also often generalize from "he
who did the evil deed is a member of a group," to "all members of his group
are evil as well." Therefore vengeance will be wreaked on the collective rather
than on the individual. The perpetrator's family, ethnic group, or nation are
held culpable for the sins of one or a few of their members. This is another
reason why revenge and punishment are best taken out of the hands of the
victim and transferred to more objective enforcers of justice.

Although the Bible discourages personal revenge against "insiders," it often
encourages group revenge against outsiders, especially non-Israelite tribes or
nations that, from the perspective of the Israelite narrator of the events, unjustifiably harmed the people of Israel. Sometimes this is expressed as a human
desire or prayer for revenge. At other times, it is expressed as a divine command to take revenge.

One example of the latter is the commandment to annihilate the tribe of

Amalek, which according to the biblical tradition, gratuitously attacked a weak and faltering Israel wandering in the wilderness. The Israelites' hatred for this tribe is projected onto God himself. In one passage, we read, "Then the Lord said to Moses, 'Write this as a reminder in a book and recite it in the hearing of Joshua: I will utterly blot out the remembrance of Amalek from under heaven. . . . 'The Lord will have war with Amalek from generation to generation' " (Exod. 17:8–16).

Elsewhere, the Bible places the responsibility for avenging what Amalek had done directly upon the Israelites themselves.

> Remember what Amalek did to you on your journey out of Egypt, how he attacked you on the way, when you were faint and weary, and struck down all who lagged behind you; he did not fear God. Therefore when the Lord your God has given you rest from your enemies on every hand, in the land that the Lord your God is giving you as an inheritance to possess, you shall blot out the remembrance of Amalek from under heaven; do not forget. (Deut. 25:17–19)

God, through the prophet Samuel, directs King Saul to annihilate the Amalekites and all of their possessions. Saul kills the people as instructed but spares the possessions and Agag, the Amalekite king. He is severely condemned for his failure to do precisely as he had been told, and loses his dynasty as a result (1 Sam. 15).

The authors of these texts considered it justifiable to bear grudges for misdeeds of yore and to avenge them many generations later on an entire population. We do not know whether these events really took place as described or simply reflect fantasies of revenge, but in either case the texts consider enemies of the Lord, and of his people Israel, to be worthy of severe punishment.[26] Moreover, guilt is tribal or national and transgenerational. All members of the offending group, including women and children, are absorbed into the collective guilt and are destroyed along with the male warriors. This unforgiving vengeance directed against external enemies is in sharp contrast to the notion that "you shall not take vengeance or bear a grudge against any of your people" (Lev. 19:18).

Many Christian and Jewish exegetes have been troubled by this and analogous biblical texts that mandate transgenerational collective vengeance and punishment. It is difficult to harmonize the literal sense of the biblical passages and their implicit values with the notion of individual guilt and responsibility and a just God.[27]

Within the Hebrew Bible itself we see a developing unease at the concept of harming children for the sins of their parents. Thus Deuteronomy 24:16 stipulates, "Parents shall not be put to death for their children, nor shall children be put to death for their parents; only for their own crimes may persons be put to death."

In 2 Kings (14:5–6) special attention is called to the fact that King Amaziah, who "did what was right in the sight of the Lord," upon consolidating his power,

> killed his servants who had murdered his father the king. But he did not put to death the children of the murderers; according to what is written in the book of the law of Moses, where the Lord commanded, "The parents shall not be put to death for the children or the children be put to death for the parents; but all shall be put to death for their own sins."

This stringent limitation on the permissible extent of revenge or retribution exacted by humans is also applied to God by the prophet Ezekiel, who elaborates at length on the theme of strict individual responsibility for sin. Ezekiel, prophesying to the Jewish exiles in Babylon, was trying to counter their despair. They had been raised on a theology that taught that sins of the fathers are visited on their children. They believed, therefore, that there was nothing they could do to extricate themselves from exile and its sufferings if God operated on the principle of transgenerational rather than strict individual responsibility. To refute this theology, Ezekiel describes a man who is a murderer, adulterer, idolater, oppressor of the poor, and more, and asks rhetorically,

> Shall he then live? He shall not. He has done all these abominable things; he shall surely die; his blood shall be upon himself.
> But if this man has a son who sees all the sins that his father has done, considers and does not do likewise . . . he shall not die for his father's iniquity; he shall surely live. . . . The person who sins shall die. A child shall not suffer for the iniquity of a parent, nor a parent suffer for the iniquity of a child; the righteousness of the righteous shall be his own, and the wickedness of the wicked shall be his own. (Ezek. 18:13–14, 20)

This new principle of retributive theology was meant to supplant the earlier one that had considered it appropriate to kill children for what their parents or ancestors had done.

The Talmud discusses one of the early biblical accounts of transgenerational retribution.[28] When the Israelites settled in Canaan their leader Joshua vowed to the local Gibeonites that the Israelites would allow them to remain in the land forever. Centuries later, King Saul tried to wipe out the Gibeonites, putting some to death and violating the ancient oath. After David succeeded to the throne, there was a famine in the land. When David inquired of the Lord as to the cause of the famine, he was told that it was a punishment for what Saul had done, that there "was bloodguilt on Saul and his house, because he put the Gibeonites to death." This guilt had to be expiated just as Abel's blood "cried out from the earth" demanding justice and expiation for his brother Cain's murder of him. When David approached the surviving Gibeonites to ask them what they would accept as expiation they replied, "It is not a matter of silver or gold between us and Saul or his house; neither is it for us to put anyone to death in Israel. . . . The man who consumed us and planned to destroy us . . . let seven of his sons be handed over to us, and we will impale them before the Lord" (2 Sam. 21:4–5).

David handed over seven of Saul's sons and grandsons. The seven were impaled and died. With the expiation completed, the famine ceased.

From the perspective of the narrator of this story, the Gibeonites had a right to demand the death of Saul's progeny, and David is not condemned for handing them over. However, later rabbis were troubled by it. They embellish the biblical narrative with imagined conversations and scenarios through which they impart their values. David is depicted as reluctant to acquiesce to the Gibeonite request for two reasons. Sons should not be put to death for the sins of their fathers, and mercy should override justice. Why then does David hand over Saul's progeny? The importance of establishing the inviolability of an oath and a commitment to protect vulnerable outsiders, as the Gibeonites were, overrode the principle of individual responsibility and set aside considerations of mercy for Saul's progeny. For these same reasons, the bodies of the impaled victims were left exposed, notwithstanding the biblical prohibition against this. In this particular instance, it was essential that the people be taught how much they must protect the foreigner from abuse and persecution. Seeing the impaled bodies of princes put to death for their father's sin was a way of effectively communicating that message. According to the rabbinic interpretation, although the Gibeonites had the right to demand justice, they should have accepted a lesser, more merciful expiation. Because they did not, David prohibited Israelite intermarriage with them. Israelites, he said, are to be characterized by mercy and not only by justice.

The rabbinic interpretation reveals an ambivalence about the biblical story. The Bible does not condemn David or the Gibeonites. The killing of the sons expiated Saul's shedding of innocent blood, as witnessed by the termination of the famine. On the other hand, rabbinic law and moral sentiment could not countenance a court or king or any human putting children to death for their father's crime or sins, even if God might do so. Their uneasy resolution of this dilemma was to introduce another moral–religious value, protecting the vulnerable—the alien, foreigner, stranger, convert—from oppression and persecution. On a one-time emergency basis, this value justified the application of a strict law of talion that relied on more primitive conceptions of retribution. Saul had killed innocent family members, so innocent members of his family had to be killed. Only thus could the demands of justice be met. Yet even as David reluctantly acquiesced to this harsh "justice" demanded by the Gibeonites, he distanced his own people, the Israelites, who were to be schooled in compassion, from them. Perhaps too David's motive in acquiescing was benevolent and utilitarian—let the progeny of Saul die so that all of Israel can be saved from the much greater number of deaths that would ensue from continued famine. (David might also have been motivated by a desire to eliminate possible contenders for his throne, but this motive would not be attributed to him by the rabbis, who considered David to be deeply pious and ethical.)

The vengeful desire to kill children for the sins of their parents is a motif in the novel by Alan Dershowitz, *Just Revenge*, that describes the moral struggle of Max, the protagonist who is a Holocaust survivor who wants to avenge the murder of his entire family by a Lithuanian Nazi collaborator, Prandus. After World War II, Prandus had entered the United States by providing false information on his visa application, and he lived a very pleasant, remorseless, satisfying life in the United States for fifty years. There was no prospect that he would be brought to justice for his crimes before his anticipated death from cancer in a few months' time. Max felt that he had the moral right and the emotional need to exact as much proportional revenge on Prandus as he could. He decided to kill Prandus's grandchild, the apple of his eye, to avenge Prandus's murder of Max's son on Passover eve a half century before. At the last minute, just as he is about to run the child over with his car, he holds back from doing so. He realizes that he would be repeating the same crime that Prandus had committed, killing children because of who their ancestors were.[29] In real-life conflicts, this urge is unfortunately often unchecked. It has become almost commonplace that groups in conflict deliberately target innocent children as victims.

· · ·

How does the God of the Bible respond to insult and injury?

The Hebrew Bible's most important elaboration of God's attributes attests to both his patient forbearance and his ultimate punitive judgment for those who abuse his patience.

After the people of Israel sinned in the wilderness by forging a golden calf and worshipping it, notwithstanding the prohibition in the decalogue against constructing and worshiping graven images, God in his wrath decided to destroy the people and create a new nation from Moses' line of descent. Moses implored God to contain his wrath, which he did. He punished but did not destroy the Israelites. Moses, who had to continue leading the people was afraid of God's "moods," so to speak, and wanted a better understanding of him and his ways. He requests of God, "Now if I have found favor in your sight, show me your ways that I may know you and find favor in your sight."

The Lord responds with a self-description.

> The Lord, the Lord,
> a God merciful and gracious,
> slow to anger,
> and abounding in steadfast love
>   and faithfulness,
> keeping steadfast love for the
>   thousandth generation,
> forgiving iniquity and
>   transgression and sin,
> yet by no means clearing the
>   guilty,
> but visiting the iniquity of the
>   parents
> upon the children
> and the children's children,
> to the third and the fourth
>   generation.[30]

Judaism and Christianity teach that people should imitate God. God's response to Moses, in which anger and punitive judgment are tempered by forbearance and mercy, is often cited as a model to follow.

What exactly was God's response to Moses' plea that he pardon Israel? One interpretation is that God changes his mind about destroying her, and defers Israel's punishment until later generations. He maintains his original covenant with Israel that he will bring her to Canaan and continue his relationship with her, although he doesn't totally wash away her sin, which later generations will have to bear. This is the response of divine mercy and grace.[31]

This interpretation, though perhaps true to the original meaning of the text, was not the preferred one. According to it, children who had not themselves sinned would suffer for their ancestors' evil deeds (and would be rewarded for many more generations for their ancestors' good deeds). Once Ezekiel's view, that reward and punishment should be individual and not transgenerational, became the preferred one, a different sense was given to God's response, and it was closer, though not identical, to what Ezekiel had taught. God requites the sins of ancestors *only on descendants who are themselves sinners* (Exod. 20:5; Deut. 5:9), up to four generations. And God's love is much deeper than his anger. He rewards righteous children for the merits of their righteous ancestors for a thousand generations.[32]

Here, and throughout the prophetic books of the Bible, God is depicted as controlling his anger in order to give the wicked an opportunity to repent. This is one way in which he tempers justice with mercy and compassion. If, however, the wicked do not repent, they will not be forgiven. Like God, we should be patient and forbearing with those who wrong us, and give them a chance to repent. If, however, they do not, they need not be forgiven and can be punished.[33]

Unlike human anger, divine anger always serves justice, as explained by the theologian Abraham Heschel.

> It is divine anger that gives strength to God's truth and justice. There are moments in history when anger alone can conquer evil. It is after mildness and kindness have failed that anger is proclaimed. . . . it is never a spontaneous outburst, but rather a state which is occasioned and conditioned by man. . . . It comes about in the light of moral judgment rather than in the darkness of passion.[34]

Jewish sages took note of what appears to be an inconsistency between God's command to the people of Israel that they not bear grudges or take revenge, and the description of God in the prophet Nahum's oracle against the city of Nineveh, the capital of Assyria. Assyria had devastated northern Israel and exiled many of its inhabitants (the "ten lost tribes of Israel"). Using the same Hebrew words for revenge (*nkm*) and angry resentment (*ntr*) as are used in "You shall not take vengeance or bear a grudge," Nahum (1:2–3) says,

> A jealous and avenging God is the Lord,
> The Lord is avenging and wrathful;
> The Lord takes vengeance on his adversaries

And rages against his enemies.
The Lord is slow to anger but great in power,
And the Lord will by no means clear the guilty.

The midrashic author imagines the people of Israel pointing out to God
the contradiction between how he himself behaves and what he demands of
them.

"So said Israel before the Holy One Blessed be He." Master of all the
worlds, you wrote in the Torah, "You shall not take vengeance or bear a
grudge," yet of you it is written, "The Lord is avenging and wrathful; the
Lord takes vengeance on his adversaries and rages against his enemies."
Shouldn't God practice what he preaches?

> The Holy One Blessed be He said to them, "In the Torah I wrote, 'You
> shall not take vengeance or bear a grudge' against Israel ['against any of
> your people']. However with respect to the nations [I have written,] 'The
> Lord spoke to Moses, "Avenge the Israelites on the Midianites" ' [who had
> earlier corrupted the Israelites with idolatry and promiscuity]."[35]

God, in this midrashic rendering, does practice what he preaches. He
preaches to the Israelites that they should overcome resentment toward their
fellow Israelites but wreak vengeance on wicked non-Israelites. Similarly, God
is patient and forbearing with Israelites when they sin, but much less so with
nations who attack or otherwise harm them, as did the Assyrians. (Although
even with respect to the Assyrians, Nahum describes God as "slow to anger.")
A biblical writer who lived after the prophet Nahum was uncomfortable
with God's harshness towards Nineveh. He felt that God's compassion and
mercy are extended even to wicked gentiles. Not that their sins would be
forgiven if they persisted in them, but that that they would be invited to
repent before God punished them, and if they did they would then be forgiven. This anonymous writer composed the book of Jonah, whose teachings
are in stark contrast to the oracles of Nahum. God tells Jonah to preach to
the inhabitants of the city of Nineveh, the infamous capital of infamous
Assyria, that their wickedness has reached the point that they will be destroyed. Jonah would prefer that they be destroyed for their sins, unsuccessfully tries to flee from God, and reluctantly preaches to the Ninevites this
oracle of their impending doom. To his dismay, the king and the inhabitants
repent and are saved from destruction.
Ironically, Jonah expresses his anger and frustration at God's compassion

toward the enemy of Israel by paraphrasing God's self-description as told to Moses. "But this was very displeasing to Jonah, and he became angry. He prayed to the Lord and said, 'O Lord! . . . That is why I fled . . . for I knew that you are a gracious God and merciful, slow to anger, and abounding in steadfast love, and ready to relent from punishing' " (Jon. 4:2).

God has to explain and demonstrate to Jonah that he loves all of his creatures and will not hasten to punish or destroy them. He prefers that they repent so that he can forgive them.

What is remarkable is the willingness of the author of Jonah to come to the defense of Nineveh, capital of one of the most brutal empires of the ancient Near East, from whom the people of Israel suffered so much and for so long. No less remarkable was the inclusion of the book of Jonah in the Jewish canon of sacred scriptures. How often does a nation preserve in its sacred history a story about the merits and righteousness of its enemies?

The author of Jonah, and the rabbis who included it in the biblical canon, felt that there had to be some critique of the dual ethic ascribed to God in other biblical narratives. If he was a just God, as they firmly believed him to be, then he had to treat even the enemies of his chosen people with mercy and forbearance and give them too an opportunity to repent.

It was hard for Jews who suffered so much from hostile nations to think benevolently of them, and they often didn't. Yet, as we see in the book of Jonah, they struggled with the tension between the understandable and even justifiable animosity that they felt toward enemies and their belief in the redemptive value of repentance for everyone. Thus while the midrash justified God's vengeance on Nineveh as expressed by the prophet Nahum, other sages established the tradition still practiced by Jews today, that the book of Jonah is read in its entirety in the synagogue on the most solemn day of the Jewish year, Yom Kippur, the day of repentance and atonement.

· · ·

The belief that Hell is a place reserved for the punishment of sinners in the afterlife is found in many cultures and religions. Authors of Jewish and Christian apocalypses developed the theme and described tours of Hell by saints such as Enoch, Peter, Paul, and Mary.[36] The motif was further elaborated in medieval sermons, literature, art, and devotional and theological writings.[37] Its best known literary formulation is in Dante's *Inferno*. Dante portrays a woman hanging helplessly by her nipples while her adulterous lover dangles by his penis. Vats of boiling semen pour over them, compounding their pain and humiliation. Those who had deprived the poor and hungry of nourishment suffer the agonies of thirst and starvation. To intensify their agony, delectable and aromatic food and drink are placed almost within their reach, but the sinners are not allowed to partake of them to assuage their suffering. The torments of the damned in Hell are eternal. The lurid and terrifying descriptions of sinners in Hell conjured up by the fertile imaginations of some preachers can compete with the fantasies and deeds of brutal sadists.[38]

According to the doctrine of Hell, these penalties for vice are willed by God and usually implemented at his command by creatures under his control. Punishments are exacted in due proportion to the effects of sins—"measure for measure", and are often designed to match them in form and method.

The doctrine of Hell has presented problems for Christians who believe in it literally. How can a compassionate and just God inflict eternal punishments on people whose sins were committed for a limited time? Isn't eternal damnation an instance of divine vengeance rather than divine love and forgiveness, especially since sinners, once consigned to Hell, no longer have an option to repent?[39] Many theologians argue, therefore, that descriptions of the torments of Hell are metaphors. The greatest punishment for sin is not externally imposed suffering, but rather the alienation from God, the source of eternal life, that sin produces in the soul of the sinner.

Whatever might be the theologically correct understanding(s) of the doctrine of Hell, for centuries its depiction in popular preaching and in religious art was vivid and graphic, and it was understood quite literally by the masses (and many theologians), and still is in some religious communities today.

The doctrine of Hell serves several functions. It provides a place for God to wreak vengeance on sinners in the service of justice. Given the fact that in this world we see that many wicked people prosper and righteous people suffer, it would appear that God is unjust, and that there is no ultimate justice or moral order in the universe. Hell and Heaven are meant to balance the scales of justice and affirm God's justness. The torments of Hell also have a deterrent effect on believers. A meditation on Hell is one of the spiritual exercises recommended by St. Ignatius of Loyola, the founder of the Jesuit Order, so that the fear of punishment will help one avoid sin. The meditator is to invoke all of his senses in vicariously experiencing Hell to "see in the imagination the great fires . . . to hear the wailing, the screaming, cries . . . to smell the smoke, the brimstone, the corruption, and rottenness . . . to taste bitter things . . . with the sense of touch to feel how the flames surround and burn souls."[40]

Belief in Hell also vicariously satisfies the innocent victim's thirst for revenge without entailing any effort or danger on his part. He can rely on God to do it for him, as promised in his sacred religious literature. Moreover, Hell depicts God as not only avenging the sins committed against innocent human beings, but also avenging sins committed solely against him. It restores to God the respect and esteem that the arrogant sinner denied God by flouting his will. The doctrine of Hell probably also functioned as a sublimation of some people's sadistic impulses.

Many prayers in the Hebrew Bible and the New Testament beseech God to avenge evil that was done to the person praying, or assert that God will do so. During the Crusades, many Jewish communities were massacred by Christian crusaders. The Jews were, for the most part, helpless victims who could barely defend themselves or bring the murderers to justice. They were a tiny, despised minority in a majority Christian society that was steeped in anti-Semitic stereotypes, theology, and behavior. The Jews felt a desire for revenge and believed fervently in justice. Since they were powerless either to take revenge upon or bring their Christian oppressors to justice, they expressed their feelings, and their hope that God would act as their avenger, in a prayer. The prayer, which is essentially a compilation of verses from the Hebrew Bible, reads as follows:

May the merciful Father who dwells on high, in his infinite mercy, remember those saintly, upright and blameless souls, the holy communities who offered their lives for the sanctification of the divine name [i.e., for steadfastly remaining committed to Judaism and refusing to convert to Christianity even under the threat of torture and death]. May our God remember them favorably among the other righteous of the world; may he avenge the blood of his servants which has been shed, as it is written in the Torah of Moses: "Rejoice peoples, His nation, for He will avenge the blood of His servants. He will take vengeance on His [nation's] foes, and cleanse [from the sin of bloodshed] His land, His people." (Deut. 32:43, my translation). And by thy servants, the prophets, it is written: "I will avenge their blood which I have not yet avenged" (Joel 4:21). And in the holy writings it is said: "Why should the nations say, 'Where then is their God?' Let the vengeance for thy servants' blood that is shed be made known among the nations in our sight." (Ps. 79:10). And it is said: "The avenger of bloodshed remembers them; he does not forget the cry of the humble." (Ps. 9:13). And it is further said: "He will execute judgment upon the nations and fill [the battlefield] with corpses; he will shatter the [enemy's] head over all the wide earth (Ps. 110:6–7). (Birnbaum, 1949)

Similarly, the souls of Christian martyrs, slaughtered by the Romans, are depicted as crying out with a loud voice, "Sovereign Lord, holy and true, how long will it be before you judge and avenge our blood on the inhabitants of the earth?" (Rev. 9:10).

The New Testament also threatens with divine punishment and vengeance those "heretics" who left the faith, probably referring not only to lapsed Christians but to Jews as well, who, Christians felt, should have known better than to reject Christ as savior since, according to New Testament belief, Christ's coming, passion, and redemptive sacrifice for sin was foretold in the Hebrew Bible that the Jews held sacred.

> For if we willfully persist in sin after having received the knowledge of the truth, there no longer remains a sacrifice for sins, but a fearful prospect of judgment, and a fury of fire that will consume the adversaries. Anyone who has violated the law of Moses dies without mercy "on the testimony of two or three witnesses." How much worse punishment do you think will be deserved by those who have spurned the Son of God, profaned the blood of the covenant by which they were sanctified, and outraged the Spirit of grace? For we know the one who said, "Vengeance is mine, I will repay." And again, "The Lord will judge his people." It is a fearful thing to fall into the hands of the living God. (Heb. 10: 26–31)

Unfortunately for the Jews, during the Crusades, and on many other occasions, Christians didn't leave vengeance on Jews in the hands of God but elected to take it into their own hands, leading to the Jewish prayer we cited above.

· · ·

We have seen that the Bible prohibits holding a grudge, at least against a kinsman. Why is it wrong to hold a grudge? The most obvious reason is that holding on to a grudge might eventually result in an unjustifiable act of revenge. This is why the prohibition on bearing a grudge and taking revenge are juxtaposed in Leviticus 19:17–18.

However, there is a deeper problem with grudges, even a grudge that never produces a vengeful deed. When I hold a grudge against someone, it adversely affects my relationship with him or her. It is a barrier to sustaining or developing friendship and love. I might not even be aware that my grudge is causing me to hold back in a relationship, preventing the development of goodwill. Our reactions to even relatively minor offenses that we file away as grudges can sour what might otherwise have been satisfying bonds with family or friends. Grudges can be "banked" for decades. Too often, when we look back on our life, we regret how by holding on to a grudge we lost opportunities for meaningful relationships.

Once, my teenage son was out walking with a friend when it began to rain heavily. The father of the friend drove to pick up his son, but, for a reason that I still cannot fathom, did not offer my son a ride home. By the time my son arrived home, he was drenched. I was very annoyed by what I interpreted as the insensitivity and selfishness of this man, who had been a neighbor, acquaintance, and someone toward whom I felt some friendship. From the time of this episode, however, I was unable to think about or see this man without my memory of that event and my grudge being triggered. I never did or said anything to hurt him, but for many years I avoided him when I could, even though he was a nice and charitable person. I never asked him why he hadn't given my son a lift in the downpour, and so I never was able to find out why he did what he did. (There may have been some plausible explanation of which I was unaware.) The grudge just sat with me for many years. I knew that I was wrong for having this feeling, but decided that it would be trivial to "make an issue" out of such a relatively insignificant "harm." (My son was much less bothered by the episode than I was.)

In fact, though, the harm of this episode was significant—not the harm to my son, who merely got drenched—but the harm to me (and perhaps to the man) for my carrying this negative feeling for so long, and not benefiting from what might have developed into a warmer friendship.

Around fifteen years after this incident, I was at the airport waiting to pick up my baggage and then take a cab home. In the baggage claim area was this gentleman, who had come to pick up another son of his who had been on the same flight with me. He greeted me warmly and offered to give me a lift home. It took an unusually long time for me to retrieve my baggage, yet he graciously waited for me rather than excuse himself, as he could have properly done. This made me feel very good because it enabled me to let go of the fifteen-year grudge. I felt that the man had in a certain sense "repented" (although I doubt that he was even aware of his "sin"). Here he was in a situation analogous to the one that had occurred 15 years earlier—an opportunity to go out of his way to give someone a lift—and unlike 15 years ago, he now demonstrated helpfulness, to a significant degree of inconvenience. I came home and told my wife how happy I was that I could feel more positive about this man, because I never really was proud of myself for bearing the grudge and would have always preferred to have been on friendlier terms with him.

This incident illustrates my pettiness. I think that I am not unique in such pettiness. If we can hold grudges over minor offenses for so long, imagine our capacity for maintaining them over more serious offenses, real or perceived.

A friend told me the following story. Many years ago she needed a few hundred dollars to carry her over a difficult period. She asked her brother for a loan. Given her close relationship with her brother, she was surprised and deeply disappointed when he refused on the grounds that he did not think she would spend the money wisely. This incident has colored her relationship with her brother for several decades. Although they are on good terms, she remembers and still resents his refusal to assist her when she was under pressure. She has never told him how much he hurt her. This grudge has prevented her from maintaining the deep relationship of affection with her brother that she had before the incident, and which she would have wanted, indeed still wants, to have, not only for her sake but for the sake of her children.

In both of these cases the "offenders" probably did not perceive themselves to be guilty of any offense, even though they were perceived as guilty by their "victims." They might not even have been aware that their "victims" felt that something wrong was done to them. One of the reasons for the biblical command not to hate your brother in your heart, but instead to rebuke him, is to give your brother a chance to reflect upon his behavior and the hurtful effect that it had on you so that he can improve himself. This is in addition to the law's interest in keeping you from festering resentments and vengeful responses.

The book of Samuel tells the story of King David's children, Tamar, Amnon, and Absalom. Amnon raped his half-sister Tamar and then cast her out of his home. She went to live in shame and disgrace with her full brother, Absalom. David, though deeply angered over the rape, did not punish Amnon "because he loved him because he was his firstborn." Absalom didn't rebuke Amnon, but hated him in his heart. Two years later he arranged for Amnon to be assassinated, and then fled. David thus was bereft of two of his beloved sons, one dead, the other in exile. One of the lessons learned from this story is the danger of failing to rebuke and of hating in the heart. Had David rebuked and punished Amnon for the rape, Absalom might not have harbored his hatred and murdered him.

Why do we hold grudges? How can we overcome them when we know that they are morally or emotionally undesirable? Here we will address the first question, leaving the second one for our later discussion of forgiveness.

Sometimes a victim can benefit by holding a grudge against the person who offended him. This is especially the case where the offender is aware of and acknowledges his offense, and feels guilty about it. To forget or forgive the offense would deprive the victim of a means with which to extract some material or other benefit from the offender. For example, when a husband cheats on his wife and she finds out, she might prefer to use her husband's offense against her to coerce him into doing things for her that he would not otherwise do. If she were to forgive or forget, she would be forfeiting this power. The wife is not necessarily holding the grudge with the intention of taking revenge, but rather to derive some advantage.

The wife might also hold the grudge so as to justify her taking revenge against her husband, or to justify her doing something else, such as having an affair, which she would not do if she didn't feel aggrieved. If she forgave, forgot, or simply decided that she would act toward her husband as if he hadn't offended her, she wouldn't do these things.

Some people get gratification from revenge, and holding on to a grudge keeps open to the victim the option of exacting "sweet revenge" on the offender.

Sometimes holding on to a grudge and repeatedly reminding the offender of his misdeed is satisfying because it makes the victim feel morally superior to the offender. "You were disloyal, but, unlike you, I am not."

Holding on to a grudge and letting the offender know that what he did to you is never far from your consciousness can act as a deterrent to his repeating the offense, or committing other ones. Were you to forgive, forget, or ignore the offense, he might forget how much it hurt you and think that he can get away with it again. The unfaithful husband will be much less inclined to have a second affair if he knows that his wife hasn't forgotten the first one, and that, were he discovered again, the consequences would be drastic, perhaps including divorce. When the wife gives her husband "a second chance," it implies that she and he always remember that he failed the first time.

Usually, serious offenses cause long-lasting suffering to their victims that makes it difficult to let go of a grudge. How can I forget my enmity when every moment of my life I suffer for what was done to me, even though the offensive act took place years ago?

Some people enjoy the role of suffering victim, and holding a grudge feeds in to this need. If I forgive or forget, then the pain isn't there anymore, so I am no longer the victim I like to be.

Another motive for holding grudges is pride. When someone hurts or injures me, there is usually a blow to my self-esteem or honor that may be even more important to me than any physical or material pain or loss that the offender caused. Unless I value humility to a very high degree, I will be reluctant to be "put down" or shamed. Therefore I will not forgive or forget but will hold on to the grudge at least until the offender has done something that will restore my self-esteem and honor.

Finally, the victim might feel that the offense is so grave that he will not forgive or forget it because it would be morally wrong to do so. I might bear a grudge against an offender who injured me because of a despicable motive, such as his racist hatred, or out of sheer evil, such as his unrestrained lust, greed, or envy, because I feel that it would be immoral to forgive, forget, or ignore the offense. If I don't hold him accountable, it can be perceived by him and by others as condoning what he did, or at least minimizing its wrongfulness.[41]

Notwithstanding the reasons for which we hold grudges, there are often good reasons for not doing so, which we will discuss in the contexts of forgiveness and repentance.

We have explored anger, resentment, and revenge, and their relationship to retribution and justice, because it is necessary to understand these before we consider other ways of responding to evil, insult, or injury. Resentment and revenge are not the best ways to assuage pain and they do not mend fractured relationships. Personal healing, as well as reconciliation between individuals and between groups, is better accomplished by forgiveness and repentance, to which we now turn.

The Essence of Forgiveness

A lonely and bitter friend of mine and his three adult, married children have not spoken to one another for years, ever since he remarried following the tragic early death of his first wife, their mother. From the children's perspective, he remarried too soon after their mother's death, and he showed more concern for the emotional needs and feelings of his second wife than for those of his children. He in turn perceived his children as selfish, not appreciating his loneliness as a widower and his need to forge a satisfying relationship with his new wife, even if it meant paying more attention to her than to his children. He is now deprived of the pride and pleasure he could have in their accomplishments and barely knows his grandchildren because of the mutual anger, recrimination, and blame that has destroyed what once were beautiful parent–child relationships. My friend was a doting, self-sacrificing father, a man to whom family was of prime importance. Here he is entering his senior years, devoid of the family joys and satisfactions he worked so hard for and deserved. His children, who loved their father before the rupture that resulted with his remarriage, are deeply hurt as well and are embittered that they have essentially lost a father, and their children have lost a grandfather. The situation is pathetic and tragic because neither father nor children are schooled in the arts of empathy, forgiveness, and reconciliation. They are caught in a no-win bind of emotional and moral foolishness, unable to extricate themselves from their mutual blame and recrimination for hurtful words and actions of the past. How sad it is to witness them living out their lives, unforgiving and unforgiven.

Forgiveness in family relationships is complicated by the ambivalent emotions we feel toward significant others, our love–hate relationships with them. For example, it is often the case that sexually abusive fathers violate their daughters for the first time when they reach puberty or early adolescence. Until that time they may have been loving, nurturing fathers who established strong emotional ties with their daughters. An adult woman whose father began to abuse her sexually only after her early childhood years, and continued to be protective of and affectionate toward her while having an incestuous relationship, might be torn between the love for her father that had developed when she was a child and the deep anger she now experiences as an adult. How does she disentangle her emotions? Does he deserve to be forgiven? Must she forever submerge her love to her hate?

Death adds another dimension of complexity to forgiveness. Expressions of remorse and sorrow make it easier for us to forgive someone who has hurt us. Yet it is often in our best interest to forgive parents, children, siblings, or friends who caused us pain but who have since died, and hence cannot apologize, confess, express remorse, or rectify what they did that injured us so deeply. What can we do to reconcile ourselves with someone no longer alive but whose earlier actions still shadow our lives, ignite our anger, and stalk our memories? A woman had great difficulty forgiving her mother's favoritism toward her younger sister. The mother had showered the sister with much more affection and encouragement than she had received. Her deep resentment toward her deceased mother produced in her both self-pity and guilt, and marred her relationship with the envied sister. But there was no longer any way for her to discuss her feelings with her mother or to ask her why she had done what she did and whether she had realized how hurtful it had been. In the course of therapy, she became able to empathize with her mother—to see the family from her mother's perspective. She realized that although her mother was wrong and insensitive in her favoritism, she had not been malicious in her intent—and indeed hadn't even been fully aware of her favoritism and how it had affected the patient. The mother had felt that because the older daughter was brighter and more attractive than the younger one, she needed less attention and support. The type of anger and resentment described here often arises in families in which one child is seriously ill or disabled and hence receives much more attention from the parents than do her healthy siblings.

Another useful healing strategy is based on the notion that we must see those we judge in their totality and must not focus exclusively on the harm they might have caused us, as we too often do. Bishop Joseph Butler, a leading eighteenth-century Anglican moralist, explained this idea.

Anger may be considered as another false medium of viewing things, which always represents characters and actions much worse than they really are. . . . Thus in cases of offense and enmity, the whole character and behavior is considered with an eye to that particular part which has offended us, and the whole man appears monstrous, without any thing right or human in him: whereas the resentment should surely at least be confined to that particular part of the behavior which gave offense: since the other parts of a man's life and character stand just the same as they did before.[1]

When the daughter was able to see her mother in this new light and realized that, notwithstanding the pain her mother had caused, she had also been devoted and generous to many in her life, it eased her resentment and enabled a measure of forgiveness that made the daughter feel more kindly toward her mother. By learning how to forgive, the daughter was also able to overcome her guilt at having felt such ill-will toward her mother.

It is easier to preach glibly the virtues and pragmatic value of forgiveness and reconciliation than it is truly to understand why, when, whom, and how to forgive. Forgiveness is a complex phenomenon. It is affected, among other factors, by the nature and extent of the injury we have suffered, our relationship with the person who has hurt us, our sense of self, and whether or not the person whom we contemplate forgiving has expressed remorse for his deed or sought to repair the emotional, physical, or material damage he has wrought upon us. Mature forgiveness entails difficult emotional and intellectual work. It is a skill that needs to be cultivated, a virtue that needs to be acquired by self-training. When practiced thoughtlessly or simplistically, it is ineffective and counterproductive and can even be dangerous to oneself, to the person forgiven, and to society.

· · ·

I have been using the terms *to forgive* and *forgiveness* as if their meanings are self-evident and shared by everyone. However, this is far from the case. These words denote and connote different things to different people, both in popular usage and in sophisticated theological and philosophical discourse. My first task, then, is to explain the varieties of meanings of "to forgive." It is also necessary to distinguish "to forgive" from other terms that share some overlapping concepts and emotions with it. The differences between "to forgive" and the infinitives below, which I will explain after defining forgiveness, are morally, psychologically, and legally significant.

To be merciful
To pardon

> To condone
> To excuse
> To justify
> To exonerate
> To forget
> To atone
> To reconcile

In defining forgiveness, it is necessary to make a critical distinction between two types. One is internal, referring to a victim's feelings and attitudes toward the perpetrator, and does not necessarily require that the victim in any way interact with the perpetrator or inform him that he is forgiven. The second type of forgiveness is interpersonal in nature. It refers to something the victim does or says to the perpetrator, directly or indirectly.

> To forgive someone means to cease feeling angry or resentful over the transgression. . . . In this sense, it is even meaningful to speak of forgiving someone who is dead or absent or who, for other reasons, would have no way of knowing whether he or she has been forgiven. . . . On the other hand, forgiveness is a social action that happens between people. It is a step toward returning the relationship between them to the condition it had before the transgression. Forgiveness signifies that the victim will not seek further revenge or demand further reparations.[2]

Let us refer to the first type of forgiveness as private and the second as interpersonal. There are four possible combinations of these two.

1) It is possible to forgive in the private sense while not forgiving in the interpersonal sense.

For example, suppose that my business partner embezzled a substantial sum of money from me, money that I needed to pay for my son's college tuition. I am deeply angered at and resent my partner for that. I am also hurt by his betrayal of my trust and friendship. However, when he was apprehended I found out that, unbeknownst to me, he had been under severe financial pressure due to expensive medical treatment for his wife's cancer. He had embezzled the money not to use it for his personal pleasure, but to care for a loved one. I still feel that what he did was wrong—he should have sought financial assistance by legal means, maybe even by approaching me for a loan, rather than depriving me of money that I need and worked hard for, and breaching the relationship of trust. But I may partially or completely overcome the anger and resentment that I initially felt toward him. However, I still feel that he has to be punished in some way for what he did, and so I press charges against him, not only to reclaim my money but to "teach him a lesson," albeit without anger. I may not even want him to know that I "understand" the pressure he faced lest he interpret my "understanding" as excusing him for what he did. I also permanently sever our business relationship and the friendship we shared prior to his crime.

2) It is possible to forgive in the interpersonal sense while not forgiving in the private sense.

For example, in the case above, even though I know why my partner embezzled my money, I cannot (or choose not to) get over my anger since he has caused me harm that is more than monetary. My son, who had dreamed of attending Yale, had to settle for an inferior education at a mediocre state university. Every time I think of this, my anger at my partner is aroused. However, I decide not to press criminal charges against him since I feel that, given his wife's illness, he has enough suffering in his life and that if he were to be imprisoned, not only would he suffer, but his wife and family would suffer as well. So I forgo the right I have to see him punished. Moreover, I tell him that I am still hurt and angered by what he has done to me and to my son, but that out of compassion for him I am not going to pursue the matter any further, and that I expect him always to bear his guilt in mind and to pay me back if and when he acquires the funds to do so.

3) It is possible to forgive in both the private and the interpersonal sense.

For example, in the case above, I can both overcome my anger and resentment and not press charges. Moreover, if my compassion is deep or if I feel a religious obligation to forgive, I might tell my business partner that I am willing to give him a second chance, and renew both our friendship and our business relationship.

4) It is possible to not forgive in either the private or the interpersonal sense.

For example, in the case above, I might continue to harbor my anger and resentment, insist on pressing criminal charges, and completely terminate our relationship.

Although forgiveness has been of interest and concern to theologians and philosophers for millennia, it is only recently that the fields of clinical, personality, and social psychology have "discovered" forgiveness as a human experience worthy of serious and sustained empirical research. Some of the impetus for this interest has come from several psychologists with committed Christian backgrounds who, aware of the centrality of forgiveness in Christian thought and the Christian ethos, have sought to introduce the study and appreciation of forgiveness into the discourse of secular psychology.[3] They have done this in a scientifically sophisticated manner, aware that in order for their work to make a contribution to society in general they cannot make explicit Christian theological assumptions the basis for their research and writing.[4]

It is interesting, however, to see some of their definitions of forgiveness, which do reflect an underlying Christian understanding of the phenomenon. Enright et al. (1996), for example, have defined forgiving

> as a willingness to abandon one's right to resentment, condemnation and subtle revenge toward an offender who acts unjustly, while fostering the undeserved qualities of compassion, generosity, and even love toward him or her. . . . therefore, a forgiver may unconditionally offer this gift regardless of the other's current attitude or behavior.

This definition, and therapeutic programs based upon it, see forgiveness as a "gift" of "love" given by the offended victim to a perpetrator who has behaved in an unambiguously "unjust" way toward his victim and has not expressed remorse or repented for it.

Enright advocates this kind of forgiveness as emotionally healthy and therapeutic.

This definition of forgiveness makes no mention of God, of Jesus' passion in which he bore his suffering with patience and forgave those who tortured him to death by crucifixion, of the New Testament teachings "love your enemy" and "turn the other cheek," or of the Christian belief in God's gracious gift of forgiveness—which he grants even to not-yet-repentant sinners because of his love and compassion for all of humankind. If, as Christianity teaches, we are to imitate Christ, then it is obvious that Enright's definition of forgiveness is derived from the distinctly Christian view and understanding of God's forgiveness and man's imitation of it. Enright, writing here as an academic psychologist, and not as a specifically Christian psychologist, does not say that we are *obligated* to forgive those who offend us (which is what many Christian theologians would say), but that it is strongly advisable that we do so. Enright does maintain that there are situations in which forgiveness is not advisable or desirable; most proponents of forgiveness, whether theologians or psychologists, oppose forgiveness in cases in which it might seriously endanger the victim's well-being to do so, as, for example, in forgiving a violently abusive spouse to the point of continuing to live with him. However, this caveat refers to aspects of interpersonal forgiveness rather than to private forgiveness.

Worthington has developed a model of forgiveness based upon a definition of forgiveness similar to Enright's. He used this model to help himself privately forgive the teenagers who brutally sexually assaulted and murdered his mother, and he has trained hundreds of people to apply the model in their lives.[5] We will examine his "Pyramid of Forgiveness" approach in a later section, looking here only at his definition of forgiveness.

We define interpersonal forgiving as the set of motivational changes whereby one becomes
a) decreasingly motivated to retaliate against an offending relationship partner,
b) decreasingly motivated to maintain estrangement from the offender, and
c) increasingly motivated by conciliation and goodwill for the offender, despite the offender's hurtful actions.[6]

The latent Christian value system implicit in Worthington's approach to teaching people how to forgive—in helping them bring about the three motivational changes—will be seen in the way he construes and utilizes empathy, altruism, and humility to induce forgiveness.[7]

A very different view of forgiveness is one that sees it not as a "gift" of overcoming resentment and forgoing the right to demand punishment in the case of an unremorseful offender, but as either a "gift" to a remorseful one, or, as we shall see in Judaism, an *obligation to a repentant offender*.

Forgiveness is multidimensional in that it includes feelings, thoughts, and where possible, behaviors. Although some people report a sudden surge of forgiveness toward an offender, more commonly it is a process that takes time. It can involve vacillation between thoughts and feelings that are conducive to forgiving, and thoughts and feelings that either divert the victim from the forgiveness trajectory—such as repressing or denying the hurt—or that reignite hatred, resentment, or a desire for revenge, such as ruminating about the offense and the hurt it caused. It is also simplistic to think of someone as either forgiving or not forgiving a person. Each of the dimensions of forgiveness or non-forgiveness, the emotional, the cognitive, and the behavioral, can vary in intensity and in range. Anger, hatred, compassion, and love, though difficult to measure, are not all-or-nothing emotions.

In addition, the circumstances in which you experience these feelings, or the stimuli that trigger them, can be few or many. One person's animosity toward an offender may be aroused by the mere thought of him, whereas another person's will be aroused only by seeing him or by being physically close to him. The process of forgiveness that these two people undergo will differ.

Some people assume that victims of injustice and injury are either vengeful or forgiving, as if the only ways of reacting to or dealing with offenses are these polar opposites. In contrast to this, Worthington enumerates more than 20 ways by which people, while not forgiving an offender according to Worthington's own definition of forgiveness, may become less resentful or vengeful.[8] He refers to these as ways of reducing unforgiveness without actually forgiving—although some people might think that they have forgiven the offender when they do these things. Since Worthington considers active forgiveness a highly desirable virtue, merely reducing unforgiveness is not, for him, as desirable as actual forgiving. However, from a non-Christian perspective, some of the methods he lists for dealing with one's anger and hatred in response to injustice may be considered more morally and psychologically desirable than forgiving a perpetrator, particularly an unrepentant one.

What are some of the ways we become less unforgiving?

As we discussed earlier, *some* people who seek revenge or justice, whether through human or divine agents, may find their anger lessened once their goal is accomplished. Worthington understands the desire to seek restorative justice, in which the offender makes amends, and to let go of anger only after restoration has been made. But he considers it spiritually inferior to forgiving him privately in one's heart without his having made amends. Moreover, revenge and justice do not seek love and concern for the well-being of the offender, even after he has been punished.

Sometimes people get bored with the grudges they hold or they realize that the hurts haven't had a long-term adverse impact, so they ignore them.

People may use defense mechanisms such as denying that they were indeed hurt—a black eye isn't such a tragedy, or "money comes and money goes." They may rationalize what the offender did, often because it is too painful to admit the full meaning of the offense. The husband whose wife suddenly picked up and left him after years of what he had assumed was a loving marriage may prefer to believe that she became emotionally disturbed rather than that she did not love him as he had always thought she did. Many abused women blame themselves for their husbands' violence, and young children in particular may blame themselves when a parent beats or punishes them severely. They reason that if my mother or father, who claims and seems to love me and who knows more about right and wrong than I do, sees fit to punish me so severely, then I must have done something wrong to deserve it. They thus direct their anger against themselves rather than against their parent. This isn't forgiveness, since the child doesn't acknowledge that an injustice was done to him. There is nothing the parent has done that needs to be forgiven. When the child matures, however, he might reassess his child-hood experiences and develop hostility toward the parent whom he now per-ceives as having victimized him.

Some people are submissive to pain and hurt, preferring to absorb it rather than to fight it, emotionally or behaviorally. This lessens their "unforgiveness," even though they don't actually forgive.

· · ·

Now that we have considered several definitions of forgiveness, let us con-sider how forgiveness differs from related concepts.[9]

Sometimes we may *forget* the wrong that someone has done to us because of the passage of time, memory loss, or aging. We may become so involved in life activities that are more immediate than the hurt we once suffered that, without any decision either to forgive or to forget, the hurtful event fades from our consciousness. It is insignificant to our present life, and remember-ing the offense and its pain isn't worth the emotional effort that we would rather expend on what is important to us now.

A woman had been deeply hurt by her husband, who used to humiliate her regularly in front of his friends. She decided that it was in her and her children's interests not to dissolve the marriage on this account. Eventually, he stopped this behavior when one of his friends told him that he was making a fool of himself, but he never apologized to his wife. Now, 20 years later, the woman is preoccupied with her career and her children; she never thinks about and can barely recall those episodes. She doesn't feel resentment because the past events are simply not on her mind. However, she never forgave her husband, and if her memory of those events is triggered by her husband's humiliating her again, the recollections will be emotionally painful and might even induce her to remind him of how he had behaved back then and that he still owes her an apology. She might tell him that he deserved a divorce for his insensitive and cruel behavior toward her, but she had decided against it for pragmatic reasons, not because she loved him. These words would hurt him deeply.

To forget is not to forgive and to forgive is not to forget. If you totally forget that you were once hurt by someone, you can't forgive them. Of course, you may not need to forgive them since you no longer remember the pain. Often, though, forgetting isn't permanent. The memory isn't eradicated, and it can be resurrected. In order to forgive, you have to first remember. Perhaps after you have forgiven, you can then forget, maybe permanently. But the two processes are distinct, not to be merged. To forget, especially to forget a wrong done to someone else (or to presume the right to forgive a wrong done not to you but to a third party), is considered by many not to be a moral virtue but rather a morally reprehensible condoning of evil.

Sometimes we *condone* a wrong that was done, usually to others but sometimes even to ourselves. In this case we decide not to hold the perpetrator accountable because we may benefit from doing so, or because we are afraid of the consequences of confronting him. Your employer who promised you a commission of 25 percent of your sales arbitrarily and retroactively reduces it to ten percent. You "let him get way with it," even though you feel that he wronged you, because you still need the job. We may condone a wrong done to others because we want to conform socially, and no one else seems to be objecting or punishing the wrongdoer. In both of these cases we may feel anger and resentment, but we still don't punish the offender. Even if they are in position to chastise or punish the wrongdoer, people sometimes condone an evil because they are glad to see the victim suffer because of some animosity of their own toward the victim. Many Germans who were not themselves members of the Nazi party, who felt that the Nazis were morally wrong in murdering Jews, and who could have protested effectively against Nazi actions, nevertheless condoned what the Nazis did because of their own dislike of Jews. For a similar reason, many Germans condoned Nazi persecution of homosexuals. Although they didn't hold the Nazis accountable for their misdeeds, they could not be said to have forgiven the Nazis.

Sometimes a person who feels that he is a sinner who deserves to suffer as punishment for his own evil will condone offenses committed against himself. He doesn't forgive the person who unjustly hurts him but is willing to let the offender do so without protest because, feeling guilty and unworthy, he is eager to see himself suffer. Sometimes one sees this psychology in Christians who are so convinced of either their innate sinfulness or of the sinfulness of their thoughts and behaviors that they welcome the slings and arrows of outrageous aggressors because they feel that their pain atones for their sins. This psychology of condoning can be especially dangerous when applied to others. If someone believes that all people are vile and corrupt sinners, then they may be passive in resisting evil: in other words, they may condone evil because the suffering that is an effect of human evil purges and purifies corrupted humankind.

Sometimes we *excuse* persons for the evil they did. We do not say that what they did was morally appropriate but that we understand the pressures, temptations, or other mitigating circumstances that influenced their behavior. We hold them morally responsible but are willing to lessen their punishment and feel less angry and resentful toward them than we would have in the absence of excuses. It isn't easy, however, to draw the line between excusing someone because we understand the mitigating circumstances and exonerating them completely from all responsibility.

When, however, we *justify* a behavior that on the surface appears to be unjust, we find reasons to believe that at a deeper level, the behavior was not morally wrong. Even though it hurt me or someone else, I have no claim against the person who did it and have no "right" to feel resentment or anger or righteous indignation, even though I might actually feel these emotions. When you justify a hurtful behavior, you are in effect saying that it makes no sense to speak of forgiveness of it—it was "just," so there is nothing to forgive. Conflicts between individuals and between groups often center around the antagonists' different perceptions of whether a hurtful action has been just or unjust. A father might sincerely believe that it is just for him to impose a curfew on his teenage son because he hadn't studied sufficiently for his school exams. The father believes that it is his moral responsibility to see to it that his son gets the best education possible and takes his studies seriously. Moreover, the father may feel that by being lax in his studies, the son is showing a lack of gratitude for all that the father has invested in his son, in time, resources, and nurturance. The son, on the other hand, feels that he is old enough to be responsible for his own life choices and doesn't owe his father gratitude. It was his father's decision to have sex and have a child, a choice obligating him to provide for and invest in the child. The son maintains that his father has no moral right to impose a restrictive curfew on him and hence for him to do so is unjust. This conflict can lead to animosity between father and son. Each one believes that he is "right." Each one is hurt by the other, and if neither comes to accept the other's viewpoint, each will feel wronged. If the conflict remains unresolved, then the anger and resentment will persist for many years. One way of overcoming the mutual resentment would be to learn how to forgive. However, if the father comes to see the son's perspective as just, then it is only the son who can forgive his father. The father who now accepts that he was wrong cannot forgive the son, because the son was right. If the son concludes that his father was right, the father might forgive his son, but it is not for the son to forgive his father. This is a hypothetical case. In many real life situations, both antagonists will often behave in ways that combine justice and injustice. The father might have justly imposed a curfew, but unjustly imposed it too frequently or restrictively. The son may have justly felt that he had the right to decide how much time he wanted to devote to his studies, but he unjustly expressed ingratitude for the sacrifices that his father had made for him, sacrifices that went beyond what a moral or legal system would agree are the responsibilities of fatherhood. One role of value-oriented therapy or family counseling is to help clarify family conflicts in the light of moral principles.

In intergroup conflict, too, the party that feels an injustice was perpetrated against it wants this to be acknowledged and an apology and reparation made before considering forgiveness; often both parties feel this way. According to those who understand forgiveness as a "gift" tendered by a victim to an offender even if the offender doesn't acknowledge his guilt, the party that feels aggrieved can forgive. However, if forgiveness is considered to be morally appropriate not as a "gift" to a recalcitrant offender, but either as a a "gift" or an "obligation" to a remorseful offender, then until the antagonist admits guilt, the self-perceived victim need not, and maybe should not, forgive. Be that as it may, justifying is different from forgiving and is logically incompatible with it.

When we *exonerate* someone we say that the harmful act that initially appears to have been performed out of malicious intent or gross negligence was not really done in that manner. The driver who fell asleep at the wheel and crashed into another car, killing its occupants, was exonerated when it was discovered that he had a rare adverse reaction to a medication that does not typically make people drowsy, and that he had been told by his doctor that there was no danger in driving. Once we find this out we will not punish him and will not be angry at him, but for this to happen we did not have to forgive him.

In the legal system, certain officials have the right to *pardon* an offender. This means that he will not receive the punishment that the court decided he deserves. There are several reasons for the legal institution of pardon, including a concern that there may have been a flaw in the functioning of the legal system, or that abiding by the strict letter of the law can sometimes violate its spirit. Often pardons are granted out of political considerations, the rationale being that even though the criminal is guilty, it is in the long-term interests of the state to free him—perhaps in order to assuage a discontented significant constituency. Sometimes the pardon includes expunging all mention of the offense from the criminal's record. He is to be treated henceforth by the legal system as if the crime were never committed. When a criminal is pardoned this does not imply, as forgiveness would, that the person who pardons him no longer resents or is angry at him for his crimes.

Atonement of a sin is similar to the secular legal concept of pardon. When God atones, he declares that he will not punish the sinner for his sin; usually the sinner must first perform or participate in a prescribed ritual. Atonement often means, in religious terms, that the sin is "washed away" or the stain of the sin is removed as if the sinner had never committed the sin. He can start anew, so to speak, with a clean spiritual slate. Atonement is similar to forgiveness in that God forgives humans or accepts their prayers or rituals as effecting atonement. Usually atonement is the divine response to a sinner's repentance. In secular discourse, we also speak of certain acts as atoning for sins or crimes, so that the criminal can be forgiven. A man who battered his wife to death, but after his release from prison devoted the remaining years of his life, at great personal sacrifice, to educating violence-prone men on how to control their violent impulses and to helping establish shelters for abused women may be said to have atoned for his sin. However, this does not necessarily mean that his children, whose mother he killed, have forgiven him.

When we are *merciful* toward someone, we either lessen or forgo his punishment or debt. Mercy, unlike forgiveness, implies that the merciful person not only feels a certain way about the offender, but also undertakes action with regard to him as well. This need not be the case when you forgive, because you can forgive by overcoming your anger, even if there is nothing you can do. You can forgive your abusive parent who is now dead, but you can't show mercy to him. If you believe in divine reward and punishment after death, you may believe that God can have mercy on your parent's soul as he decides how to punish him for having abused you. If you have forgiven him, you might pray to God to be merciful to him. This points to a second distinction between mercy and forgiveness. Mercy (unlike pity) is an emotion we feel and act upon toward someone over whom we have some authority, especially the authority to punish. We can, however, forgive people irrespective of their relationship of power to us, although the relationship can influence our inclination to forgive.

Finally, although forgiveness can often lead to *reconciliation* between the offender and his victim, it need not necessarily do so. The victim, though willing to forgive in the sense of forgoing the right to punish the offender or to have others punish him, and in the sense of dissipating his hatred or anger toward the offender, might not want to reestablish any intimate or even close relationship with him. Christian understandings of forgiveness and, to a significant extent, Judaic ones as well, see reconciliation as an ultimate goal of forgiveness, indeed as an overriding human goal in general even though it may not be realizable in specific cases. A secular notion of forgiveness, which doesn't posit a utopian goal of universal harmony or assume that it is possible and desirable that all humans love one another, does not consider reconciliation to be the ultimate objective of forgiveness, although it is to be appreciated when it occurs. Just as forgiveness doesn't necessarily imply reconciliation, reconciliation doesn't necessarily imply or depend upon forgiveness. Given the difficulty of forgiving, it is good that it does not, or else there would be little reconciliation in human relationships. People and groups will often reconcile even after decades or centuries of enmity because it is pragmatic to do so. The American and the Japanese nations effected a political reconciliation after World War II. This resolution does not mean that Americans have forgiven the Japanese who bombed Pearl Harbor and who killed and tortured hundreds of thousands of soldiers and civilians in the war. Nor does it mean that the Japanese have forgiven President Truman and his advisers who ordered the atomic bombings of Hiroshima and Nagasaki, which from the Japanese perspective were not "legitimate" military actions, but horrible, racist-motivated crimes against a civilian population.

· · ·

We have spoken of forgiveness as a process and also as a constellation of feelings, thoughts, and behaviors in response to injury. In addition to these senses of the concept, some psychologists, theologians, and philosophers refer to forgiveness as a relatively stable personality trait, disposition of character, or virtue. Robert Roberts, a philosopher/theologian interested in the psychology of Christian virtues, has coined the term *forgivingness* to describe this virtue, and recently several psychologists have tried to measure this trait and to see if it is correlated with other traits, attitudes, or values.

Roberts[10] considers the ability to overcome one's justified anger at an offender and replace it with emotions such as love and compassion to be the critical components of forgiveness. People differ in their ability to do this and in the frequency with which they do it. The person who has the virtue of forgivingness tends to react to injuries with an attitude of forgiveness. Where does this tendency come from? Why do people differ in their possession of this trait? Why consider it a moral virtue? Forgivingness is a moral virtue, claims Roberts, because unlike anger, it encourages harmonious relationships between people.

I would suggest, however, that, as Aristotle and many others have maintained, some anger is morally justifiable, and the absence of anger at injustices toward oneself or others is a vice rather than a virtue.[11] "A person is praised who is angry for the right reasons, with the right people, and also in the right way, at the right time and for the right length of time. . . . It is a slavish nature that will submit to being insulted or let a friend be insulted unresistingly" (*Nichomachean Ethics* 4.2).

Although Catholicism considers anger a capital sin, St. Thomas Aquinas and other theologians generally agreed with Aristotle that anger is righteous when it is aroused in response to evil and directed toward rectifying injustices. There were dissenting views among the ancients, such as that of the Stoic philosopher Seneca, and within Christianity. These held that anger is never justifiable, and this attitude characterizes some contemporary Christian advocates of radical forgiveness. However, there is a long and venerable Christian defense of justifiable anger, when this anger is controlled and does not itself lead to injustices. Jeremy Taylor, the Anglican bishop, instructs:

> Such an anger alone is criminal which is against charity to myself or my neighbor; but anger against sin is a holy zeal, and an effect of love to God and my brother, for whose interest I am passionate, like a concerned person; and if I take care that my anger makes no reflection of scorn or cruelty upon the offender, or of pride and violence . . . anger becomes charity and duty.[12]

Roberts is aware that critics of forgiveness, construed as the forgoing of all anger, maintain that it is a vice rather than a virtue because it is in effect indifferent to or tolerant of evil. Roberts argues, however, that "forgiveness is virtuous because one's anger is given up without abandoning correct judgment about the severity of the offense and the culpability of the offender."[13]

He analyzes several factors that facilitate forgiving an offender, among which are compassion for his suffering and a sense of moral commonality with him. Forgivingness, as a virtuous trait, is the tendency deliberately or unconsciously to evoke anger-reducing and love-inducing values and attitudes in the face of injury. These forgiving skills can be learned until they are second nature (perhaps people are born with innate differences in these tendencies as well), and the person who wants to acquire the virtue of forgivingness will work hard at mastering them. The person who would be a forgiving one will cultivate his empathy—his ability to see his "enemy" as a person who suffers, and his humility—his ability to see that he has within him many of the same evil tendencies that his "enemy" does. A person who has cultivated these traits of compassion and humility will more easily and regularly forgive offenders and even come to love them.

Compassion, says Roberts, is incompatible with anger, since wishing an offender well, which is an aspect of compassion, precludes wishing him punitive harm, which is an aspect of anger.

He gives an example of forgiveness motivated by compassion for an offender's suffering, taken from Tolstoy's *War and Peace*.

Prince Andrei and Natasha were deeply in love, but in Andrei's absence, the contemptible Kuragin alienates her from him. Andrei pursues Kuragin from one country to the next, bent upon avenging this injury by killing him in a duel, but Kuragin eludes him. Andrei is severely wounded in a battle, and in the tent hospital to which he is brought, he sees lying on a nearby table a man with an amputated leg, convulsively sobbing and choking. It is none other than Kuragin. Kuragin's suffering evokes in Andrei pity, tears, and love for him, even as Andrei remembers that it was Kuragin who deprived him of his beloved Natasha.[14]

What can we learn about the trait or virtue of forgivingness from Tolstoy's description of an act of compassionate forgiveness?

> An important dimension of the virtue will be an ability and disposition to take the viewpoint of sufferers, in particular of sufferers who have offended against us. It is an ability to transcend, or detach ourselves from, our own position as one who has been harmed, and take the position of the other almost as if it were our own. . . . the forgiving person is one in whom such reasons as the offender's suffering and weakness cast into the shadow legitimate reasons for being angry.

Andrei's love for Kuragin was not a result of repentance on Kuragin's part or anything that he might have have done to mitigate his offense. Tolstoy's and Robert's assumption is that it is morally desirable to love all people, even sinners.

However, why should I love everyone? Indeed, is it psychologically possible to love everyone, *in the sense of experiencing intense feelings of caring and concern for them?* Probably not for the vast majority of us, although we can love multitudes, if by love we mean treating them justly and coming to their assistance when they are in need and we have the capacity to help them. Moreover, even if it is desirable and possible to love multitudes of people, in the emotional sense of love, why should I love people who unjustly harm me or those close to me, or who harm any innocent person for that matter? The Christian response is that God has commanded us to do so. Many non-Christians who don't accept the authority of the New Testament feel otherwise.

Roberts illustrates humility, the second attitude conducive to forgiveness and hence to cultivating forgivingness, with the story about a robber, Moses, who later became a monk at Scetis.

> A brother at Scetis committed a fault. A council was called to which Abba Moses was invited, but he refused to go to it. Then the priest sent

someone to say to him, "Come, for everyone is waiting for you." So he got up and went. He took a leaking jug filled with water and carried it with him. The others came out to meet him and said to him, "What is this, Father?" The old man said to them, "My sins run out behind me, and I do not see them, and today I am coming to judge the errors of another." When they heard that, they said no more to the brother, but forgave him.[15]

Abba Moses is echoing the themes of the Lord's Prayer, which says that we will be forgiven only if we forgive others, and that we must not judge others lest we be judged. We should also not be eager to punish sinners by casting the first stone at them, since we too are sinners.

Abba Moses is inviting the council to see themselves as on the "same level" as this offender. In anger we judge others for having done wrong, so anger is undercut by the recognition that one is guilty of offenses similar to the offender's and this recognition is a reason for forgiving the other. This is why humility is closely allied with and supports forgiveness. One who is inclined to insist on the moral difference between himself and offender—a haughty or self-righteous person—will be unsusceptible to this consideration and more likely to remain angry.

The person who wants to nurture the virtue of forgivingness will always look upon offenders and himself with this attitude in mind.

Although I agree that in judging others we should be aware of our own moral weaknesses and of the innate moral weaknesses of all humans, which can make us more understanding and even merciful in judgment, I find Abba Moses' approach to be socially and morally dangerous, and even offensive. To advocate forgiving *all* offenders and *all* offenses because everyone commits *some* offenses blurs all distinctions between degrees of sin, evil, and crime.

Are all of us *equally* sinful or vicious? Is St. Paul as sinful as Hitler? Is the Dalai Lama, a man of compassion and moral virtue, as sinful as Pol Pot, the Khmer Rouge Cambodian dictator whose "killing fields" soaked up the blood of millions of innocents? Is Mother Teresa as sinful as the perpetrators of the Rwandan genocide? Is there to be no distinction between saints and sinners? Is there to be no distinction between one sin and another? Does the wife who insulted her husband verbally bear the same degree of moral guilt as her husband who beat her senseless in response? Is he as deserving of her love and forgiveness as she is of his?[16] This is not the view of Catholic moral theology, of Judaism, or of moral philosophy.

Shall we eliminate the judicial system because no human has a right to sit in judgment against another? What would be the social consequences of forgiving and loving rapists, muggers, embezzlers, murderers, and perpetrators of crimes against humanity?

Many Christians would respond to my objections by saying that to forgive someone does not preclude punishing them as a means of moral education or as a deterrent. Yet even as you incarcerate or punish an unrepentant, unremorseful sinner or criminal you can and should love him. Your love should be directed toward encouraging and supporting his spiritual rehabilitation. The devout Christian tries not to hate his enemy and struggles with the natural inclination to want to see his enemy suffer. The devout Christian also believes that, in the long run, an attitude of love for one's enemy will bring about his repentance and transformation into a better person, whereas hatred of him will serve no positive purpose. Forgiveness, in many Christian writings, is also advocated because it frees the forgiver from the self-destructive and self-corrosive emotions of hate, anger, and desire for revenge; this freedom is said to be spiritually edifying and therapeutically satisfying. The less bitterness, anger, and hostility you harbor against people, even those who hurt you deeply, the happier and more religiously pure you will be.

The emotionally daunting demands of radical Christian forgiveness are well illustrated in the life stories described by Arnold.[17] These people, who struggled mightily with anger and forgiveness, often vacillating between the two, felt that their forgiveness eventually triumphed over their anger and hatred. They had experienced intensely painful hurts, such as loss of a child at the hands of a murderer, infidelity of a spouse, physical, sexual, and psychological abuse by a parent, and betrayal by a trusted business partner. Not only did many of these people cease hating those who had hurt them, but they took active steps to develop compassion for their "enemy" and, when possible, to develop friendships with the perpetrators and assist them on the road to rehabilitation.

It seems to me that underlying the views of advocates of radical forgiveness, though not always explicitly stated, is the Christian doctrine of original sin. As a consequence of Adam's disobedience of God in the Garden of Eden, his nature was corrupted. This corruption was transmitted to all humans; we are all sinners from birth. Yet, notwithstanding our innate sinfulness, God loves us all and forgives our sins (or at least the sins of those who convert to Christianity). We should imitate Christ by loving and forgiving sinners too.

While a non-Christian may not agree that we are all equally sinful and guilty, he can still agree that moral humility is a virtue worth cultivating and that it can facilitate an attitude of forgiveness, or at least a strong caution against unreflective hatred of those who hurt us. Murphy's[18] view is that the purpose of moral humility should not be to lump everyone together as equally evil or to preclude all retribution to evildoers but rather

> to force . . . people to face honestly the question of why they have lived in such [a legally and morally correct] way. Is it . . . because their inner characters manifest true integrity and are thus morally superior to those of people whose behavior has been less exemplary? . . . Perhaps . . . their favored upbringing and social circumstances, or the fact that they have never been placed in situations where they have been similarly tempted, or their fear of being found out has had considerably more to do with their compliance with the rules of law and morality than they would like to admit. . . . the lessons of moral humility . . . should make all morally reflective persons pause and at least think twice about their hatreds and the courses of action on which these hatreds tempt them to embark.[19]

Some people seem to be more forgiving than others. Tangney and her associates studied individual differences in the propensity to forgive and personality and attitudinal correlates of such a propensity.[20] They compared the scores of 285 undergraduate students on a Multidimensional Forgiveness Inventory (MFI) with their scores on other personality variables. The MFI presents a series of everyday situations involving transgressions, which the respondents are instructed to imagine were perpetrated against them. For example:

> Imagine that your dentist misreads his own notes and pulls out the wrong tooth.
> Imagine that your cousin borrows a large sum of money from you to pay bills. The next day, you find out he spent the money on an expensive CD player.
> Imagine that on your way home from work, a driver runs a stop sign and totals your new car.
> Imagine that you find out that your best friend has been gossiping about you to mutual friends.

For each imagined situation, the students were asked four questions:

How hurt would you be?
How angry would you be?
How likely would you be to forgive him/her?
How long would it take you to forgive him/her?

The answer to the first three questions can range along a five-point scale, from "not at all" to "extremely" for the first two, and from "not at all" to "very likely" for the third. Answers to the fourth question range from "immediately," to "days," "weeks," "months," "years," and "never."

The researchers wanted to find out what emotional and intellectual qualities help nurture forgiveness and which qualities impede it. This information could then be used for practical ends such as to help foster a propensity to forgive in our children.

The students were scored on their propensity to forgive and their scores were compared with their scores on measures of their "moral emotional styles" of empathy, guilt, and shame. What they found, not surprisingly, was that there was a positive relationship between the propensity to forgive and to be empathetic. Empathy has always been considered one of the most important emotional skills and attitudes for "forgivingness," as we have already seen.

They also found that people who are forgiving of others tend to be more guilt-prone, whereas unforgiving people tend to be more shame-prone. Guilt-prone people, in general, tend to focus their self-criticism on a specific behavior of theirs, whereas shame-prone people tend to focus on their personhood as a whole.[21] How might people's tendency to feel ashamed of themselves be related to their unwillingness to forgive others for transgressions against them?

Tangney et al. suggest that shame-prone people find it difficult to forgive because they tend to project blame onto others and have high levels of anger. This makes it more difficult for them to forgive others than it is for guilt-prone people, who are more inclined to accept some of the responsibility for unpleasant interactions and are less easily angered by them.

Extrapolating from this study to the moral education of our children, if we value forgivingness as a character disposition, we should teach our children how to be empathetic, for example, by cultivating their ability to imagine the pain or pressures that another person is experiencing. Also, when they do something wrong we should not shame them globally—"You are a bad child"—but have them feel guilty about and assume responsibility for their specific misdeed. Telling a child that he is a bad person doesn't give him concrete guidance on how to improve himself. Despairing of doing so, he will resort to projecting blame onto others, and to becoming angry, which will make him less amenable to becoming a forgiving person. Probably the best way to socialize our children to be empathetic and forgiving is for us to model these attitudes and behaviors for them.[22]

Having looked at the essence of forgiveness, we will now consider in more depth what Judaism, Christianity, and moral philosophy teach about why and when to forgive those who have hurt us.

THREE

Why & When to Forgive

In the 1980s, a crime committed in New York City was widely publicized. Two men brutally raped a nun. But they didn't stop at rape. The assaulters also cut 27 crosses into her body with a nail file.

Notwithstanding the public outrage, the rapists could not be charged for rape and aggravated assault but only for lesser crimes for which they received relatively light sentences. This was so because the nun, claiming that she had no desire for revenge, refused to testify against the men. She hoped that her forgiving attitude would lead her attackers to become aware of and sensitive to the harm they had done.

Did the nun do what her Christian faith requires of Christian women who are raped and tortured? If you are a Christian woman, would you do the same if you were raped and tortured? If you are a Christian man and your wife, mother, sister, or daughter were a victim of such a crime, would you think that they, like the nun, should not press charges? Do you feel that what the nun did was unethical because, though she might have *personally* been able to forgive those who assaulted her, from the *societal* point of view she had no right to do so? Jacoby argues that

from a public perspective . . . this expression of religious compassion—
"private forgiveness" . . . is troubling. Had the victim testified, her assailants
would undoubtedly have received much longer prison terms. . . . As
the sentence stands, one of the rapists could be released from prison in
only five years. This, of course, is likely to pose a new danger to the
community.

Beyond the question of individual deterrence, though, there is [also] the matter of justice and retribution. It simply defies commonly understood standards of decency and justice that men who raped and tortured a woman for an hour-and-a-half—with nail files, broomsticks, crucifixes, candles—should receive anything less than the maximum sentences prescribed by law for the crimes they actually committed. . . . the victim herself was responsible, by virtue of her refusal to testify, for the relatively light penalty meted out to her attackers.[1]

As a contrast to the nun's perspective, let us consider a second-century rabbinic text from the Mishnah.[2] The Hebrew Bible prescribes capital punishment for certain sins and crimes, such as adultery and murder. According to the rabbinic interpretation of biblical law, in order for the death penalty to be inflicted, an elaborate set of due process procedures had to be implemented, one of which was the requirement that there were two direct eyewitnesses to the crime. Hearsay or circumstantial or indirect evidence of any sort was not acceptable. The text describes what the Jewish court would say to witnesses who came to testify against the accused in a capital case, before they were permitted to officially give their testimony.

How do they admonish witnesses in capital cases?
They would bring them in and admonish them [as follows]: "Perhaps it is your intention to give testimony (1) on the basis of supposition, (2) hearsay, or (3) of what one witness has told another;
You should know that the laws governing a trial for property cases are different from the laws governing a trial for capital cases.
In the case of a trial for property cases, a person pays money and achieves atonement for himself. In capital cases [the accused's] blood and the blood of all those who were destined to be born from him [who was wrongfully convicted] are held against him [who testifies falsely] to the end of time."[3]

This first part of the admonition is meant to make witnesses fully aware of the solemnity of their responsibility and the grave implications of their testimony. To be the cause of putting someone to death wrongfully is akin to murder. And to kill a person unjustly is also to deprive him or her and the world of the potential for creating new lives, which inheres in every individual.
The Mishnah continues:

For so we find in the case of Cain who slew his brother, as it is said, "The bloods of your brother cry" (Gen. 4:10). It does not say, "The blood of your brother," but, "The bloods of your brother"—his blood and the blood of all those who were destined to be born from him.

Here the Mishnaic sage is buttressing his point with a creative interpretation of the Hebrew word for *the blood of,* which could be either *dam,* which is the singular, or *dmay,* which is the plural. The original Hebrew text uses the plural form, *dmay.* Why? In order to teach us that in murdering one person, we really murder many.

The Mishnah goes on to reflect on an interesting feature of the biblical account of the creation of humankind in contrast to the creation of the animal world. In Genesis 1, God creates animals in bulk, so to speak, entire species at once. However, in Genesis 2, God creates Adam, one single human being, (and later adds Eve), who eventually generates all of mankind. Why this difference in approach? Or to put it a little differently, what would have been the implications for the world if Adam had died or been killed by an animal? It would have been the end of mankind. The death of a single person would have been equivalent to the death of all.

In light of these reflections, the Mishnah says that the witnesses are further told:

Therefore man was created alone, to teach you that whoever destroys a
single soul is deemed by Scripture as if he had destroyed a whole world.
And whoever saves a single soul is deemed by Scripture as if he had saved
a whole world.

But these solemn and frightening admonitions to the witnesses can have adverse consequences as well, as they might deter them from coming forth with their testimony lest they bear the responsibility for causing wrongful death by giving tainted testimony, even if inadvertently or unconsciously. The judges now have to emphasize the other side of the moral coin, how essential it is for justice and for the moral social order that those who have witnessed crimes testify against the perpetrators of them.

The Mishnah continues:

Now perhaps you [witnesses] would like now to say, "What business have
we got with this trouble?"

But it already has been written, "He being a witness, whether he has seen
or known, if he does not speak it, then he shall bear his iniquity"
(Lev. 5:1).
And perhaps you might want to claim, "What business is it of ours to
convict this man of a capital crime?"
But has it not already been said, "When the wicked perish there is rejoicing"
(Prov. 11:10).

Here the judges tell the witnesses that not to testify when you have observed a crime is itself a sin. And lest you feel that you prefer the sin of "not
testifying" to a presumed "sin" of bringing about the death of a human being—although a criminal—know that Proverbs teaches that to destroy the
wicked is a cause for joy rather than for guilt.

The rabbinic view in this Mishnaic text is clearly at odds with the raped
nun's interpretation and understanding of the New Testament teaching that
one must forgive sinners and turn the other cheek, even if they have not
repented or shown remorse for their sin. Of course, not all Christian theologians would argue that the nun was acting properly from a Christian perspective by not testifying against her assailants, and they would disagree with
her interpretation of Christian teachings on forgiveness. After all, Christian
societies had courts which punished criminals. They didn't just forgive and
pardon them. However, as we have seen, there is a strong strain in Christian
teaching that emphasizes forgiveness of even unrepentant or at least not-yet-
repentant sinners, which could lead to laxity in justice.

In Judaism there are many teachings about the importance of *midat ha-
rahamim* (the measure of compassion or mercy), when judging people, especially in one's private, interpersonal relationships. Moreover, many Mishnaic
sages, though accepting the right in principle of a court to sentence a duly
convicted sinner or criminal to death, preferred to abolish capital punishment
in practice.

Notwithstanding the existence of a range of opinions within both Judaism
and Christianity as to how and when to temper justice with mercy, and when
and whom to forgive, and under what circumstances to do so, Judaism overall
is more concerned with guaranteeing justice than with forgiving incorrigible
sinners, whereas Christianity, at least in its foundational prayer and creeds, if
not in its actions, talks more of forgiveness as an act of grace, given even to
the undeserving and not-yet-repentant, than of justice.

The theologian L. Gregory Jones, in his analysis of forgiveness from his
particular Christian perspective, illustrates with the following example the

lengths to which he believes Christians should love their enemies and forgive them.

A Turkish officer raided and looted an Armenian home. He killed the aged parents and gave the daughters to the soldiers, keeping the eldest daughter for himself. Some time later she escaped and trained as a nurse. As time passed, she found herself nursing in a ward of Turkish officers. One night, by the light of a lantern, she saw the face of this officer. He was so gravely ill that without exceptional nursing he would die. The days passed, and he recovered. One day, the doctor stood by the bed with her and said to him, "But for her devotion to you, you would be dead." He looked at her and said, "We have met before, haven't we?" "Yes," she said, "we have met before." "Why didn't you kill me?" he asked. She replied, "I am a follower of him who said 'Love your enemies.' "[4]

I refer to this version of Christian forgiveness as *radical forgiveness.*
Jones considers this a "shining example" of Christian piety.

Many non-Christians (and Christians as well) would not consider the nurse's behavior to be noble or admirable. They might agree that she should have nursed the Turkish officer as she did, but not for the reason that she did. Her professional responsibilities as a nurse might override her moral right to allow him to die by refusing to administer to him. Why, however, is it noble to love and take care of evil people?

Some Jews view Christian preaching of radical forgiveness of enemies and of the wicked as somewhat hypocritical. For many centuries, Christians persecuted and murdered Jews in the name of Christian faith. They never forgave the Jewish nation for the participation of a few Jews in the arrest and handing over of Jesus to Pilate, who had him crucified, and for the adamant refusal of Jews to believe that Jesus was the Messiah, and later, that he was God incarnate.

Moreover, many Christians who glibly preach forgiveness of enemies are no less prone to anger and resentment than are non-Christians.

Some time ago a Christian biblical scholar, upon learning that I was researching the topic of forgiveness and that I was a Jew with strong connections to Israel, asked me if I didn't think it was about time for the Israelis to forgive and forget the atrocities perpetrated against them by Palestinian terrorists. I asked him whether he had ever held in his arms the bloody body parts of his dead child killed by a grenade thrown into a schoolroom by a Palestinian terrorist.[5] What amazed me, moreover, was that but a few minutes after his "preaching of forgiveness," when the conversation had shifted to mundane academic matters, he expressed deep hurt and lingering resentment toward a colleague who had failed, many years before, to give him what he felt was due credit for an article he had written. I don't think he was even aware of the incongruity between his own inability to forgive a relatively minor offense to his ego some decade or so ago, and his preaching to victims of terror that they should forgive and forget.

Many Jews also see in Jones's and other Christians' advocacy of radical forgiveness a violation of justice. They view it as presumptuously arrogant when someone who is not the victim proclaims that he or she forgives an offender. Only the victim herself has the moral right to forgive an offense against her, which makes murder a crime that no human can forgive, since the victim is dead.[6]

In August of 1997 the pastor at a church service in Martha's Vineyard held up a picture of Timothy McVeigh, the man who bombed the federal building in Oklahoma City, killing 168 people, wounding hundreds more, and emotionally traumatizing thousands. " 'I invite you to look at . . . Timothy McVeigh and then forgive him,' " the Reverend . . . said in his sermon. 'I have, and I ask you to do so . . . we as Christians are asked to do so.' "

What does this request mean?

Is the pastor saying that McVeigh be released from prison?

Is he saying that if McVeigh had been a multimillionare (which he wasn't) the families of the victims should not sue him for civil damages?

Is he saying that the widows and orphans and bereaved parents of the 168 dead victims, and the amputees and paralyzed and blinded and brain-damaged among the wounded should not be angry or resentful?

Is he saying that the families impoverished by the loss of their breadwinner should love McVeigh?

Is he saying that the victims who, according to his Christian belief, are in heaven and looking down on the ongoing suffering of their loved ones should nevertheless forgive McVeigh?

Is he saying that the people in the church, and he himself, who though emotionally hurt and morally offended by the bombing, should not be angry or resentful toward McVeigh?

Is he saying to his congregants that it will make them feel better if they overcome their anger, and that this is healthy, physically or psychologically? (If so, hasn't he demeaned forgiveness to narcissistic self-help at the expense of moral indignation and pain at evil?)

Perhaps the pastor is saying all of the above, or perhaps only some. He doesn't make it clear to his congregants what he means when he asks fellow Christians to forgive. The call to radical forgiveness often uses the phrases "forgive your enemy" and "love your enemy" without clarifying precisely what is meant by them, why one should follow these commands, or how to get oneself to love and forgive those whom one naturally reviles and hates.

Another objection to radical forgiveness and love of one's enemies, especially unrepentant ones, is that it can erode an offender's sense of moral responsibility. Moreover, it can be psychologically *unhealthy* for some victims. The victim will continue to feel demeaned by the injury she suffered, and by the offender. She might feel guilty for not forgiving, and though uttering the words "I forgive you," she knows that she is untrue to what she really feels. It puts her in the emotionally and morally compromising position of saying one thing while feeling another—an absence of inner integrity.[7]

What are the theological and psychological assumptions behind Christian calls for radical forgiveness and love of enemies? They seem to be based upon or influenced by the following premises:

1) Human beings are created in the "image of God."

2) The "image of God" confers upon humans a special status, dignity, and irrevocable value, so that no matter how evil an act or set of acts a person might perform, he never loses the fundamental, divinely conferred, human dignity with which he was born (created).

3) People are born corrupted with sin. Yet this state of sinfulness is removed by the sufferings and death of Christ on behalf of mankind, for those who believe Christian doctrine. Christ was willing to suffer so as to bring about the atonement and forgiveness of believers in him.

4) We are to imitate Christ. Just as Christ was willing to absorb suffering and pain in order that sinful mankind be forgiven, (or at least, those sinners who believed in him), so too must humans be willing to absorb pain and injury perpetrated by offenders and forgive them. This forgiveness does not necessarily preclude bringing them to justice and punishing them, although a victim who forgoes her right to have offenders punished is particularly noble and spiritually heroic.

5) God has created the world and mankind with the hope that all will ultimately be reconciled with all. We have to do our share in bringing about this redemptive state of love and conciliation by reconciling with others, even as we live in an unredeemed, hate-filled world of sin and corruption.

6) An important Christian argument for forgiving sinners *who do not repent,
   or have not yet, repented* is that when they see Christian love expressed
   in forgiveness freely given, this will induce them to repent. A similar
   claim is made for the use of non-violence in resistance to evil. The
   redneck sheriff who is forgiven by the blacks whom he beats, or who
   hears them declare their love for him as he brutally strikes them, will be
   so moved by their non-violence, their love, and their forgiveness that he
   will eventually realize how evil he has been, repent, and change his ways.[8]

In this vein, the Christian philosopher Jean Hampton says that it is precisely when "*moral* hatred" is justifiable, for example, when the offender hasn't
repented, apologized, or acknowledged that he did something wrong that the
"gift" of forgiving should come into play.

The central notion she develops is that we should not judge people in their
totality on the basis of the specific injuries they caused us. There is more to
most offenders than just their being offenders. Their humanity is broader
than their evil acts, and so to forgive is to allow this focused awareness of
their general humanity to determine how you will feel about and relate to
them. If to continue your relationship with them is not dangerous, then
reconciliation and forgiveness is called for. Among the benefits of such a
forgiving attitude, she claims, is that by affirming the human dignity of the
offender, notwithstanding his offense and his lack of apparent remorse, you
will increase the chance that he will eventually change his ways for the better.
She says that many offenders have such low self-esteem that they are in despair
of possibilities for self-transformation. When they see that their victims, and
society at large, consider them to be of fundamental worth, it will help them
overcome their despair and induce self-change.[9]

This claim, which doesn't seem to be confirmed by *most* human experience
with evil, needs to be studied empirically (as do all religious or other claims
about human behavior) to see how frequently and under what conditions it
might be true, if it is to be a basis for advocating forgiveness in the absence
of repentance by the offender.

There are significant differences between rabbinic Judaism and these Christian views. Rabbinic Judaism, like Christianity, considers humans to be unique
among all living things, in that they are created in the "image of God."[10] The
sages of the rabbinic period, however, express little respect, love, or tolerance
for malicious, chronic, unrepentant evildoers, whether or not they retain their
"divine image." In the rabbinic view, when one reaches the age of maturity
and responsibility, one has to *earn* the respect and love of others and of God

on the basis of how one leads one's life. There are limits to how patient and forbearing one must be in dealing with the wicked. If the evildoer persists in his evil deeds and refuses to repent, he will be held accountable and not be forgiven for his sins, no matter how ardent his belief or trust and faith in God might be.

Rabbinic Judaism does not assume that we are born inherently evil, corrupted with sin even before we reach the maturity of moral responsibility. However, it assumes that we do have a strong propensity to violate God's expectations of us—an "evil inclination" or "evil impulse" (*yetzer hara*). We can easily become arrogant, lustful, envious, angry, slothful, greedy, gluttonous, and more, and may rebel against God and injure others if we fail to control our evil impulses. We are, however, empowered to overcome those impulses. The burden of responsibility is on us. A life of Torah study and performance of the commandments is one of the more effective means of overcoming the *yetzer hara*.

Although we are to imitate God, who is slow to wrath, forbearing, and merciful, there is no doctrine that God suffered in order to atone for our sins, so there is no expectation that we should suffer repeated insult and injury and forgive those who injure us. We have to imitate God, and God, for the most part, punishes unrepentant sinners and forgives repentant ones.

Another difference between Christianity and rabbinic Judaism in their assumptions about human nature is that Christianity views man as so intrinsically "fallen" and flawed that he is highly dependent on divine mercy, grace, and forgiveness to raise him from the morass of his sinfulness. He can rarely "save" himself by his own initiative. Rabbinic Judaism tends to be more optimistic about man's ability to engineer his own self-improvement. This in turn places more responsibility on him to do so, and more accountability when he fails to do so. Therefore repentance is emphasized as a precondition for forgiveness, in both the human–divine relationship and in interpersonal relationships.

Some of the differences between rabbinic Judaism and Christianity are ones of emphasis rather than of the absolute presence or absence of a particular concept or value. Repentance and justice *are* values in Christianity, just as forgiveness *is* a value in rabbinic Judaism. But the former are emphasized more in rabbinic Judaism and the latter in certain Christian denominations. The different emphases can have important psychological, behavioral, and ethical consequences for the adherents of the respective faiths.

There are many agnostics or atheists in our society who do not believe that we are commanded by God to forgive, or that we are all created in a divine image and hence deserve to be loved even when we do evil. To the extent that they too value forgiveness, their rationales for it are not based upon religious premises but upon appeals to reason and to personal or group interests. We will now consider some non-theological grounds for interpersonal forgiveness.

. . .

To object to *radical forgiveness* is by no means to object to the value of forgiveness and of reconciliation in many contexts. There are many good reasons to forgive, or to at least dissipate one's anger, *when it is either morally or psychologically desirable to do so.*

When we think about forgiveness, it is useful to distinguish between three different emotions.

1) Forgiving, as reduction or dissipation of anger and resentment toward an offender.
2) Forgiving, as having compassion on an offender.
3) Forgiving, as loving an offender.

Even when an offender has expressed remorse and fully repented which includes reparations for the harm or damage that he caused it is very difficult for a victim to give up her anger against him and to have compassion for him. If all of us learned how to do this, the world would be an immeasurably better place. Some of us might be able to go a step beyond having compassion for the *repentant* sinner, and even come to love him as well.

However, to *demand* of a victim that she forgive the *unrepentant sinner* who has harmed her is considered by many non-Christians to be morally wrong. It can also be emotionally damaging to her. If, upon reflection, the victim concludes that the offender was, for one reason or another, not morally responsible for the injuries he caused, then anger reduction, compassion for him, and even love of him, are possible and realistic, although not easy. However, if the victim does for some reason see fit to exonerate the perpetrator, she is not really forgiving him in the moral sense of the term, since in the absence of culpability there is nothing to forgive.

We may forgo our anger against an offender and develop compassion for him if we believe that he is mentally ill to the point that he was unable to control his violent or aggressive behavior. Often we read of apparently horrific crimes in which a man or woman "murdered" his or her entire family, including infants and children. Our anger is aroused, and we want justice and punishment for the vicious criminal. Later, however, we find out that the killer had been suffering from a deep depression. In his pathological state of mind, life was a horror chamber of perpetual emotional or physical torture. When he looked upon his wife and children and ruminated upon the sufferings they were destined to endure, he couldn't bear to contemplate the dark future that awaited them. Out of compassion, he decided to help them escape, by locking them in a car in his garage and leaving the motor running. He had intended to die with them but by chance survived.

On the assumption that sometimes a profound depression can distort rational and emotional processes to this degree, neither the law nor logic holds the killer morally responsible for what he did. Relatives of the victims will experience sorrow and pain at the losses, perhaps even compassion for the killer, but little or no anger.

As we noted earlier, an effective way to avoid or dissipate anger against an offender, no matter how vicious he has been, is to adopt the philosophical stance of the strict determinist who denies that humans have free will. If everything a person does is a result of internal and external forces, whether recent or distant, over which he has no control, then why hate him, be angry at him, or hold him responsible for his deeds? We may have to incarcerate him to protect ourselves, or punish him so as to instill fear, guilt, or shame to deter him from committing additional offenses, but we needn't resent him.

Our legal and moral value systems have difficulty with a determinist position; our laws and morality are premised on the assumption that we are free, autonomous moral agents. However, they constantly grapple with determinism when they try to assess "degrees" of culpability acknowledging that we aren't as "free" as we might like to believe. As many judges and jurists have noted, while we should not exonerate young criminals because they were raised in love-deprived, abusive, and impoverished environments, we—a society that could do more than it does to help these youths—are partially to blame and bear some responsibility for what these offenders have done. How angry should I be at a sixteen-year-old, cocaine-addicted murderer who never experienced love, was never taught self-control or moral values, and was first introduced to the drug at the age of eleven? When I think of him in those terms, my anger might dissipate, my compassion might be aroused, and I might be able to imagine the possibility that he too could have been or might yet be entitled to my love.

Ironically, an atheist who is a strict determinist might find it easier to radically forgive the vicious, unrepentant sinner than would the devout Christian who believes in free will. Strictly speaking, the determinist atheist is not "forgiving" the sinner because he doesn't blame him in the first place, but the effects of his determinist attitude on his feelings toward the offender, on his judgment of him, and on the nature and extent of the punishment he might impose, can be quite similar to the radical demands that some Christians make of victims.

Another reason to forgive is the repentance of the offender. There are several arguments for this, and here Judaism maintains that a victim is *obligated* to forgive the offender if he has sincerely and fully repented. As we shall see in our discussion of repentance, the penitent offender can be considered to be, in effect, a different person from who he was when he committed the offense. Why then continue to be angry and resentful toward him, and to withhold from him the compassion you would readily render to one who has not harmed you or others?

One justification for moral hatred or resentment and punishment of an offender is that he has, by his offense, *implicitly* declared that he does not accept the moral standards of society, religious or secular, and that he is contemptuous of his victim, who he considers to be inferior to him. Consequently, another argument for forgiving the offender who repents is that he is repudiating these implications of his offensive behavior. He is affirming that what he did was wrong, that he wants to repair—to the extent that he can—whatever damage he did, and that he respects you and your right not to be hurt by him. In effect, then, by sincerely repenting, he has on his own initiative brought about the outcomes that were to have been served by retribution, and eliminated the grounds for your resentment of him (Murphy and Hampton 1988, 26).

Two other reasons to forgive a repentant sinner are that it will contribute to harmony and reconciliation in society and will also encourage the ex-sinner not to sin again.

If we acknowledge that none of us is perfect, we might also decide to forgive some offenders who haven't repented. We all commit some offenses. Just as we would want those whom we hurt, deliberately or through negligence or insensitivity, to give us another chance, so too should we be willing to forgive others who have hurt us. This is especially important for people who are in close relationships with us and with whom we continue to live after they have hurt us. Do we really want to be angry and resentful for a long time at the parents, spouses, and children whom, notwithstanding the pain that they have caused us, we still love and who still love us? If we do not learn how to dissipate our anger and forgive offenses, we will be unable to make room in our hearts for the mutual intimacy, tenderness, caring, and sharing that are so essential to our happiness.[11]

To forgive loved ones does not mean that you should never tell them how much they have hurt you. On the contrary, if you really love them, you want them to be good, and if you don't apprise them sensitively of the wrong they did, they will not be able to become better. We should chastise our loved ones even as we forgive them.

Forgiving can sometimes be therapeutic. If your anger and resentment are debilitating to you, and if there is no way you can assuage them by bringing the offender to justice, it is in your own self-interest to remove them. Certain forgiveness strategies can be helpful, as we shall later see. Many people feel a deep sense of relief when a long-standing anger is dissipated and they are free at last from the perpetrator's control over their emotions. When you hold on to an anger that consumes you without satisfying you in any way, you are, in effect, allowing the individual who hurt you to injure you continuously. Often, anger and a desire for revenge or for justice so dominate a victim's consciousness that they prevent her from pursuing a satisfying and constructive life. To dissipate anger and hatred through forgiveness allows you to resume an emotionally healthier life.

In these therapeutic uses of forgiveness, you are not necessarily forgiving the offender in a *moral* sense, but are using a forgiveness strategy to help you overcome anger that is detrimental to your well-being and to that of others whom your anger affects adversely, such as close family members. There are, of course, many strategies for dissipating anger—not all of which involve forgiveness—and they may serve the therapeutic purposes equally well.[12]

In his novel *Walden Two,* the psychologist B. F. Skinner has the protagonist, Frazier, who is teaching emotional management skills to children, explain how and why he chose some of the techniques he uses for anger control.

I began by studying the great works on morals and ethics . . . looking for any and every method of shaping human behavior by imparting techniques of self-control. Some techniques were obvious enough, for they had marked turning points in human history. "Love your enemies" is one example—a psychological invention for easing the lot of oppressed people. The severest trial of oppression is the constant rage which one suffers at the thought of the oppressor. What Jesus discovered was how to avoid these inner devastations. His technique was to practice the opposite emotion. If a man can succeed in "loving his enemies" and "taking no thought for the morrow" he will no longer be assailed by hatred of the oppressor or rage at the loss of his freedom and possessions. He may not get his freedom or his possessions back, but he's less miserable. It's a difficult lesson. It comes late in our program (pp. 105–6).

I think that Jesus, in preaching "love your enemies," was imparting a spiritual message rather than a psychological self-help one. However, the psychological process Frazier describes can be an additional effect of forgiving enemies and loving them. Of course, the oppressed might also be able to assuage some of their inner rage by imagining the punishments that their oppressors will endure in Hell, a Christian concept that seems antithetical to the teaching that one should love one's enemies.[13]

Several years ago, I met a spiritually beautiful woman, compassionate and loving. When I mentioned my interest in forgiveness, she shared with me her views about Christian love. These provide an additional rationale for loving and forgiving those who hurt us and others.

> One's capacity and ability to love, understand, and console another is not dependent upon the degree to which one's love is returned. If I could only love another human being to the degree that they returned my love, I would probably have given up loving people a long time ago. Jesus also understood this kind of love. He said if someone borrows your shirt, do not expect it to be returned (and he went further and said, "Give him your coat as well"). This may sound like a "one-way" street—one person continually trying to understand and love others and often receiving little or nothing in return. Ah, but the "reward" is not in receiving another's "reciprocity"—the "reward" is in the joy of loving itself.[14]

Another point that she made was that much of our disappointment in others results from unrealistic expectations. If we were to realize and accept that people often hurt us because of their weaknesses, insecurities, and fears, it would be easier to forgive and love them.

This woman believes, and has personally experienced, that being loving, compassionate, and forgiving, even to those who hurt us, is inherently pleasurable and joy-creating. Her argument is not explicitly theological or moral, but psychological and therapeutic, although there is a Christian value system underlying it.

I reacted ambivalently to my friend's words. On the one hand, I was moved and inspired by them. They spoke to sorrow and hurts that I have suffered. I have tried, sometimes successfully, to adopt her values, and have found them useful in assuaging some of my own sadness and pain at unrealized expectations. I am privileged to know this woman whose love and compassion are expressed not only in words but in the many good deeds she does. I pray for a world inhabited by the likes of her—giving, loving, forgiving souls. I have deep respect and admiration for the love and compassion instilled by certain Christian teachings.

On the other hand, I wonder whether her effusive outpourings of love and understanding for human frailty and wrongdoing will help "repair" our broken world. I fear that such a perspective might retard the ethical and moral improvement of people by being too understanding, too forgiving, too excusing of the wrongs that we do to one another.

Another reason for forgiving is that the offender who hurt us might have done so out of a good motive, even though what he said or did was misguided. The case of the depressed killer is an extreme example, but many common, non-pathological examples can be given, especially those in which parents (mis)treat children whose inner worlds they often do not understand. I was amazed to learn of some of the resentments that my children feel toward me for certain things I did out of misguided love and concern for them, compounded by total lack of awareness of "where they were at" at critical times in their childhood years. I hope they will forgive me for these offenses.[15]

When some humiliation that an offender has experienced has humbled him, or when, even in the absence of true remorse for what he has done, he "grovels in the dust," begging mercy and forgiveness from us, we might be inclined to forgive. One reason that we want to punish him is that he has treated us as less worthy than himself; now that he is humbled, there is no need to be retributive. Similarly, when an offender has been broken by extreme suffering, our pity for him overcomes our anger, and we see no point in punishing him. We may feel that "he is getting what he deserves," even if not because of any action of ours against him.

Sometimes we also forgive people who offend us because we remember the love we once had for them or the good that they did in the past. This is often the reason that we are willing to forgive family members or friends who have hurt us.[16] We shouldn't judge people with whom we are close by only one or a few of their deeds. We need to take a broader perspective, looking at their total relationship with us. In balance, the good they have done for us might outweigh the wrongs we have suffered.

Forgiveness prompted by the recollection of past good deeds is ascribed by the prophet Jeremiah to God, who had punished the ten tribes of Israel (symbolized by Ephraim) by exiling them from the Holy Land. When he saw the depths of Ephraim's suffering and recalled Israel's love and devotion to

him in the early phase of their covenantal relationship (for which both father–
son and husband–wife metaphors are used), his compassion and mercy were
aroused. He also saw that Ephraim (Israel) was remorseful for his (her) sins
although he (she) found it difficult to break away from them on his (her)
own initiative.

> Thus says the Lord:
> "A voice is heard in Ramah,
> Lamentation and bitter weeping.
> Rachel is weeping for her children;
> She refuses to be comforted for her children
> Because they are no more."
> Thus says the Lord:
> "Keep your voice from weeping,
> And your eyes from tears; . . .
> There is hope for your future," says the Lord:
> "Your children shall come back to their own country."
> Indeed I heard Ephraim pleading . . .
> "Bring me back, let me come back,
> For you are the Lord my God.
> For after I had turned away I had repented . . .
> I was ashamed, and I was dismayed
> Because I bore the disgrace of my youth."
> "Is Ephraim my dear son?
> Is he the child I delight in?
> As often as I speak against him,
> I still remember him,
> Therefore I am deeply moved for him;
> I will surely have mercy on him,"
> Says the Lord . . .

The days are surely coming, says the Lord, when I will make a new
covenant with the house of Israel and the house of Judah. It will not be
like the covenant that I made with their ancestors when I took them by
the hand to bring them out of the land of Egypt—a covenant that they
broke, though I was their husband, says the Lord. But this is the covenant
that I will make with the house of Israel. . . . I will put my law within them,
and I will write it on their hearts; and I will be their God, and they shall
be my people. . . . I will forgive their iniquity, and remember their sin no
more." (Jer. 31)

Earlier, even as God warned Israel of his intent to punish her for her infidelity, he foreshadows the forgiveness that will eventually be granted in part because of his appreciation of her self-sacrificial devotion to and her trust in him in the wilderness.

> I remember the devotion of your youth,
> Your love as a bride.
> How you followed me in the wilderness,
>   In a land not sown.
> Israel was holy to the Lord, the first fruits of His harvest. (Jer. 2:2–3)

On the other hand, his recollection of the intensity of their early love cuts both ways, since it deepens his disappointment in her.

> Can a girl forget her ornaments,
> Or a bride her attire?
> Yet my people have forgotten me,
> Days without number. (Jer. 2:32)

Jeremiah's (and God's) grappling with the clash between disappointment and hope, anger and mercy, punishment and forgiveness, mirrors so much of human experience. These biblical passages have inspired many "soul songs" which it is customary for some Jews to sing around the Sabbath table. They movingly express the yearning for reconciliation between man and God, and, by extension, between one person and another.

· · ·

Christian theologians are often caught in a bind about what should be their attitude toward forgiving the unrepentant sinner because there are contradictory teachings on this in the New Testament. Many biblical scholars argue that the doctrine of radical forgiveness is not what Jesus and the New Testament had in mind in his teachings about loving enemies and forgiving sinners. Moreover, what Jesus did have in mind was not unique to him but was preceded by or parallel to some post–Hebrew Bible Jewish teachings of the pre- and early Christian period. Let us trace the development of the notions of divine and human forgiveness in the Hebrew Bible, intertestamental literature, and the New Testament.

David Reimer[17] points out that a majority of Christians, theologians, clergy, and laypersons make three assumptions, namely, "Forgiveness is central to Christianity; the biblical witness on forgiveness is united [i.e., both the Hebrew Bible and the New Testament are in accord in their teachings on interpersonal forgiveness; and]; . . . Jesus develops the concept in a unique way by his actions and his teachings . . . breaking away from Jewish understandings . . . [and] lifting the idea of forgiveness to new heights."

Reimer challenges each of these assumptions.

The writings of St. Paul are the earliest in the Christian canon. It is surprising therefore that Paul's writings and Pauline traditions rarely refer to interpersonal *forgiveness*. Paul does refer to *love* as being patient, not quick to take offense, and keeping no score of wrongs (1 Cor. 13:4–8), characteristics closely related to forgiving offenses. Overall though, asks Reimer, "If forgiveness is so central to Christianity, why must we work so hard to find it discussed by St. Paul whose influence on formative Christianity can hardly be denied?" (p. 268).

In contrast with the Pauline writings, the synoptic gospels (Matthew, Mark, and Luke) frequently mention and discuss forgiveness.

In the Lord's Prayer, Jesus says, "And forgive us our debts, as we also have forgiven our debtors" (Matt. 6:12), or in Luke's version, "And forgive us our sins, for we ourselves forgive everyone indebted to us" (Luke 11:4). This suggests that God will forgive us if we forgive others, implying that if we don't forgive others, he won't forgive us. It isn't clear if God expects us to forgive others who have hurt us even if they have not apologized or repented.

In the context of teachings about how members of the Christian community should relate to one another (and not necessarily referring to people in general), Peter asked Jesus, "Lord, if another member of the church[18] sins against me, how often should I forgive? As many as seven times?" Jesus said to him, "Not seven times, but I tell you, seventy-seven times" (Matt. 18:21–22). This seems to suggest that a Christian should forgive one who offends him even if the offender repeats the offense numerous times or, in effect, has not repented.

However, another view is expressed a few verses earlier.

If another member of the church sins against you, go and point out the fault when the two of you are alone. If the member listens to you, you have regained that one. But if you are not listened to, take one or two others along with you, so that every word may be confirmed by the evidence of two or three witnesses. If the member refuses to listen to them, tell it to the church; and if the offender refuses to listen even to the church, let such as one be to you as a Gentile and a tax collector. (Matt. 18:15–17)[19]

In other words, if the Christian offender does not accept rebuke, you can exclude him from the community and presumably not forgive him for his sins against you.

The concluding verse of the chapter suggests that Christian forgiveness (whether pre- or post-repentance) is to be directed at fellow Christians. Jesus teaches, with the parable of the unforgiving slave, that God will punish the unforgiving Christian. In the parable, a king who had learned that his slave owed him a substantial sum of money had pity on the slave and forgave him the debt. However, that same slave showed no pity on another slave who owed him less than he had owed the king. Seeing that the forgiven slave showed no forgiveness to another, the king in his anger had him tortured until he paid the original debt in full. Jesus concluded, "So my heavenly Father will also do to every one of you, if you do not forgive your brother or sister from your heart"(Matt. 18:35). ("Brother or sister," in the context of the chapter, refers to members of the Christian community.)

There are many passages in the gospels in which Jesus is described as angry and unforgiving toward those who do not believe in him, such as the Pharisees. For example, all of Matthew Chapter 23 is a vituperative fulmination against the Jewish scribes and Pharisees to whom Jesus says "You snakes, you brood of vipers! How can you escape being sentenced to Hell?" (Matt. 23:33). Can this Jesus be reconciled with the Jesus who preached,

> You have heard that it was said, "An eye for eye and a tooth for tooth." But I say to you: Do not resist an evildoer. But if someone strikes you on the right cheek, turn the other also. . . . You have heard that it was said, "You shall love your neighbor and hate your enemy." But I say to you: Love your enemies and pray for those who persecute you, so that you may be children of your Father in heaven; for he makes his sun rise on the evil and on the good. . . . For if you love those who love you, what reward do you have? Do not even the tax collectors do the same? . . . Be perfect, therefore, as your heavenly father is perfect. (Matt. 5:38–39, 43–46, 48)

There is a long history of New Testament interpretation and Christian theology that tries to synthesize and harmonize the contradictory teachings about forgiveness and love and the incompatibilities between what Jesus preaches and what he practices. Often they ignore the plain sense of the texts and their historical and social contexts. The gospels and the other books of the New Testament include traditions from multiple sources that reflect different points of view about what Jesus taught and felt, and what the authors of these books themselves believed to be Christian values. Perhaps the most straightforward and honest approach is that of the Christian philosopher Jean Hampton:

> How do we reconcile Jesus' retributive-sounding anger with . . . his insistence on loving one's enemies and his encouragement of forgiveness? Perhaps we cannot. Perhaps Jesus' teachings are informed by the claims both of love and of justice, the latter prompting an anger which he cannot deny but which he is afraid to recommend or approve because it violates what love requires.
>
> And perhaps Jesus' dilemma is also our dilemma: even though we value and encourage love towards our fellow human beings, prompting us to forgive them when they wrong us, we also seem to respect the idea that the guilty deserve to pay in pain for the wrongs they cause others, a thought generally encased in an anger that drives out love. There does not seem to be any easy way to reconcile these two responses to wrongdoing, nor is it easy to give either response up. Yet they coexist uneasily within us.[20]

A propos of Jesus' threat that Pharisees would be consigned to Hell, Jones, (p. 255), who wants to reconcile the doctrine of Hell with the doctrine of forgiveness, cites 1 Cor. 5:1–5. Paul has heard that a member of the community of Christians is living with his father's wife, a grave sexual sin. He instructs the community to "hand this man over to Satan for the destruction of the flesh, so that his spirit may be saved in the day of the Lord."

Jesus, according to Jones, would consign his opponents to Hell as an act of love, in the hope that they would ultimately experience forgiveness and reconciliation.

Whatever the theological logic of such a doctrine, it carried within it a seed of evil. The idea that punishment of the body, whether in Hell or in Purgatory,[21] purges the soul was at times used by Christians to justify the torturing of humans—Christian sinners, Jews, and others—*in the here and now*. Indeed, if by torturing their bodies you could induce them to confess their sins and repent, you were actually acting out of love.

Many an abusive parent makes the same claim as did the Church. A father claims to beat his child "for his own good" because he loves him so much. It is true that we often do need to inflict pain and punishment on those who need to be corrected and that we do so out of concern for their betterment. There is a fine line, however, between justifiable and educative punishment and chastisement, and overly harsh, abusive, and demeaning punishment, which turns our victimized children into worse rather than better adults.

Theologians of Hell can hypothesize that God can be trusted to use punishment wisely and lovingly. However, the torments of Hell that Jesus (allegedly) threatened would be inflicted upon Jews and their descendents who did not believe that he was the Christ, were, to say the least, somewhat excessive, and not particularly conducive to love, forgiveness, and reconciliation. These Jews tried to live piously and ethically,[22] notwithstanding the caricature of them in the gospels as embodiments of the Devil.[23]

In sum, although interpersonal forgiveness is central to the teachings of Jesus, there seem to have been different views within the early Christian community concerning to whom it was to be directed and whether repentance was a prerequisite for it.

In contrast with the New Testament, there is very little in the Hebrew Bible about interpersonal forgiveness. A few narratives describe forgiveness and reconciliation. Esau does not exact revenge on his brother Jacob, who took advantage of Esau's thirst by pressuring him to sell his birthright, and who fooled their blind and aged father Isaac into giving him the superior blessing that Isaac had intended for Esau. When Jacob, who fled from Canaan out of fear that Esau would kill him, returns, he offers magnanimous gifts and an implicit apology to Esau, who came to meet him with four hundred men. Esau is moved and reconciles with Jacob.

Joseph, who was sold into slavery by his brothers and was now vice regent of Egypt, forgave his brothers when they pleaded for mercy. They had by then demonstrated some of the elements of repentance, among them confession, apology, and a willingness to resist a temptation similar to the one that they faced and had succumbed to when they sold Joseph. They had offered to sacrifice themselves to protect their father's "favored" son, Benjamin. This offer contrasts with their behavior in selling Joseph into slavery because they envied and hated him for being Jacob's favored one (and for insensitively flaunting his favored status).[24]

David too is depicted in a few stories as forgoing revenge and controlling his anger at Nabal, and perhaps at Saul and Absalom, all three of whom had tried to kill him.

In these stories, the forgiver is someone in power who shows mercy toward an offender whom he could have put to death. There are no instances of a powerful offender requesting forgiveness from or being forgiven by a weak victim of his, or of someone forgiving an offender no more or less powerful than the victim. These narratives enhance the reputation of the powerful party who "pardons" and acts mercifully toward an offender who is in a temporary or a permanent position of weakness. The motives for the forgiveness differ in each case. Joseph seems to forgive out of brotherly affection, respect for his deceased father, and a belief that his brothers had been God's instrument for good, even though they had intended evil. We are not informed of Esau's motive for forgiving Jacob and reconciling with him. David does not kill Nabal because he is moved by the pleas of Nabal's wife, Abigail, who appealed to David's magnanimity and self-interest, and whom he desires and indeed takes as a wife when Nabal later drops dead. There is no indication that he is in any way less resentful toward Nabal or "loves his enemy." David spares Saul's life because of David's reverence for one anointed by God, because of his deep and loving friendship with Saul's son Jonathan—who would be pained were his father killed, and perhaps out of appreciation for the love that Saul had once shown him. In each of these cases, the forgiveness or mercy is not a "free gift of love." It is grounded in self-interest or in natural emotions that are more powerful than the desire for revenge.[25]

In our discussion of revenge in the Bible, we saw that many psalms are replete with requests that God, punish and destroy the prayer's enemies or expressions of gratitude to God for doing so. The supplicant does not beseech God to forgive his enemies, nor does he himself forgive them. Christian theologians like Jones, who would like to believe that the psalms reflect their doctrine of forgiveness, offer forced Christological interpretations of them. Jones says, "There is a long tradition in Christian exegesis that the lament Psalms need to be interpreted, first and foremost, as prayers of Jesus Christ. In that context, the Psalmist's desires for vengeance are relocated in the judgment of grace wrought by Christ and thus ultimately seen in the light of Christ's reconciling work in the power of the Spirit" (p. 259).

Whatever the tradition of Christian theological biblical exegesis, few serious biblical scholars today, including Christians, would maintain that the lament Psalms are prayers of Jesus. They are the prayers of oppressed Israelites living long before Jesus, calling out for God's justice and even vengeance.

Just as there is a paucity of stories and prayers advocating interpersonal forgiveness in the Hebrew Bible (in contrast with the New Testament), there are no explicit laws or commandments to forgive someone who has injured you. The one closest to it is the admonition, "You shall not hate in your heart anyone of your kin; you shall reprove your neighbor, or you will incur guilt yourself. You shall not take vengeance or bear a grudge against any of your people, but you shall love your neighbor as yourself: I am the Lord" (Lev. 19:17–18).

This admonition prohibits concealed hatred and taking vengeance, not resentment expressed openly and channeled legitimately and fairly through the justice system (justice and due process are the general context of concern in which the passage appears). The prohibition is with respect to your "kin" and "neighbor." If "Love your neighbor" is the coda to verses 9–17 in their entirety, as some suggest, then "love" refers primarily to compassion for the poor, to honesty and integrity in matters of money, to truth and objectivity in legal judgment, and to sensitive and ethical behavior. To "love" is to act properly. It is not necessary to forgive injuries. Later rabbinic teachers broadened the meaning of "love your neighbor as yourself" beyond its narrow original sense, and Jesus expanded it even more.

Although the Hebrew Bible is relatively reticent about interpersonal human forgiveness, it is replete with divine forgiveness of Israel, especially when she repents, and sometimes even if she does not. When, in postbiblical times, a doctrine of imitation of God developed, it generated in Judaism an expectation that we too should forgive one another.

Jesus' preaching of forgiveness is not a sudden and radical break from postbiblical Jewish views. It can be found in some books of the Apocrypha[26] and other intertestamental Jewish works. For example, we read in the *Wisdom of Ben Sira* (second century B.C.E.), "Forgive your neighbor the wrong he has done, and then your sins will be pardoned when you pray" (Sir. 28:2). In *The Testament of Gad*, Joseph's brother Gad offers ethical instruction to his children before he dies. He had hated Joseph, but repented of that hatred and from his own experience learned how important it is to overcome hatred.

> Love one another from the heart, therefore, and if anyone sins against you, speak to him in peace. Expel the venom of hatred, and do not harbor deceit in your heart. If anyone confesses and repents, forgive him. . . . Even if he denies it and acts disgracefully out of a sense of guilt, be quiet and do not become upset. For he who denies will repent and avoid offending you again. . . . But even if he is devoid of shame and persists in his wickedness, forgive him from the heart and leave vengeance to God.[27]

As I have indicated, not all Christian spiritual mentors teach that forgiveness should be granted in the absence of repentance, and not all Jewish ones teach that repentance must always be a prerequisite to forgiveness. In rabbinic literature, we find several teachings that call for forgiving even the unrepentant offender, or at least praying for him.

For example, a story is told of the renowned Rabbi Meir (second century c.e.), who had been offended by villains in his neighborhood. (The nature of the offense isn't described but, presumably, it was very grave.) He prayed that the perpetrators should die. Meir, it seemed, justified his prayer by appealing to the verse "Let *htm* be consumed from the earth, and let the wicked be no more" (Ps. 104:35). The Hebrew consonants *htm* in this verse can be vocalized as *hotim*, which means sinners, or *hataim*, which usually means sins. Rabbi Meir understood the passage to refer to sinners, so he prayed that the sinners would die. Upon hearing this, his wife, Beruria, criticized and corrected him. You should vocalize *htm* as *hataim*, referring to sins, not sinners. The verse should be interpreted as saying that if sins were removed, there would no longer be sinners. Rather than pray for the sinners to die, pray that they should repent and no longer sin. Meir followed his wise wife's advice and prayed that the sinners should repent, which eventually they did (Talmud Berakhot 10a). This is the idea that God loves sinners even as he hates their sins.

This idea can be understood in several ways, but one common one is that almost every sinner also has the potential to do good, which is what God wants him to actualize. God, in his patience, defers or sets aside punishment so that the sinner can reform himself. We should treat sinners who hurt us in a like manner. One way of understanding Joseph's benevolent and forgiving behavior toward his brothers, for whom he engineered an opportunity to repent, is that he was more concerned with their spiritual well-being than with revenge or strict justice. If we didn't love the perpetrator or have compassion for him, we would not want him to repent, just as Jonah didn't want the Ninevites to repent. This is not precisely the the same as radical forgiveness—because repentance is still the focus of concern—but it comes quite close to it.

St. Thomas Aquinas's understanding of the command to love our enemies, which he takes to mean those who have sinned against us or against God, is similar. Where there is hope for their reform, we have an obligation to show them love and encourage them to repent, which is how God responds to human sin. However, when they persist in sin and fall into such a depth of wickedness that they cannot turn back, they are to be punished—even by death, in some instances.[28]

Although the predominant theme in traditional Jewish teaching about forgiveness is that you needn't forgive someone who has sinned against you and who doesn't express remorse, compensate you, and request forgiveness,[29] there appears to have been a debate about this that is reflected in two closely related texts from the second and third centuries c.e. The first is from the Mishnah.

The context of this teaching is the law of torts that specified the fines that a person who shamed another was required to pay. After specifying the monetary penalties, the Mishnah goes on to state, "Even though he (the perpetrator) pays (the victim of his insult), he is not forgiven until he requests from him [forgiveness]."[30]

The text continues with an admonition to the victim that it would be cruel for him not to grant forgiveness once the perpetrator has paid the fine and also requested forgiveness. This teaching reflects the predominant attitude of the tradition. However, another rabbinic text takes a different approach. It teaches that the victim of an assault should pray to God to have mercy on his assailant even if the assailant has not requested that he do so.[31] Later commentators who juxtaposed these two passages either accepted the fact that there were two different views, or else tried to harmonize the two texts by explaining the latter to mean that if the perpetrator has requested forgiveness, the victim should not only forgive him himself, but also pray to God on his behalf, even though he did not request that from the victim.

If we accept that the two teachings reflect conflicting opinions about whether or not to forgive an offender who has not apologized or shown remorse, we have here a debate similar to the "debate" that is implicit in the New Testament. This debate is not surprising in light of the history of forgiveness within Judaism, and considering the similar cultural milieux of the Christians and Jews of Palestine from the first through the early third centuries C.E.

The Mishnah and other rabbinic sources emphasize that the victim must forgive the offender who has appropriately repented.[32]

A more elaborate and radical Jewish version of an ethos of forgiveness, much closer to the dominant Christian one, is found in the sixteenth-century book *The Palm Tree of Deborah*.[33] This brief but influential ethical–mystical treatise by the great kabbalist (Jewish mystic) Rabbi Moses Cordovero of Safed in the Galilee applies in detail the notion of the obligation to imitate God, as a vehicle for teaching values about how one should respond to insult and injury. Cordovero cites biblical verses that describe how God behaves toward the people Israel as a model for how Jews should respond to one another.[34]

Cordovero cites the passage from Micah 7:18–20.

> Who is a God like You,
> Forgiving iniquity
> And remitting transgression;

Who has not maintained His wrath forever
Against the remnant of His own people,
Because He loves graciousness!
He will take us back in love;
He will cover up our iniquities,
You will hurl all our sins
Into the depths of the sea.
You will keep faith with Jacob,
Loyalty to Abraham,
As You promised on oath to our fathers
In days gone by. (New JPS Translation)

Cordovero analyzes each phrase for the message it can teach about forgiveness. The Jew is to act toward his fellow Jew in the same way that God is described in these passages as acting toward the people of Israel as a collective. Let us follow Cordovero phrase by phrase, focusing on the teachings he derives regarding interpersonal forgiveness.[35]

"Forgiving iniquity (or bearing sins)"
A man should learn the degree of patience in bearing his neighbor's yoke and the evils done by his neighbor even when those evils still exist. So that even if his neighbor offends he bears with him until the wrong is righted or until it vanishes of its own accord . . . (p. 50)
"Who has not retained his wrath forever"
Even when it is permitted to chastise his neighbor or his own children who suffer as a result he should, because of this, not linger in his anger but make an end and not retain his ire for ever. This applies even where such anger is permissible. . . . It is a religious duty to encourage [a sinner] lovingly, and perhaps, this way of dealing with him will succeed (pp. 54–55).
"Because He loves graciousness"
Even when he is offended or provoked, if the offender has his good points in that he is kind to others or he possesses some other good quality this should be sufficient to soothe his anger so that his heart is pleased with him and delights in the kindness he does. And he should say: "It is enough for me that he possesses this good quality." How much more so with regard to one's wife, as the Rabbis say: "It is enough that they rear our children and save us from sin." So he should say with regard to all men: "It is enough for me that he has shown me or another man kindness

or that he possesses this particular good quality." And he should delight in mercy (pp. 56–57).

"He will take us back in love"

This is how man should behave towards his neighbor. He should not feel hatred from his former anger but when he sees that his neighbor wants to love him he should show him a greater degree of kindness and love than formerly. He should say: "Behold he is to be compared to the penitents in whose place the perfectly righteous cannot stand." And he should encourage him to a far greater degree than those who are perfectly righteous, namely, those who have not offended him (pp. 59–60).

"He will cover up our iniquities"

This quality, too, a man should make his own; not to subdue the good his neighbor has done and to remember the evil he has done. On the contrary, he should subdue the evil, forget it and reject it so that evil does not dwell within him. But the good his neighbor has done should always be arraigned before him and he should remember this good so that it prevails over all the deeds his neighbor has done. And he should not deduce in his heart, saying: "If he has done good to me he has also behaved badly to me," so that the good is forgotten. He should not do this, but with regard to the evil his neighbor has done to him he should allow himself to be appeased in every possible way. But the good should never be removed from his sight and he should hide himself from the bad as far as he possibly can . . . (pp. 61–62).

"You will hurl all our sins into the depths of the sea"

Even if his neighbor is crushed through suffering as a result of his sins he should not be hated, "for after he has been disgraced, he is as thy brother." He should welcome those who suffer and are punished and have mercy upon them. On the contrary, he should save them from their enemies and should not say: "His sufferings are the result of his sins" but he should have compassion on him according to this quality (p. 65).

"In days gone by"

Even when he cannot discover any plea [on behalf of the sinner] . . . he should still say: "Behold there was a time when they had not sinned. And in that time or in former days they were worthy." . . . In this way no man will be found an unworthy recipient of goodness nor unworthy to be prayed for and to have mercy shown on him (pp. 68–69).

[Man] is to bring the love of his fellow-men into his heart, even loving the wicked as if they were his brothers and more so until the love of his fellow-men becomes firmly fixed in his heart . . . How can he love them? By recalling in his thoughts the good qualities they possess, by covering their defects and refusing to look at their faults and only at their good qualities (p. 79).

The overall perspective of Cordovero's teachings is similar to the Christian approaches that many Jews have found to be inappropriate responses to insult and injury. Be that as it may, Cordovero is solidly within the Jewish tradition of ethical teachings even though his view is a minority one. Of course, Cordovero does not say that a victim has no right to sue for monetary compensation for damages, or that offenders should not be punished by the legal system. He is dealing with how a Jew should respond emotionally and behaviorally to sinners in general as well as to offenses committed against him by another Jew. The premise is that Jews have a special obligation to strive for the highest levels of sanctity and holiness, and these require an ethic of forgiveness that goes beyond normal expectations. Indeed, Cordovero is aware that it would be unrealistic and even inappropriate to demand such forbearance, love, and compassion all the time. There are times, he says, when other emotions and reactions, more in line with justice than with compassion, are necessary. However, he says that the Jew should at least try to respond with compassion, mercy, love, and forgiveness toward evildoers on Sabbaths and other holy days and occasions on which aspirations to holiness are particularly demanded.

Now that we have considered why and when we should forgive, we turn our attention to the challenge of learning how to forgive.

FOUR

How to Forgive

Notwithstanding the differences in Jewish and Christian theologies of forgiveness, both traditions agree that when the offender has repented, the victim should forgive him and let him know that he has done so. From a secular perspective too, forgiveness in response to apology, remorse, and restitution has psychological and social value for offender and victim. It can relieve the remorseful offender from guilt that is no longer necessary because it has served its function of self-transformation. It can give some closure to the victim and free him from consuming and painful anger and hatred, without loss of self-respect and without a violation of his sense of justice, because the offender's apology and reparation have vindicated him. Forgiveness in response to repentance encourages people to change for the better and brings harmony and reconciliation into ruptured human relationships. It opens up possibilities for the renewal of friendship, affection, and love. Within the family unit, it can keep families intact and committed to mutual help and support. Forgiveness can also have physical and emotional benefits.

Although forgiveness in the absence of the offender's repentance might have some of the above benefits as well, its emotional and moral costs may outweigh its benefits. This is especially so when the offender is alive and capable of repenting, or at least apologizing and expressing remorse, but does not do so. Some people consider forgiveness in the absence of repentance to be a denigration of justice and a moral disservice to the intransigent offender. To give him a gift of love, notwithstanding his insistence on identifying with evil, is equivalent to not holding him responsible and accountable for what he has done, and thus to treat him as less than a morally autonomous human being.[1]

When the offender cannot repent because of death or some other reason, the question that faces his victim is whether to forgive or instead use other strategies for making his or her anger and resentment less burdensome.

Even when all would agree that forgiveness is morally and psychologically desirable, it is still a very difficult thing to do. The injured victim who, even if the offender has apologized and repented, will bear forever the consequences of the offense, cannot so easily overcome his or her resentment and hatred. It is difficult to face the offender and say, "I now see you as a different person from the one who injured me, and I no longer bear you animosity. I don't want you to be punished anymore and I no longer wish that you will suffer as you have made me suffer." There are many emotional hurdles that we have to overcome in order to forgive, even when we know that it is the best and right thing to do.

We will now consider some strategies for helping us forgive when we want to forgive but are unable to get ourselves to do so. Many of these are practical applications of the ideas we discussed earlier when we considered reasons for forgiving. We will look at how psychologists and marital counselors are developing and testing programs to help people work through the process of forgiveness in a variety of situations of deep hurt and conflict. Some of these programs are, for me, too Christian in their approach, in that they deemphasize or ignore the role that an offender's apology and repentance should play in encouraging victims to forgive, and they are too sanguine about our capacity to love our enemies. However, they provide important psychological insights into forgiveness as well as tactics for forgiving, both of which are applicable in many situations.[2] Of course, those of you who do believe that you should forgive those who hurt you deeply even if they do not feel any remorse will find the work of the Christian-oriented therapists indispensable in helping you implement your Christian beliefs in your personal lives.

· · ·

Robert Enright and his colleagues have been pioneers in forgiveness research and its application. As we saw earlier, Enright defines forgiveness as "a willingness to abandon one's right to resentment, condemnation and subtle revenge towards an offender who acts unjustly, while fostering the undeserved qualities of compassion, generosity, and even love towards him or her. . . . Therefore, a forgiver may unconditionally offer this gift regardless of the other's current attitude or behavior."

Enright's process model of forgiveness includes four phases. Within each phase are several units that apply to feelings, thoughts, or behaviors. The process of forgiveness is complex and differs for people as a function of the offense, the relationship between the victim and the offender, the personality of the victim, whether or not the offender has expressed remorse, and other factors. The different units within each phase and across the four phases are thus not necessarily applicable to all victims in all situations.

PHASE I—UNCOVERING PHASE—UNITS 1–8

1. Examination of psychological defenses.
2. Confrontation of anger; the point is to release, not harbor the anger.
3. Admittance of shame when this is appropriate.
4. Awareness of cathexis.
5. Awareness of cognitive rehearsal of the offense.
6. Insight that the injured party may be comparing oneself with the injurer.
7. Realization that oneself may be permanently and adversely changed by the injury.
8. Insight into a possibly altered "just world" view.[3]

Before an injured party can even contemplate forgiving the injurer, she must acknowledge that she has been hurt by him. Yet we often deny that we have been hurt, and we deny the negative feelings and thoughts about ourselves that being hurt can engender, such as shame and anger. Who among us wants to admit that we have been betrayed or, if betrayed, that we are emotionally devastated by the treachery of one in whom we placed our trust and to whom we gave our love? To do so would be to admit to ourselves that we weren't as wise or as lovable as we had perceived ourselves to be. Better, then, to deny rather than to acknowledge these unpleasant feelings and thoughts. We often are not aware of how pervasive hurtful feelings and thoughts are, whether conscious or suppressed, and how much negative energy we invest in them. We must overcome this denial so that we can address our pain.

Once we acknowledge our anger, we have to release it rather than ruminate on it, as we often do when we are hurt. A devoted mother and wife whose husband has abandoned her after years of what she thought was a mutually loving marriage, who is alone, lonely, and, now, economically vulnerable, often contrasts her plight with her former husband's current situation. While she lies lonely in her bed, weeping silently, she imagines him and his newly "acquired" younger secretary/lover cavorting joyously on the beaches of Bermuda before retiring to their suite in an upscale hotel. These ruminations and comparisons exacerbate her pain and can be obstacles to forgiving. Imagine that you have suffered a debilitating and permanent injury when struck by a car operated by a drunk driver who received a relatively light sentence. Over and over you agonize, where is justice? Is it fair that I can no longer work at my profession, but the man who incapacitated me can? Your father abused you sexually as a teenager, and you have had difficulty trusting men ever since. You seethe with anger every time you recall your father's stealthy approach to your bed. Your daughter was raped and murdered, and you have been in a deep depression ever since. The recurring thoughts and feelings of her suffering and your loss give you no rest and have deprived your life of all pleasure and meaning. The only sustained emotion you feel is a desire for vengeance.

If you, at first, denied your pain and injury, the Uncovering Phase helps you acknowledge it, become aware of how you are allowing yourself to engage in thoughts and nurture feelings that embitter and enrage you, and realize that these responses to injury are self-defeating and self-hurting. They make you a victim twice over, once at the initial injury and its natural aftermath, and a second time in the shame, anger, pain, anxiety, and deep sadness that you allow to consume you. Moreover, these negative thoughts and feelings also prevent you from contemplating the possibility of forgiving the husband who cast you aside for another, the hit-and-run driver who paralyzed you, the father who stole your innocence and your ability to love, and the man who destroyed your precious child.

Only after you are fully aware of how you were wronged, of how the wound cuts deep, and of the poisonous embrace of your anger, are you ready to consider an alternative way of dealing with it. You can now go on to the next phase, in which you will be called upon to make a conscious choice.

PHASE II—DECISION PHASE—UNITS 9–11

9. A change of heart/conversion/new insights that old resolution strategies are not working.
10. Willingness to consider forgiveness as an option.
11. Commitment to forgive the offender.

You realize that there has to be a better way, one that will help heal your own psychic pain, but also move you away from a preoccupation with your own pain into the realm of the spiritual and moral claims of a gospel of love and compassion. If you are convinced that this is the right goal, and if you accept that forgiveness is the path that can bring you to it, you now commit yourself to learning how to forgive and embark on the journey.

PHASE III—WORK PHASE—UNITS 12–15

12. Reframing, through role taking, of who the wrongdoer is by viewing him or her in context.
13. Empathy and compassion toward the offender.
14. Acceptance/absorption of the pain.
15. Giving a moral gift to the offender.

Earlier we pointed out that, in judging people who have hurt us, we should take into account the totality of their personhood and not focus exclusively on the injury they caused us. The disloyal husband, the alcoholic driver, the abusing parent, and even the rapist/murderer may have done worthy and good things in life, and may yet do more. Viewing them with a panoramic lens may make it easier to forgive them.

Moreover, in judging the offender, we have to consider the overall context in which his offense against us was perpetrated. For example, when, in a difficult marriage, one spouse hurts the other deeply, by word or deed, and the injured partner wants to forgive (in cases in which it would not be dangerous to do so), he or she might find the following four reflections to be helpful.

1) I might be partially to blame for my spouse's or partner's injuring me. Perhaps I was insensitive to his/her needs and expectations, or perhaps I inadvertently hurt him/her without my being aware of it. There might be some legitimate cause for his/her anger or resentment toward me, even though I feel that, on balance, I am more right and just than he/she is in our conflict.

2) I should try to be more empathetic. Do I understand and acknowledge my partner's fears, anxieties, and pain? Perhaps if I could better understand where he/she is "coming from" I might be more sympathetic, even if I can't justify what he/she has done to me.

3) I should be aware of extenuating circumstances or mitigating factors that might have brought my partner to behave as he/she did, for example, stress, or a history of trauma, abuse, or lack of parents who provided love or proper values. These mitigating factors do not exonerate my partner from responsibility for having hurt me, but I should take then into account as I judge him/her.

4) All people, even those who do wrong, are of intrinsic worth by virtue of their humanity, and are entitled to love and compassion. I may "hate the sin" but I should try not to "hate the sinner."

The idea that we should love the sinner even as we hate the sin is a central element of Christian ethics. St. Dominic, for example, expressed a desire to be placed over the mouth of Hell in order to save sinners from being sent there. Aquinas, basing his thoughts on Augustine's interpretation of "love thy neighbor" as referring to all humans, maintains that since sin does not destroy our essential human nature, sinners are included in the category of neighbor and must be loved with the love that is mandated by the Christian virtue of charity. This means, for example, to be concerned about their spiritual welfare, to pray on their behalf, and not to feel vindictive toward them. It also means to come to their assistance when they are in urgent need, even if they are our enemies.[4] Many parables in the New Testament, such as that of the father celebrating the return home of his prodigal son, express this value.

Not everyone, however, believes that humans have intrinsic worth forever, irrespective of their behavior, and the intrinsic worth notion will not facilitate their forgiving someone whom they feel has behaved in an egregiously evil way. Moreover, at some point, it becomes logically difficult to disconnect and differentiate the sin from the sinner, especially when the sinner is a chronic one. "Sins" do not have an independent existence—they are things done by people. The occasional sin done by an essentially good person may be considered an aberration—the sin doesn't really reflect the character of the person who did it. But when the sinner repeats the sin again and again, why should we not have negative feelings? We cannot imagine a judicial system or any social system that punishes crimes without punishing criminals, and there are times when it might not be possible or desirable to hate the sin without hating the sinner as well.

Be that as it may, if you have successfully been able to "reframe" your view of the offender, and find empathy and compassion for him, you might be willing to "absorb" your pain rather than "pass it on" to him with punitive words or actions. Your willingness to forgo your right to punish him will also save innocent others from the negative consequences of a sustained and exacerbated conflict. If couples learned the art of forgiveness, many more marriages would be "saved" and the traumatizing effects on children of seeing their parents at war, or vengeful and bitter in divorce, would be avoided. Your willingness to forgive will be a gift to your spouse, and to your children as well. This will only be the case if the forgiveness is not a pseudo-forgiveness, one in which you don't fully acknowledge the reality of your hurt and honestly work through your emotions and the deliberate choice you make to give up what is your due. If your forgiveness is only lip service, or even God service, but doesn't truly deal with your anger and your sense of having been treated unjustly, the anger will resurface, or find its way into your feelings and actions by some side door or, even worse, via the dank cellar of repressed resentment. It is, of course, sometimes desirable to restrain yourself from expressing your anger and taking punitive action, even if you don't forgive. But if you choose that course of action, do not confuse it with forgiveness, which involves much more than just restraint.

These thoughts are applicable in many other situations of conflict and hurt. Remember my friend who hasn't spoken to his once beloved children (whose loss of love he laments every day as he awakes in painful emptiness) or frolicked with his grandchildren. Remember my friend's children, who harbor resentment toward their father, and guilt for feeling that way about him. Remember the grandchildren who have no grandfather to visit, to dote on them and spoil them as grandfathers do. Would that the father and his son and daughter could decide to reframe their view of one another, to use an empathic lens, to imagine the costs of bearing grudges, to try the path of forgiveness and reconciliation. We are not talking here about sexual abuse, rape, or murder, but much lesser offenses—insensitivities, ingratitude, narcissistic preoccupation with self, and even simple misperceptions of one another's intentions. Are the anger and resentment generated by these offenses and the retention of the grudges really worth the price of destroying three generations of family love? It would be helpful if either father or children were willing to apologize to the other and ask for forgiveness. Better yet would be a situation in which both parties apologized and requested forgiveness. But even if neither were willing to acknowledge that they were at least partially wrong in the conflict, perhaps one or both could still forgive.

Let us assume it was the father who was willing to take the initiative to forgive. He should not say to his children, "I forgive you," since that would probably offend them even more, because it implies that they have done something wrong, which they aren't willing to acknowledge. What he should do, after going through all of the necessary steps in the phases we have described, is to call or write to his children, and say that he loves them dearly and wants them back in his life. Perhaps he can invite them to dinner. If they accept the invitation, he should ask them if they would bring along pictures of the grandchildren. At dinner he should give them the chance to talk about their children, which parents often love to do. He could inquire about his children's work and suggest that if he can be helpful in any way he wants them to call on him. Gestures of love and overtures of reconciliation often have dramatic healing effects. Note that the father is not being asked to say to them that he was wrong, since he doesn't believe that he was. He is not groveling or demeaning himself, because he hasn't denied to himself that justice is with him. Even if the children or an outside observer might view what he does as a weakness, it really is a manifestation of emotional and spiritual fortitude. The negative consequence it might have, if indeed the children had wronged him as he believes, is that it could reinforce their false belief that they were in the right, and thus prevent them from facing up honestly to their misdeeds. It could be an obstacle to their repentance. On the other hand, if the father's gift of forgiveness succeeds in reestablishing the relationship, then with the dissipation of anger, the resumption of communication, and the renewal of love, the children might be more open to critical self-analysis. They might reassess their role in the original conflict, assume some responsibility for it, and perhaps even go so far as to express to their father their remorse. If this is how the process ultimately unfolded, it would be an example of how forgiveness of an offender prior to his repentance can encourage him to eventually repent.

Since forgiveness is a multistage process—influenced by many factors that can extend over a long period of time, with advances, retreats, and diversions—we should not think of it as an all-or-none affair, in which you forgive or you don't. As we pointed out earlier, there are degrees of forgiveness, and *some* forgiveness is better than *none*, as long as the "some" is part of the proper process and not a "false" forgiveness. To use a metaphor: Imagine you are in a Hellish place of offensive stenches and searing blazes and you set forth on a journey whose destination is an Eden of fragrances and temperate climes. The further along your path, the less painful and foul do the fire and odors become and, at some point, you begin to discern faint wafts of perfume and gentle, refreshing breezes. The journey of forgiveness can be like this. Even though you haven't reached the Eden of love and reconciliation, you still might have moved far away from the Hell of resentment and rage.

Although by the end of this third phase of the process you have come a long way on the journey of forgiveness, some of you might discover unanticipated benefits that go beyond the dissipation of your specific anger and resentment and your willingness to forgo real or imagined punishment of the offender. What might happen is summarized by Enright and Coyle in Phase IV, the Deepening Phase.

PHASE IV—DEEPENING PHASE—UNITS 16–20

16. Finding meaning for oneself and others in the suffering and in the forgiveness process.
17. Realization that oneself has need for others' forgiveness in the past.
18. Insight that one is not alone (universality, support).
19. Realization that oneself might have a new purpose in life because of the injury.
20. Awareness of decreased negative affect, and, perhaps, increased positive affect, if this begins to emerge, toward the injurer; awareness of internal, emotional release.

When you have successfully emerged from the narrow focus on your pain and anger, and have practiced strategies of reframing, empathy, and compassion, new vistas of experience *might* open up for you. Perhaps you will now be able to look for some meaning in your suffering that you weren't able to consider until now. For example, were it not for the fact that you were mugged and thrust into the judicial process, you might not have become aware of the plight of the marginalized in our society. I surely don't recommend that the best way to become sensitized to the pain and despair of many who turn to crime is to go out and proclaim, "Please mug me so that I can learn." However, once you have suffered, you might turn that experience into a valuable one. The very process of forgiving can teach you that you have spiritual and psychological powers of which you were never aware. These can now be harnessed to other aspects of your life. Again, an analogy: Imagine that someone threatened to harm you if you didn't run the Boston marathon, a challenge you never would have considered on your own. Out of fear of being punished, you force yourself to do so. It is excruciatingly painful for you but, to your own amazement, you actually cross the finish line. Lo and behold, you now know that you have within you the power and stamina to run a marathon. You might decide to run it again the following year, not under threat, but proudly and voluntarily. One benefit of completing the difficult journey of forgiveness is the self-knowledge you will acquire that you can overcome powerful negative emotions and are capable of great self-restraint. I had a good friend who used to run the marathon. I asked what he got out of it besides exercise. He said that it revealed to him that he was capable of successfully undertaking great challenges in life that he would otherwise have avoided. The challenge of forgiveness might do this for you.

Another possible benefit of forgiveness is that, in the process of reflecting on the weaknesses of the offender, you might come to embrace the wisdom of the virtue of humility. You might find yourself thinking along these lines:

"I should keep in mind the fundamental weakness of human nature. We all have a propensity to be selfish and to thereby hurt others. It isn't easy to be good, kind, caring, and sensitive. I must be humble and realize that I too am an imperfect person, even if not to the same degree as the person who offended me. I might behave in a similarly offensive way under some circumstances.

"I should also bear in mind that someday I might be in a position in which I will have done wrong to another and will want to be treated with empathy and compassion by my victim. If, when I relate to an offender, I don't allow empathy and compassion to influence my reactions, then I should not expect others to act in that spirit toward me. I shall forgive so that I will be forgiven."

These are some of the ancillary benefits of forgiveness that Enright and Coyle suggest might deepen the meaning of it for the one who forgives. What they would hope to see in this phase is that, not only will negative affect toward the offender be decreased, but the victim might even develop positive feelings toward him. For them, the ultimate goal of the forgiveness process is the gift of love extended by the victim to the perpetrator.

When the victim and the offender are in a close personal relationship, such as husband and wife, parent and child, or siblings, it would be desirable indeed if love would resurface or grow again. I don't think, however, that forgiveness itself suffices to nurture love, although it may clear away thistles and thorns that prevent its growth. Other processes need to be involved in reinstating or creating love, and these should follow upon both repentance and forgiveness in family dynamics.[5] When the victim and offender had no prior relationship, or when love was not an element of their relationship (e.g., employer–employee), I don't see why love should be expected or desired, since I don't think everyone can love everyone, and we needn't try to do so. Everyone should treat everyone else with fairness, dignity, respect, and justice, and often, with compassion. But these behaviors are not love.[6]

The psychologists Exline and Baumeister[7] discuss several barriers to forgiving, among which are these four.

1) Fear that the transgression will be repeated
2) Fear of appearing weak
3) Fear that the principle of justice and fairness will not be served
4) Loss of benefits deriving from being a victim

If there is a realistic fear that the transgression, especially if it is a dangerous one, will be repeated, you might forgive but still distance yourself from the dangerous offender.

If you fear that by forgiving you will appear weak, in the sense of making the offender more prone to take advantage of or attack you again, then you can forgive without letting him know that you have done so, or by taking precautionary measures to protect yourself if you can. Just as you would protect yourself against a wild, vicious dog without hating the dog, so too should you protect yourself from a person who is dangerous but who you really don't want to hate. Forgiveness does not override the right and obligation to self-defense. It is important, when forgiving and attempting to repair and sustain a relationship in which you were deeply hurt, that you do not jeopardize your physical or emotional well-being. The person you are forgiving must understand that you are not giving him or her license to repeat the hurtful behaviors.

If, however, you are afraid that to forgive *is actually to be weak* and not just to *appear* to be weak, then you would have to reassess your basic attitude toward forgiveness. In the sense in which Enright and Coyle define and analyze forgiveness, it is anything but weakness. It takes great courage and strength to go through the process. Remember that, in forgiving, you are not saying that you consent or deserve to be a doormat. You are maintaining your claim to dignity and just treatment even though you don't insist upon your full rights to act upon those claims. Just as the judge who tempers his justice with mercy is not acting from a position of weakness but of strength, so are you, in forgiving, tempering the justice due to you with empathy, mercy, and compassion.

The concern that to forgive is to condone injustice, or to be perceived as condoning it, is very legitimate. Perhaps one way to avoid seeming to condone injustice is explicitly to explain to those concerned that you are forgiving the offense, including the offender himself, but that you are not condoning what he has done. It was wrong, he should repent, and if what he has done is not just a personal offense against you, but a crime as well, he will have to pay the penalty. When this is made clear, it will be safer to forgive without fear that it will be perceived as condoning. Just as to give someone "a second chance" is not to condone, but rather to hope for improvement, so too can your forgiveness be construed as a hope for improvement.

As for losing your victim status, it is probably healthier for you in the long run to have your status determined by who you really are than by offenses you have suffered. It is better for you to aspire to what you deserve because of your character, efforts, wisdom, or good deeds than to rely on having been someone's victim. Do not let the temporary benefits of victimhood prevent you from forgiving, even though forgiving would usually imply that you no longer claim the "rights" owed to you by having been your offender's victim.

· · ·

Let us now look at a second model of forgiveness, Everett Worthington Jr.'s "Pyramid of Forgiveness."[8] Worthington, a devout Christian and a psychologist whose conceptual approach to forgiveness is very similar to that of Enright, relates in a moving paper his struggle with rage and forgiveness.

> My brother's voice was shaky. "I have some bad news," he said. "Mama's been murdered. . . ."
> Mama had been beaten to death with a crowbar, her body [sexually] assaulted with a wine bottle. Rage bubbled up in me like lava. I heard myself saying, "I'd like to have that murderer alone in a room with just a baseball bat. I'd beat his brains out. . . ."
> That night . . . I fought the bed covers. Rage and sadness had stolen sleep. Imagined scenes of violence and thoughts of hatred and revenge intruded. Ironically, only days before I had finished co-writing a book on forgiveness. . . . Did I really believe what we had written about forgiveness— that empathy was a key to forgiving—or was that book just for other people? Could I empathize with the person who had murdered my mother?
> I imagined how two youths might feel as they prepared to rob a darkened house. Perhaps they had been caught at a robbery previously. This time, though, they wouldn't get caught. Standing in the street, they were keyed up. The house was dark, no car in the driveway. . . . They couldn't know that Mama didn't drive. A quick rap of the crowbar and they were in, emptying drawers, dumping the contents on the floor. I imagined the intruder's shock when he heard a voice behind him. "What are you doing here?" Oh, no, he must have thought, I've been seen, I'll go to jail. She's ruining my life. He lashed out with the crowbar, slamming my mother three times. Panicked, the youths went crazy, trashing the house, angry at having their plans ruined and overcome with the shame of having murdered.
> I felt I understood better what had happened. The youth who murdered my mom did a terrible thing. Nothing will change that. Through empathy, I understood that he had lashed out in fear, surprise, guilt, and anger. My mind flashed back to hours earlier when I had talked about beating him to death with a baseball bat. I was willing to do what the youth did, only with more forethought, more naked malice than he.
> "Whose heart is darker?" I almost said aloud. When I saw the evil I was

capable of plotting, I was humbled. I saw my own guilt over plotting revenge. As a Christian, I knew that even as I confessed it, I would receive
Divine forgiveness for my evil intent. I felt that forgiveness flood me. I
knew that the youth, too, needed forgiveness. How could I withhold what
the youth needed?

So, I forgave him, and I have since felt peace.

In my case, I worked through five steps up a Pyramid of Forgiveness,
and I was able to forgive within a single night. Most of the time, it takes
longer to forgive—sometimes years. Even though I was able to forgive
quickly on that night, my forgiveness did not shorten my grief. For over a
year afterward, I would periodically be overcome by grief. The blessing was
that at least I did not have to deal with my own hatred and bitterness.[9]

In further elaboration on his experience he relates:

Blessedly, I was not left to wallow in the gooey stain of revenge. I recognized quickly that Jesus had died that I might have forgiveness and be
washed clean of that stain. I thought, *if I have received forgiveness for the
stain in my heart, then who am I to withhold forgiveness from this youth.* With
that thought I released my desire for revenge, my bitterness, my desire for
punitive justice. I forgave and paradoxically the chains that bound me to
the youth in hatred fell from my heart and set us both free.[10]

Worthington does not recount whether his mother's murderer was apprehended and tried for his crime and, if so, what he did and felt at the trial.
Nor do we know whether there was any personal interaction between him
and the murderer. This information would be useful in helping us better
understand Worthington's views about the relationship between forgiveness
and justice, and what he means when he says that he forgave the youth. Did
he or would he tell the youth that he forgave him? What would he want or
expect the youth to do with that knowledge? Would Worthington want the
youth to empathize with him the way that Worthington empathized with
him? Would he want the youth not to feel guilt?

When he speaks of forgiving, is Worthington referring only to his own
feelings, or to some actions he took with respect to the youth, such as pleading,
perhaps, for a lenient sentence? I assume that, even if he felt that the youth
should be "punished" in some way, the purpose of the punishment should be
strictly rehabilitative and educative (and deterrent), but in no way retributive.

Worthington's decision and ability to forgive the murderer is formulated within his specific Christian belief system. What would he say about forgiving to someone like me? I don't believe that Jesus died so that I might be forgiven and be washed clean of the stains of my sins. I don't believe that the desire for revenge in such a situation is evil. It is a natural reaction which, however, has to be channeled through a judicial system, lest anarchy prevail. I do not think that my sins (and I confess that I have committed many) are in the same category as those of the youth who murdered his mother. I don't understand how one person's forgiveness of another "sets the other free." From what is the murderer being set free? Is he free from sin, from guilt, from responsibility, from the need to repent? I don't think this is what Worthington means, since, as we shall see, he places great importance on repentance when he encourages forgiveness in therapy. Moreover, for what is he forgiving the murderer? The murderer killed his mother but, in doing so, deeply injured Worthington and many members of his family, and society as well, by breaching its rules of social order. He may have committed only one crime in the strictly legal sense, but he has committed multiple moral sins. I assume that, at most, Worthington can forgive the murderer for the sin he committed against him, but not for the crime and the sins he committed against others. In what sense then does the forgiveness set the murderer free if only Worthington forgives him?

Notwithstanding my many questions and reservations about what it means for Worthington to forgive (beyond assuaging his own hate and rage), and whether in doing so he might be excusing or condoning crime (he says he is not, but there is a very fine and often imperceptible line between *extreme* empathy and condoning or excusing), I believe that we do have to temper our hatred and anger at offenders with the help of empathy and humility.

In fact, Worthington has much of great value to say to people like me about forgiveness.

Worthington's pyramid model of forgiveness called REACH, has five steps to it:

Recall the Hurt (R)
Empathize (E)
Altruistic Gift of Forgiveness (A)
Commit to Forgive (C)
Holding on to Forgiveness (H)

One of the unique features of Worthington's model is its assumption that an unforgiving person has been neurobiologically conditioned to experience many negative emotions about the offender, especially fear, which leads to either avoidance or retaliatory behavior. Any stimulus that reminds the victim of the offense or the offender will automatically trigger these responses. In order to forgive, the victim has to be re-conditioned to associate positive emotions with the offender. The most important way of doing this is by training him to empathize. What is particularly interesting and unique in this second, step of the pyramid is that it tries to create in the forgiver a *state of empathy* with the offender. This step involves more than just teaching him to think several general, empathetic thoughts about the person who injured him. For example, Worthington suggests that the potential forgiver might be asked to:

> Speculate about what the offender might have been thinking or feeling during the hurtful event.
> Write a letter of explanation, assuming reasonable motives on the offender's part.
> Recall good experiences with the offender.
> Actively imagine interacting with the offender during more pleasant times.
> Breathe deeply and slowly during the memory or imagery.

Worthington differentiates between at least three kinds of empathy. *Empathic accuracy* means being able to ascertain correctly what another person thinks or feels. *Empathic identification* is the ability to share with another person similar mental or emotional states. *Empathic compassion* combines empathic accuracy and empathic identification with feeling compassion for another person and caring for him or her. The goal of step two of the pyramid is empathic compassion.

Even if you cultivate empathic compassion toward an offender, you still might not be willing to forgive him. To advance the injured person along the trajectory of forgiveness, the model tries to induce in him a state of humility, which comprises the experiences of guilt, gratitude, and gift, the elements of the third step, the Altruistic Gift. Much of Worthington's work has been with couples whose marriages are troubled by conflict and mutual resentments. In such contexts, more than in situations in which one is injured by a stranger, it is usually the case that both partners have contributed something to the deterioration of the relationship. Therefore, it is possible to expect both of them to assume some measure of responsibility for the unhappy situation. Guilt is the "healthy sense of one's own wrongdoing" and can be invoked in couples therapy to encourage each partner reciprocally to acknowledge that he/she has harmed the other and to apologize for having done so. In other words, repentance is incorporated into this model as a precursor and facilitator of forgiveness. In an earlier paper on forgiveness, particularly in marriages and families, Worthington and his colleagues write:

> No married couple can live together without hurting each other. Thriving marriage must be founded on forgiveness. We have found that forgiveness is best promoted by helping partners to confess their own offenses rather than on forgiving the partner who has hurt them. If partners can humbly say "I'm sorry I hurt you. Please forgive me," more forgiveness seems to occur than when they say, "You hurt me, I forgive you." Confession must be accompanied by sincere repentance if trust is to be rebuilt. While sinless perfection isn't possible and the confessing partner will eventually hurt again, there must be evidence of sincere turning away from deliberate hurtfulness.
>
> Forgiveness in marriage in not promoted by a single intervention, a single confession, or a single profession of good intention. Forgiveness is granted in mercy when a partner believes a sincere confession, and commits to being a force for healing rather than for hurting. (pp. 360–61)[11]

Worthington goes even further in his use of guilt as a "humbler," so that it is not only the real offenses that you committed that should humble you and make you more amenable to forgiving the other but, in addition, "the person should come to experience that he or she is capable of inflicting . . . harm, *or even capable of desiring to inflict . . . harm* (my emphasis). The person might even realize that he or she has harmed others in very different ways— perhaps more severely" (1998, p. 124).

One can clearly discern here echoes of Jesus' teaching "Blessed are the pure in heart" (Matt. 4:8) and "You have heard that it was said, 'You shall not commit adultery.' But I say to you that everyone who looks at a woman with lust has already committed adultery with her in his heart" (Matt. 4:27–28).

Evil thoughts and desires are condemned by Judaism as well as Christianity, and a case can be made, even on non-religious grounds, that they are morally wrong and undesirable in certain circumstances.[12] The significant distinction between an evil capacity that is not exercised or an evil desire or thought that is not executed, and actual evil deeds is important, however, and tends to be glossed over by some Christian writers. I question whether using "the desire to inflict harm" as a guilt inducer is a healthy use of guilt (to which, in general, I am sympathetic), or whether it is "fair" as a means of humbling the victim who, whatever his thoughts or desires might have been, did not act upon them, as did the perpetrator upon his.

After the potential forgiver has reflected upon his own guilt, he is asked to consider if and when he was ever forgiven for a transgression of his own.

> The person recalls and describes aloud, in writing, or in both, a specific time that a parent, employer, teacher, friend, or acquaintance offered forgiveness for a clear transgression. Then the person dwells on the sense of release, freedom, and relief that was experienced upon receiving that forgiveness, as well as the gratitude that he or she has for having been forgiven. (p. 124)

Here we have an echo of the parable of the servant unwilling to forgive those in debt to him but wanting to be forgiven the debts he owed his master, which teaches that just as God forgives you, you should forgive others, and if you don't forgive others, God won't forgive you.

If and when the potential forgiver experiences a sense of gratitude, three things will probably occur, according to Worthington's analysis of the forgiving process. His emotional state will reflect positive emotions such as joy and love, and these will become associated with the offender because they were aroused in the context of a treatment meant to promote forgiveness of the offender. Second, the potential forgiver will project these good feelings empathically on to the offender and, third, he will be motivated to see the offender as in need of forgiveness, and will offer it to him as a gift.

Even if the potential forgiver has, by now, forgiven the offender in his heart, he might have second thoughts because the original conditioned fear which made him unforgiving might reemerge. Relying on several social–psychological theories that suggest that public commitment to private thoughts and feelings can reinforce them, Worthington includes commitment as the fourth step of his model. In order to encourage this commitment, the forgiver is taken through a series of five exercises:

1. We ask the person to talk about his or her experience of forgiveness.
2. Then, the person is invited to write a certificate stating the date of granting forgiveness. That certificate is retained for later reference.
3. The person is invited to write a letter of forgiveness explicitly forgiving the person for the harm *as if* the person were going to send the letter.
4. The person is invited to read the letter aloud to the psychoeducational group . . . the therapist, a family member, or a partner.
5. The person is asked to consider whether it is possible and wise to send

the letter or some edited version of it to the offender. This fifth step, though, begins reconciliation, because it involves a step that might lead to the rebuilding of trust; therefore it can be a continuation of forgiving within the reconciliation process—but it is not necessary to forgiveness. (pp. 126–27)

In the final, fifth step of the pyramid, the forgiver is taught a variety of techniques to help him maintain the forgiveness over time, such as emotional management and refocusing thoughts when emotions and thoughts that might weaken the forgiveness recur.

Based upon his work as a family therapist, Worthington suggests that empathy, humility, a public commitment to forgive, and confession will restore and enhance marital love, whose three major components are intimacy, passion, and commitment between husband and wife. They will also improve other troubled dyadic (two-person) family relationships, such as those between parent and child and between siblings.[13]

The positive effects of confession in inducing forgiveness and reconciliation are illustrated by a family he was treating. The husband had become an alcoholic (but didn't admit to it) shortly after his mother's death. He was locked in bitter dispute with his wife, who constantly complained about the effect his drinking and the verbal abuse that accompanied it were having on their adolescent children. The man's feud with his sister over their mother's estate and the ruptured relations that resulted caused guilt, grief, and disruption in the two families, who had been close prior to the feud. Each member of the family was blaming and accusing others for having wronged them. With the therapist's guidance, eventually each one admitted that they had also done things that were wrong and expressed hostile emotions to others in the family constellation.

As members who were present confessed their part (often tearfully) in the continuing estrangement, the man's sister eventually began to cry. She granted forgiveness and also asked for forgiveness for her greed. She said that the confession of the oldest daughter [that she had blamed her father and aunt for poisoning her childhood], and seeing her so willing to forgive [them] had "melted her anger." She also said that she could finally see how much they all needed to forgive each other for the many things that had occurred over the previous three years. . . . Although this session of tearful confession and forgiveness did not resolve all of the family's problems, it was a turning point. The husband drank less, the wife complained less and their children experienced fewer problems. The couple also reported that they felt that within their own nuclear family, and between their family and the aunt's family, forgiveness and reconciliation had begun. (p. 73)

There are many intriguing elements and hypotheses in Worthington's pyramid model, which has been used by hundreds of people reporting significant success. However, as Worthington himself admits, there is much in the model that is speculative, and controlled research studies of its effectiveness are needed. It might work better for devout Christians (although it is meant as a general model applicable beyond just a Christian clientele) than for other people. On the face of it, it would seem more appropriate to forgiveness within a marital or family setting in which there are reservoirs of positive, loving experiences, from which memories and imaginings conducive to empathic compassion can be drawn, than to settings that lack such a reservoir. Another fact that might influence its effectiveness is the relative severity and number of offenses committed by each party, when both are called upon to forgive reciprocally.

Although it is often useful and sometimes necessary to have the expertise of a therapist to guide people along their forgiveness journey, you can apply on your own many of the ideas and techniques used by therapists in your personal struggle with anger and forgiveness.

· · ·

Michael McCullough, a student and colleague of Worthington, has developed a Forgiveness Manual used in an eight-session forgiveness workshop.[14] Over the course of the workshop, participants analyze the processes involved in hurt, anger, and forgiveness, and they are presented with thoughtful and challenging questions and exercises. For example, they are asked to assess the hurts they experienced with respect to eight categories:

Disappointment
Rejection
Abandonment
Ridicule
Humiliation
Betrayal
Deception
Abuse

When we are hurt, we often have diffuse, undifferentiated negative thoughts and feelings. This fact makes it difficult for us to understand exactly what we are experiencing. But emotional self-understanding is a necessary first step toward dealing intelligently and constructively with our emotions, and McCullough's materials excel in providing people with insight into the psychology of their emotional reactions.

Participants are first taught about each of the stages in the "process of experiencing interpersonal hurt," which usually includes shock, denial, recognition of the offense, and a cycle of negative emotions. They are then taught about the stages of forgiveness, and how to prepare the way for reconciliation.

The section "Nurturing the Hurt," for example, includes the following explanation and discussion questions:

> Although your needs for security and significance have been threatened by the serious emotional hurts you have received, some of the effects that the hurts have had on your thought life and emotional life may "nurture the hurt," or cause it to recycle and re-inflict damage. This may be a way your memory works in order to prevent yourself from [experiencing] future hurt. Additionally, when we are hurt by the behavior of others, we sometimes make things worse by the ways in which we act towards them. Some of our actions can create even more destruction.
>
> Discussion Questions:
> 1. Are there any ways that you are possibly nurturing the hurt in your minds now? Can you think of any ways that you think about the events that happened to you that may serve to continue your pain?
> 2. What are some of the payoffs of nurturing your hurt?
> 3. What are some of the costs of nurturing your hurt?

McCullough has also developed a six-session marital forgiveness workshop, "Building the Forgiving Marriage."[15] The goal of this workshop is preventive rather than therapeutic. It is geared to couples functioning at high or moderate levels who would like to develop skills that will help them avoid marital difficulties in the future. It is also appropriate for premarital counseling and for newlyweds whose marriages have shown initial signs of distress.

The program focuses on cultivating a disposition to forgive. Spouses who successfully develop what Roberts (1995) calls the virtue of "forgivingness" will have mastered skills that facilitate forgiving and will also be more inclined to forgive than to be resentful when they are hurt by their partner. They will thus enjoy "forgiving marriages."

McCullough uses Gottman's (1989, 1993a, 1993b)[16] "cascade theory of marital dissolution" to understand how forgiveness skills can prevent the disintegration of marriages. According to Gottman, three factors contribute to cascading, which eventually results in the breakdown of a marriage. In the first phase, as hurtful behaviors increase, there is a gradual change in the overall ratio between negative and positive marital behaviors until a critical threshold is reached at which there are more negative than positive behaviors. This changes the initial positive perceptions that spouses had of one another, and of the quality of their marriage, into negative emotional perceptions. The high rate of negative behaviors and negative perceptions results in chronic physiological arousal. Eventually the spouses become so overwhelmed by the pain of conflict and the constant criticism and expressions of negative feelings that they

> distance themselves from one another. They share fewer activities together, develop friendships that they do not share with their partners, and eventually find it easier to manage their marital problems on their own rather than in tandem. . . . Spouses find it more difficult to remember the reasons they got married, how they became attracted to each other, and the potential incentives for staying together. As these relational memories (which form a basis for commitment to the relationship) erode, the perceived incentives for staying married become fewer and fewer until the couple ends up separating and, eventually, ending the marriage through divorce. (pp. 82–83)

When, for example, a wife has come to perceive her basic relationship with her husband as a bad rather than a good one, she might respond to a new hurtful behavior on his part by feeling herself to be an innocent victim, in which case she will tend to further withdraw from contact with him, as a mechanism of self-defense. Or she might respond with righteous indignation, in which case she will more likely retaliate in order to protect her self-esteem. Neither of these responses will resolve the hurts but will instead prolong or exacerbate their effects (p. 83).

The earlier in the "cascade" that measures can be taken to halt the decline in the couple's relationship, the greater the chance that the marriage will be saved. McCullough hypothesizes that a forgiving disposition can be useful in preventing the cascade effect. Among the ideas, exercises, and discussion topics included in the six sessions are the following:

Session 1

After the spouses have been educated about the meaning of forgiveness, they are asked to think of three incidents in which their spouse hurt them that they need to forgive. These should include a minor, a moderate, and a very painful hurt. They then learn about the cascade theory and the way it describes the key elements that erode a marriage. They can now look at the list of their hurts and the anger and other emotions they experienced in response to these hurts and think about how they might feed into the "cascade triad" of a high ratio of negative to positive experiences, the development of negative perceptions, and distressful emotional arousal.

Session 2

This session begins with a discussion of the psychology of interpersonal hurts, including discussions of the natural reactions to being hurt by another, such as the rupturing of bonds that had existed between them, that caused psychological distancing, produced negative physiological reactions, and engendered a desire to retaliate.

Although these reactions may be natural or normal, they aren't conducive to happy marriages. The husbands and wives are asked to reflect regularly on whether they want a marriage that is "bitter or better?" Discussion ensues about why it is difficult to forgive, including automatic thoughts and feelings spouses often have such as "I won't forgive because my spouse never accepts responsibility for what he/she does," "I would be a hypocrite if I forgave, because I do not feel like forgiving," and "Forgiving is only for weak people." At the end of the session, the leader introduces the empathy model of forgiving in which "empathy is defined . . . as a psychological highway that leads to forgiveness," followed by an exercise in which each participant is asked to recall times when he/she felt empathy for his/her spouse.

Session 3

Here the participants delve more deeply into the role of empathy in forgiveness. They also learn about "two-way" and "one-way" channels for developing empathy. Two-way channels involve a change in the offender's behavior which induces a change in the victim's perception of the offender. Apologies and positive behavior change, for example, are two-way channels. An important skill that spouses need to develop is how to elicit apologies with a sensitive reproach.

> Sincere apologies are most easily elicited when the offended spouse uses "I messages" that specify the offending behavior, a feeling associated with the offending behavior, and the reason why the behavior was perceived as hurtful ("I was hurt by your late arrival home from work because I felt neglected and taken for granted"). This form of reproach is most likely to cause the offending spouse to develop empathy for his or her injured partner, which may also facilitate a contrite apology. (pp. 86–87)[17]

In this session the spouses practice the art of apologizing and of eliciting apologies using the list of offenses that they recalled.

Session 4

The session begins with a discussion of the distinction between hard and soft disclosures, since another two-way channel to encourage empathy involves the use of soft rather than hard disclosures when accounting for one's behavior.[18] When we try to explain something we did that hurt another person, we might reveal motives such as disgust, anger, hatred, annoyance, or frustration, which are "hard." Or we might indicate that our hurtful behavior was motivated by feelings such as fear, disappointment, sadness, or doubt and uncertainty, which are "soft." Soft disclosures elicit empathy from the victim, whereas hard ones do not. Couples practice soft disclosure, using the moderate hurts from their personal "hurt list" as material for the exercise.

Session 5

Here the concept of one-way channels to empathy and forgiveness is introduced. One-way channels that develop empathy do not require any interaction between the offender and the victim. The offended spouse uses them privately. Among the most important of these channels is one in which you change the attributions you make concerning the motives and the responsibility of the offender. In order to encourage empathy for the offending spouse, McCullough encourages "causal agnosticism" and "expanding the attributional repertoire" of the victim. No one is aware, or capable of, taking into account all of the factors that influence another person's choices. Therefore, whenever we judge another person's responsibility for an action, our judgment should be tentative rather than final. Spouses rarely recognize that their judgments of responsibility can be more flexible and subject to revision than they typically tend to be. To facilitate this attitude, the therapist guides the spouse who has been hurt in making a list of influences, such as environmental, developmental, and relationship ones, that might have caused the offending partner's behavior. "The goal here, of course, is to help a client widen his or her attributional repertoire so that it becomes possible to see a spouse's hurtful behavior as a complex, ironic mix of the spouse's goodness and badness and the susceptibility of human choice to the external factors that shape who people are and the choices they make" (p. 89).[19]

These concepts are explained to the participants, and they are asked to apply them to marital relationships in general and to their own "marital hurts" list.

The rest of the session is devoted to recalling instances in which each participant needed forgiveness and was granted it, and the role that gratitude and humility can play in developing empathy and a forgiving disposition. The couple's homework assignment for the final session is to prepare themselves to ask forgiveness for the severe offenses against their spouses, integrating apology and soft disclosure in their requests.

Session 6

In this final session, spouses seek forgiveness from each other, and the group leader integrates for the participants the major ideas and skills of forgiveness-seeking that they have learned. Then three additional ideas are introduced and discussed. Forgiveness has its limits, and, for especially serious issues such as marital violence, infidelity, or abuse and neglect of children, other interventions may be necessary. Forgiveness is not a panacea for all marital difficulties. There are problems in communication or conflicts that may not be a result of one spouse wronging the other but of differences in habits, opinions, or preferences. Finally, spouses must be willing to adjust their behaviors to accommodate the needs and sensitivities of their partners if they want their marriages to succeed and be a source of mutual joy and happiness.

McCullough concludes his description of his marital forgiveness workshop with a call for more research into the effectiveness of all forgiveness-based marital therapies and workshops, including his own. He is aware that some proponents of forgiveness make claims for it that have not been substantiated. He also advises "pro-forgiveness" advocates not to dismiss the possibility that sometimes forgiveness might create rather than solve problems. He notes that some mental health professionals have expressed serious reservations about forgiveness. "We need to take them seriously. The best way to give these reservations the respect that they deserve is to direct some resources toward a deliberate search for the dark side of forgiveness"[20] (p. 94).

•   •   •

Eric Lomax, a British soldier captured by the Japanese in World War II, wrote a moving memoir.[21] This book should be read by all who want to understand the power of deep, sincere repentance to induce forgiveness and to transform a victim's desire for revenge into compassion for and reconciliation with an offender. It also provides insight into the power of forgiveness to provide respite to the repentant offender from his guilt and fear of divine or karmic punishment.

In 1943 Lomax was one of several hundreds of thousands of prisoners of war forced to work on the construction of the notorious Burma–Siam railroad under extremely brutal and inhumane conditions. The project took the lives of 250,000 men, and after the war several of the Japanese involved were convicted as war criminals and executed. During a period of his captivity in Kanburi, Lomax was subjected to prolonged interrogations and horrific torture. The Japanese soldier who acted as English translator/interpreter during his interrogations was Nagase Takashi. Lomax did not learn his name until decades later but could never forget his voice and face.

For fifty years after the war, Lomax harbored dreams of revenge against his interlocutors and the translator and felt a deep hatred for Japan and the Japanese. Although after the war he resumed a "normal" life, the emotional and psychological scars of his experiences were deep and pervasive—"there is no statute of limitations on the effects of torture" (p. 200). He was plagued with recurring nightmares.

> I would be left in a cell of my own, with no food or water, starving and suffocating and crying out for release. . . . and I knew I was never going to be released. . . . I would fall endlessly and painfully down the iron staircase covered in disgusting sores. . . . Outram Road kept coming back, night after night. Silence, disease, hunger, fear, and above all the intensity of the uncertainty and fear. (pp. 209–10, 221)

By night it was nightmares, by day it was fantasies of revenge.

> In the cold light of day my anger was more often turned to the Japanese who had beaten, interrogated and tortured me. I wanted to do violence to them, thinking quite specifically of how I would like to revenge myself on . . . the hateful little interrogator. . . . with his dreadful English pronunciation. . . . I wished to drown him, cage him and beat him and see how he liked it. (p. 210)

Lomax became obsessed with finding out more about the Japanese who had tortured him (and other prisoners of war).

> Physical revenge seemed the only adequate recompense for the anger I carried. I thought often about the young interpreter. . . . There was no single dominant figure . . . on whom I could focus my general hatred, but because of his command of my language, the interpreter was the link; he was the centre-stage in my memories; he was my private obsession . . . he gave voice to the big torturing NCO: he represented all of them; he stood in for all the worst horrors. (pp. 225–26)

In January 1985 Lomax wrote an article for a newsletter for ex-prisoners of war appealing for information about the events in Kanburi in 1943. He wanted to identify the men who had beaten him, and their interpreter. The psychic toll of memories of torture and repressed but periodically flashing anger had contributed to the dissolution of his first unhappy marriage. Now it was adversely affecting his second, happy one. He agreed to seek the help of the Medical Foundation for the Care of Victims of Torture in London, making the six-hundred-mile roundtrip journey from Scotland once a month with his wife, Patti. For the first time in a half century, he felt that he could talk about the torture he experienced and the psychological toll it had taken with people who could understand and empathize. The director of the foundation, Helen Bamber, had worked for two and a half years after the war in the concentration camp at Bergen-Belsen where she had learned how important it was to give people who had suffered torture and related traumas the opportunity to talk, and to listen patiently and sympathetically to their testimony.

In response to his letter, Lomax received a copy of an article from the *Japan Times* about a Mr. Nagase Takashi, a frail seventy-one-year-old Japanese veteran of World War II. After the war, Nagase had been assigned by the British the task of accompanying a team from the Allied armies to translate for them as they tried to identify alongside the railway line the thousands of obscured, hidden, and unmarked graves of Allied POWs who had died at the hands of the Japanese. Nagase said that until this experience he had not been aware of the fate that awaited the trainloads of POWs whom he had seen in 1943 being shipped from Singapore to Thailand to work on the railway. As a result of this experience of seeing thousands of corpses in graves alongside the tracks, he said that he decided to dedicate the rest of his life to memorializing these victims of the Japanese.

The article had a picture of Nagase, and upon seeing it Lomax recognized him as the man who had been the interpreter for his torturers.

Nagase had suffered ill health and recurrent cardiac attacks for many years. He was quoted as saying that with each such attack he had "flashbacks of Japanese military police . . . torturing a POW who was accused of possessing a map of the railway. One of their methods was to pour large amounts of water down his throat. . . . As a former member of the Japanese Army, I thought the agony was what I have to pay for our treatment of POWs" (p. 239).

The article described how Nagase visited the Allied cemetery that had been established in Kanchanaburi in Thailand many times to atone for his guilt by laying wreaths there, and said that he had established a foundation for surviving Asian forced laborers, vast numbers of whom had also died working on constructing the railroad.

Lomax continues, "I had apparently found one of the men I was looking for. . . . The years of feeling powerless whenever I thought of him and his colleagues were erased. Even now, given the information about what he had done since the war . . . the old feelings came to the surface and I wanted to damage him for his part in ruining my life" (p. 241).

Lomax made inquiries about Nagase and learned that he was a staunch opponent of resurgent Japanese militarism but,

> what I could not tell was whether his expressions of remorse were genuine or not. I needed to see that for myself. The thought was entering my head, distantly at first, that perhaps I should try to meet this man, to make up my mind with that face in front of me again. . . . I wanted to see Nagase's sorrow so that I could live better with my own. . . . One or two people suggested that perhaps it was time for me to forgive and forget. . . . The majority of people who hand out advice about forgiveness have not gone through the sort of experience I had; I was not inclined to forgive, not yet, and probably never. (p. 241)

Lomax learned that Nagase had published a small book, which had been translated into English in 1990, describing his experiences during and after the war. He eagerly sent for a copy of it, hoping it would reveal details about the events of 1943 with which he was obsessed. Sure enough, he read about the events that led up to his interrogation and torture: "Suddenly it's as though he [Nagase] steps out from behind a screen and I am a looking at a scene familiar to me distanced as though in a dream."

Nagase described the interrogation of a prisoner who had been suspected of spying because a search of his belongings revealed a sketch of the Thai–Burma railway with names of its stations. The prisoner stubbornly denied the charges. Had he confessed, he would have been put to death. Nagase continued:

> The fierce questioning continued from morning till night for over a week, which exhausted me as well. . . . The MP beat him with a stick. I could not bear the sight, so I advised him to confess to avoid further mental and physical pain. He just smiled at me. Finally, the policeman applied the usual torture. First they took him to the bathtub. . . . Then his broken right

arm was placed in his front and his left arm behind his back, tied with a cord. They laid him on his back with a towel loosely covering his mouth and nose. They poured water over his face. The soaking cloth blocked his nose and mouth. He struggled to breathe and opened his mouth to inhale air. They poured water into his mouth. I saw his stomach swelling up. Watching the prisoner in great torture, I almost lost my presence of mind. I was desperate to control my shaking body. I feared that he would be killed in my presence. I took him by the broken wrist and felt the pulse. I still remember clearly that I was relieved to feel an unexpected normal pulse.

With the prisoner screaming and crying, "Mother! Mother!" I muttered to myself, "Mother, do you know what is happening to your son now?" I still cannot stop shuddering every time I recall that horrible scene. (pp. 247–49)

Eighteen years after the war, Nagase visited the Allied war cemetery and offered a wreath at the base of the white cross in its center. He writes,

The moment I joined my hands in prayer . . . I felt my body emitting yellow beams of light in every direction and turning transparent. At that moment I thought, "This is it. You have been pardoned." I believed this feeling plainly. . . . The sense of guilt had lain in my mind for a long time. The moment I visited the graves, I felt the sense of guilt vanish. (p. 251)

The experience of pardon did not result in Nagase's forgetting the war and the suffering it caused. He continued to support surviving Asian slave laborers who, unable to return to their native lands, lived out their miserable lives in Thai villages along the rail line. He opened a temple of peace and courageously criticized militarism.

How did Lomax respond to Nagase's autobiography? "It all seemed admirable . . . but I felt empty. And I wondered at his feeling that he had been forgiven. God may have forgiven him, but I had not; mere human forgiveness is another matter" (p. 252).

Lomax's wife Patti also read the book, and Nagase's description of his experience of pardon while laying a wreath at the cross in the cemetery made her even angrier than it did Lomax himself. "She wanted to know how Nagase could feel pardoned. How could his sense of guilt simply 'vanish' if no-one, and me in particular, had pardoned him?" (p. 252).

Patti wrote to Nagase telling him that the prisoner who was tortured was her husband, who would like to correspond with him in order to receive more information about the events leading up to the episode Nagase described. She included a picture of Lomax. Patti also wrote:

My husband has lived all these years with the after effects of the cruel experiences he suffered and I hope that contact between you could be a healing experience for both of you. How can you feel "forgiven," Mr. Nagase, if this particular former Far Eastern prisoner-of-war has not yet forgiven you? My husband does understand the cultural pressures you were under during the war but whether he can totally forgive your own involvement remains to be seen and it is not for me, who was not there, to judge. (p. 253)

Nagase wrote back:

Dear Mrs Patricia M Lomax

I am now quite at a loss after reading your unexpected letter. . . . The words you wrote to me "If this particular former Far Eastern Prisoner of War has not forgiven you" has beaten me down wholely, reminding me of my dirty old days. . . . Please tell your husband that if I am a bit useful for him to answer any questions that he has had in mind, I am willing to answer him. . . . Looking at the picture, he looks healthy and tender gentleman, though I am not able to see the inside of his mind. Please tell him to live long until I can see him. . . . The dagger of your letter thrusted me into my heart to the bottom. (p. 254–55)

Lomax describes Patti's and his own reaction to Nagase's letter.

Patti thought this was an extraordinarily beautiful letter. Anger drained away; in its place came a welling of compassion for both Nagase and for me, coupled with a deep sense of sadness and regret. In that moment I lost whatever hard armour I had wrapped around me and began to think the unthinkable: that I could meet Nagase face to face in simple good will. Forgiveness became more than an abstract idea: it was now a real possibility.

As the days went by it seemed that Nagase's sincerity might be utterly genuine. I began to appreciate more fully how damaged he must be by what he had done, however unwillingly; an interrogator suffering in retrospect with his victims. Nor was his concern to make reparation some occasional thing; it was truly almost a way of life. . . . He had also become a devout Buddhist. (p. 255)

Lomax and Nagase arranged to meet in Thailand together with their wives, in Kanburi where Lomax had been imprisoned. At the designated site, Lomax saw Nagase approaching him, and as he came closer

> I remembered him saying to me again and again, "Lomax, you will tell us," and other phrases he had recited in the voice I hated so much . . .
>
> He began a formal bow, his face . . . agitated. . . . I stepped forward, took his hand and said "Ohayo gozaimasu, Nagase san, ogenki desu ka?" "Good morning, Mr. Nagase, how are you?"
>
> He looked up at me; he was trembling, in tears, saying over and over "I am very, very sorry . . ." I somehow took command, led him out of the terrible heat to a bench in the shade; I was comforting him, for he was really overcome. At that moment my capacity for reserve and self-control helped me to help him, murmuring reassurances as we sat down. It was as though I was protecting him from the force of the emotions shaking his frail-seeming body. I think I said something like "That's very kind of you to say so" to his repeated expressions of sorrow.
>
> He said to me "Fifty years is a long time, but for me it is a time of suffering. I never forgot you, I remember your face, especially your eyes". He looked deep into my eyes when he said this. . . . He was kind enough to say that compared to my suffering his was nothing; and yet it was so obvious that he had suffered too, "Various sufferings, various sufferings in my heart and mind." (pp. 264–66)

Lomax and Nagase spent several days together in Thailand. Lomax realized that, although by now he had forgiven Nagase for his involvement in his torture, Nagase needed to receive from him a "formal" expression of that forgiveness.

> I still needed to consider the matter of forgiveness, since it so concerned him. Assuming that our meeting, in itself, constituted forgiveness, or that the passage of time had made it irrelevant, seemed too easy; once someone raises forgiveness to such a pitch of importance you become judicial. I felt I had to respond to Nagase's sense of the binding or loosening force of my decision.
>
> A kind Thai woman who we met that week tried to explain the importance of forgiveness in Buddhism to me; I understood that whatever you do you get back in this life and if what you have done is tainted with evil and you have not made atonement for it, evil is returned to you in the next

life with interest. Nagase dreaded hell. . . . Even if I could not grasp the theology fully, I could no longer see the point of punishing Nagase by a refusal to reach out and forgive him. What mattered was our relations in the here and now, his obvious regret for what he had done and our mutual need to give our encounter some meaning beyond that of the emptiness of cruelty. It was surely worth salvaging as much as we could from the damage to both our lives. The question was now one of choosing the right moment to say the words to him with the formality that the situation seemed to demand. (p. 269)

Lomax and Nagase had arranged that after their meeting in Thailand, Nagase was to accompany the Lomaxes on a trip to Japan. During his stay in Japan, Lomax "never felt a flash of the anger I had harboured against Nagase all those years, no backwash of that surge of murderous intent I had felt on finding out that one of them was still alive."

As the time for his return to Scotland neared, Lomax decided that the time to "formally" forgive could not be deferred. He asked to meet Nagase privately in the hotel room in Tokyo where Nagase was staying.

There in that quiet room . . . I gave Mr Nagase the forgiveness he desired.

I read my short letter out to him, stopping and checking that he understood each paragraph. I felt he deserved this careful formality. In the letter I said that the war had been over for almost fifty years; that I had suffered much; and that I knew that although he too had suffered throughout this time, he had been most courageous and brave in arguing against militarism and working for reconciliation. I told him that while I could not forget what happened in Kanburi in 1943, I assured him of my total forgiveness.

He was overcome with emotion again, and we spent some time in his room talking quietly and without haste. (pp. 274–75)

The next day Nagase and his wife accompanied Lomax and his wife to the airport.

As the plane tilted us over the bay of Osaka, I held my wife's hand. I felt that I had accomplished more than I could ever have dreamed of. Meeting Nagase has turned him from a hated enemy, with whom friendship would have been unthinkable, into a blood-brother. If I'd never been able to put a name to the face of one of the men who had harmed me, and never discovered that behind that face there was also a damaged life, the nightmares would have always come from a past without meaning. And I had proved for myself that remembering is not enough, if it simply hardens hate. . . . Sometime the hating has to stop. (p. 276)[22]

Forgiving Oneself & Forgiving God

Does it make any *logical* sense to talk of "forgiving oneself" or "self-forgiveness?"

If it does, what is the *psychological experience* of forgiving oneself?

In addition to questioning the logical and psychological sense of "self-forgiveness," do we also need to clarify whether it is *morally* appropriate to forgive oneself?

The answers to these three questions depend in large measure on how the word "forgiveness" is used in the expression to "forgive oneself," and what we mean by the "self." Furthermore, what is it that the self-forgiver is forgiving him/herself for?

As is often the case, differences of opinion result from the imprecise use of terms, and "self-forgiveness" is an ambiguous term. It is no surprise therefore that we find the following contrasting assessments of the propriety and value of self-forgiveness. On the one hand,

> it is not uncommon for people to say that they have forgiven themselves
> for their past transgressions, but such forgiveness is hollow and self-serving.
> Those who seek to take responsibility for their past failures must seek for-
> giveness from the person or persons they wronged. . . . The idea that we
> can forgive ourselves our own trespasses violates all traditional conceptions
> of forgiveness.[1]

On the other hand,

whatever one offers to another in interpersonal forgiveness is offered to oneself now in self-forgiveness . . . [which] may be defined as a willingness to abandon self-resentment in the face of one's own acknowledged objective wrong, while fostering compassion, generosity, and love toward oneself.[2]

Until now we have used the expression "to forgive" when a perpetrator has injured a victim unjustly. As a result, the victim harbors justifiable resentment against the perpetrator, and the perpetrator has incurred a moral and/or legal debt to the victim, such as to apologize, make reparation, or be punished. When the victim forgives the perpetrator, he no long harbors anger or resentment toward him (and may even come to love him, according to some) and "forgives" the private debt due (even though the legal punishment might, in some cases, still be implemented). Moreover, we are not legally or morally obligated to forgive an unrepentant perpetrator (unless we are a certain kind of devout Christian).

Amnon has raped Tamar. Tamar has not forgiven Amnon. Can Amnon forgive himself for what he has done to Tamar? How could he have the right to do so? If he does forgive himself, does that mean he no longer needs to repent, apologize, or make reparation to Tamar?

When formulated this way, self-forgiveness is neither logical nor moral. It is not logical because it refers to the perpetrator forgiving the perpetrator, rather than to the victim forgiving the perpetrator, which is what forgiveness is about. It is not moral because perpetrators don't have the moral authority to forgive their own crimes or sins. Moreover, it is the victim's resentment that has to be dissipated, and Tamar is still angry. If Tamar still has a claim on Amnon and still resents him, what substance is there to Amnon's self-forgiveness? It hasn't accomplished any of the things that forgiveness is supposed to accomplish.

It seems, however, that the advocates of self-forgiveness are using "forgiveness" in an analogical rather than in the traditional, conventional sense in which one person forgives another who has hurt him or, theologically, in which God forgives a human for offending him.[3]

Amnon is not only the perpetrator of an injury against Tamar, but, by raping her, he has perpetrated an injury against himself as well, because to hurt an innocent other is to demean yourself. More than this, if Amnon now feels guilt, shame, and anger at himself for his crime, then he too is a "victim," or at least a "sufferer" as a result of his own sin or crime because guilt, shame, and anger at oneself are painful experiences. If Amnon feels guilty, he may also demand of himself that he do penance (in addition to what he "owes" Tamar, or in the case that Tamar is no longer available). When Amnon forgives himself, he is dissipating the anger he was feeling about himself, and letting go of his painful feelings of guilt and shame and of his "demand" of himself that he should be punished for what he has done. Seen this way, we can talk "logically," even if only "analogically," about self-forgiveness.

Sometimes, moreover, a person may feel angry at herself, guilt-ridden, and ashamed even though there is no moral or rational reason that she should feel that way. The alleviation of this neurotic self-directed anger, guilt, and shame is also often referred to as forgiving oneself. Here the term forgiveness is even further removed from its traditional sense. If you didn't do anything wrong, you don't have to forgive yourself, but because you believe and feel that you did do something wrong, you might find it useful to go through the process of self-forgiveness. Similarly, it might be easier to alleviate your guilt effectively if a priest or therapist were to assign you some penance that would allow you to feel that you had atoned for the sin you believe you have committed than to convince you that you really aren't guilty of anything in the first place and don't need to perform any penances.

A central idea in self-forgiveness is that the offender learns to differentiate between the specific offense(s) he committed and his overall estimate of his worth as a human being. This is similar to what happens in interpersonal forgiveness in Enright's model. The victim allows his appreciation of the intrinsic human worth of the offender, and his right to love and compassion, to overcome his hostility toward him for the specific unjust acts he committed. So too in self-forgiveness, you don't judge yourself solely, or primarily, on the basis of your specific sins, crimes, or offenses. You acknowledge the wrongs that you did and hold yourself responsible for them and their consequences, but you also look upon yourself with love and compassion, which dissipates your guilt, your shame, and your anger at yourself.

However, the moral question remains: Is self-forgiveness in this analogical sense morally justifiable or desirable? There are arguments for and against forgiving oneself in such a circumstance. Let us consider the pros and cons.

Enright (1996), an advocate of self-forgiveness, addresses five rational and moral objections to it.[4]

1) "The self-forgiver will be unmotivated to alter offensive behavior if he or she is resigned to self-acceptance before a change in that behavior."

To this, Enright responds that the self-forgiver is not condoning or excusing his behavior. Moreover, as a consequence of forgiving himself, he can develop feelings of positive self-worth, which may induce rather than inhibit improved behavior.

2) It is irrational to expect a person to be an objective judge of his own behavior.

3) "Self-forgiveness is the . . . new opiate that not only blinds us to our faults, but makes those faults all the more likely to occur without guilt."

Marino, a critic of self-forgiveness, puts it this way:

> The person who forgives himself usually does so on the basis that . . . he has experienced the pain of guilt. And now, after a time, which is for some long and others short, the self-absolver concludes that the amount of guilt he has suffered is sufficient to pay for the suffering that he has caused. But . . . who am I to decide that the pangs of conscience that I have suffered are sufficient penance. . . . Indeed, if I could really assume the roles of both judge and defendant and so set my own penalties, there would not be any need to plead for forgiveness. I could decide the whole matter myself without ever coming under the examination of another; I could sentence myself to so much guilt, serve my sentence of knit brows, and then go my morally self-assured way.

Enright's responses to these criticisms are that in self-forgiveness we are not pardoning ourselves but "welcoming ourselves back into the human community," and since self-forgiveness originates from guilt, remorse, and shame, leading us out of pain via a prior path through pain, it is not an opiate.

4) and 5) Self-forgiveness may easily turn narcissistic, and the excessive preoccupation with oneself will discourage attempts to seek out forgiveness from those you offended, and reconcile with them.

To these objections, Enright argues that proper self-forgiveness does not stand alone but is part of a "triad of forgiveness," which includes "seeking forgiveness" and forgiving others, and as such is not narcissistic. Since self-forgiveness is seen as part of this triad, it is not incompatible with repentance ("seeking forgiveness") and reconciliation.

The debate between the advocates and the critics of self-forgiveness has been conducted primarily from the "armchair" of speculation or from therapists' anecdotes, with almost no rigorous research on what actually are the attitudes of self-forgivers and the consequences of their self-forgiving for their future behavior and feelings. My intuitive feeling is that there is greater moral danger than moral promise when self-forgiveness is encouraged in someone who has a weak conscience, with low levels of guilt and shame after having transgressed. Such a person needs more guilt and shame, not less. On the other hand, when the guilt and shame are intense and excessive (admittedly a subjective judgment, and one best made not by the offender himself but by an "outsider," such as a morally sensitive therapist or clergy, or anyone schooled in ethical and moral thought), the benefits of guiding the offender through self-forgiveness may outweigh the risks. But even when allowing for self-forgiveness, it must not be at the expense of demanding sincere remorse and repentance. Only after repenting has the sinner earned the right no longer to be as guilt-ridden and angry at himself as he was before repenting (although residual guilt, shame, and self-anger would still be appropriate, since even the best repentance cannot retroactively obliterate the pain and injury that the offense caused the victim).[5]

A psychologist colleague of mine proudly told me of a program he developed for hardcore violent criminals that encourages them not to think about their past, so that they can free themselves from its mire and hope for and work toward a better future. My response to this was that I would think that what these criminals needed was precisely the opposite—to think more, not less, about the injuries they had caused, so that perhaps they could develop a conscience and the feelings of guilt and shame that they lacked. I had been taught, I continued, that someone who has no remorse for the wrongs they committed is a psychopath, and that he seemed to be encouraging psychopathy.

This psychologist was a devout Christian, and my sense was that he and some of the other proponents of self-forgiveness were transferring to "secular" psychology their understanding (or misunderstanding) of the Christian notion that if the sinner professes his faith in Christ, his sins will be forgiven and he will experience a spiritual rebirth, even though he bypasses repentance. By repentance I mean not only confession of guilt, but remorse, apology, attempts at reparation, and resolve not to sin again. I say that the psychologist might be misconstruing Christian teaching, because many Christian theologians do not believe that God forgives sinners who convert to Christ but who don't repent in the above sense and do not believe that repentance is secondary to forgiveness.

Marino, a believing Christian who criticizes self-forgiveness, suggests a different explanation for the popularity among some psychologists of the notion of self-forgiveness:

Though I have twice heard the heretical invocation to self-forgiveness come from the pulpit, it is one thing for me to pray for and have trust in God's forgiveness and quite another for me to imagine that I can forgive myself. In this point, I have the strong sense that the idea of self-forgiveness is a symptom of the secularization process. People for whom the idea of a personal God has become an offense often wish to retain some of the ethico-religious ideas associated with faith, such as forgiveness. So, fantastically enough, they take this power upon themselves. . . . I am not suggesting that we should burn ourselves at the stake for our transgressions. . . . I am, however, insisting that not everything is permitted by the understandable desire to get on with our lives.

The Christian theologian Jones[6] opposes self-forgiveness because it shirks responsibility and the call for repentance. Here he criticizes Lewis Smedes's (1984) "therapeutic forgiveness," which privatizes and internalizes forgiveness.[7]

There is no sense in which [in Smedes's book *Forgive and Forget*] we are obligated, or even encouraged, to go to those whom we have wronged and seek forgiveness. Indeed, the one place where Smedes does acknowledge a person's need to be forgiven only reinforces this internalization: Smedes thinks that persons need to be forgiven as they forgive themselves. As he puts it, "To forgive yourself is to act out the mystery of one person who is both forgiver and forgiven. You judge yourself; this is the division within you. You forgive yourself: this is the healing of the split" (p. 77). Smedes seems to think that all that is needed is a kind of therapeutic will: I think I can forgive myself, so I can. But what if, as the Christian doctrine of sin at its best suggests, one of humanity's most intractable problems is self-deception? . . . Underlying Smedes' internalization and privatization of forgiveness is its preoccupation with individual feelings and thoughts at the expense of analyses of culpability, responsibility and repentance. (p. 50)

Jones agrees that Christians can gain insight from psychology and psychotherapy "particularly as we seek to learn the complexities of human sin and evil and the ways in which forgiveness needs to be embodied and understood" (p. 68) but not at the expense of what he considers to be the core Christian theological understanding of forgiveness. Christian forgiveness, as he understands it is not "primarily . . . absolution from guilt; the purpose of forgiveness is the restoration of communion, the reconciliation of brokenness. . . . It involves a way of life in fidelity to God's Kingdom" (p. 5).

Psychotherapists, too, differ on the desirability of guilt and self-forgiveness, as reflected, for example, in the following interchange between some professional therapists in a psychotherapy Internet forum in which this issue was raised.

1) When a person is suffering from guilt, and this suffering leads to mental anguish, so much so that s/he must seek inpatient psychiatric treatment, where does one begin with the concept of "forgiveness?" Patient cannot forgive him/herself. I would appreciate any/all feedback/recommendations.

2) My hypothesis is that individuals who . . . do not forgive themselves . . . engage in irrational, blaming.

To blame is not to merely hold oneself accountable for one's action, which is highly desirable, but to rank a person's worth accordingly. It is to put oneself . . . down for how [he] behaved. Typically this type of behavior substitutes the rational feelings of sadness and remorse for either depression, guilt, anger and/or vengeance. It is important to help the individual gain acceptance for [himself] . . . without holding a negative view. You want to fully accept that the individual has made a mistake, a screw up, or has botched things. This in fact might be reality. What is not reality is that because of this screw up, the individual [has] less worth. [He has] merely acted humanly which includes being imperfect. You support sadness and remorse while ablating guilt.

3) Guilt, allows us to exist in a world where we cannot run wild. It tells us that we have done something wrong. Now sometimes we act and feel as if we have committed a wrongdoing when we haven't. I use Cognitive Therapy with my patients where I . . . help them assess whether or not their belief is realistic.

When someone has done a wrong, however, a good dose of guilt serves a very useful purpose. Let us not discount the usefulness of a healthily functioning superego.

4) I fully agree with your thoughts here. I think where the pathology begins is when a person takes on false guilt, guilt that is not related to an actual wrongdoing but a perceived wrongdoing.

5) The argument that forgiveness of self . . . is not necessarily the best outcome to a situation and that guilt is useful and important, I think, is flawed. While I do agree that guilt at times does lead to a cessation of poor behavior, I think more times than not it leads to poor self image, depression, feelings of worthlessness, anger, vengefulness toward self or others and a

continuation or worsening in behaviors. Being angry at yourself and not liking your self tends to lead to punitive and self deprecating behavior. This does not serve you the individual nor the community. I believe that disliking your behavior and feeling sorry or regretful for how you have behaved allows for change and growth.

6) My thoughts about this subject have been shaped, too, by a scene in the movie "The Mission." Robert DeNiro plays a conquistador who mindlessly slaughters natives in the Amazon jungle. He feels excruciating remorse when he realizes the wrongfulness of his actions, a pain that is not alleviated by the priest offering him God's forgiveness. He requests and is given a penance to complete; he is to carry a full-sized cross on his back until such time as the priest indicates he can remove it. He suffers greatly, carrying the cross in a trek through the wilderness. Another member of the party, seeing his distress, says to the priest, "can't you tell him to remove the cross? He has suffered enough." The priest replies, "you know that and I know that, but he doesn't know it yet." As therapists, we sometimes work with people who are undergoing a penance of their choosing; in such cases our pronouncements that they don't deserve the suffering they are inflicting accomplish little. Perhaps we can, though, help them decide how much is enough.[8]

Given that some psychologists use "self-forgiveness" in therapy, and some religious thinkers advocate it, even where an actual, and not just an imagined, wrong has been committed, what are the stages of self-forgiveness and what does it feel like?

Enright (1996, pp. 125–26) applies, with the appropriate variations, his four-phase model of forgiving others to the process of forgiving oneself.

By the end of the Uncovering Phase, the person has acknowledged that he hurt another, realizes that he is imperfect, criticizes and may condemn himself, and might experience lowered self-esteem. By the end of the Decision Phase, he is committed to forgiving himself, which means that he will no longer condemn himself or engage in any form of self-revenge or self-abuse. The Work Phase includes becoming aware of his past habits, patterns of responding, and pressures to which he was subjected. This work is not intended to transfer blame from himself onto others or to external factors, but to enable him to accept his vulnerabilities and imperfections. In so doing, he will become more aware of how he has suffered from his behavior. He will be capable of loving himself notwithstanding his prior actions and the suffering they caused.

The final Outcome (or Deepening) Phase includes "realization that self has forgiven others and received forgiveness from others in the past; thus one could offer this now to the self . . . realization that one is not alone. There is social support and others have had to forgive themselves . . ." The culminating experience is a sense of release that results from "relief from excessive guilt and remorse."

The psychologist Steen Halling and his students and colleagues explored the phenomenology of forgiveness, including self-forgiveness.[9] For them the essential affective experience in self-forgiveness is movement from a sense that "something is fundamentally wrong about one's life, and a feeling of estrangement from self and others" to a feeling of being at home with one's self in the world. The self-forgiver moves from "an attitude of judgment to embracing who one is." The sense of estrangement is deeply painful and "often accompanied by intense feelings of self-recrimination . . . wracked with confusion, guilt, anxiety and despair." The self-forgiver moves from these dark and painful feelings into the light. For Halling, self-forgiveness cannot be achieved in social isolation. On the contrary,

> it is particularly important to experience some kind of loving acceptance from others, especially of those parts of ourselves that we find disturbing: our anger, hatred, inadequacy, mistakes, ignorance, hurtfulness, alienation, irresponsibility. . . . It may not be too strong a statement to say that 'self'-forgiveness always takes place in the context of some variation of loving relationships with others. (p. 155)

The self-forgiving process often requires determination and faith in the idea that, notwithstanding one's present state of "brokenness," healing is ultimately in the offing. It includes moments of "grace," some experience of an unexpected gift "almost out of nowhere," which facilitates the movement from the darkness of despair to the light of new hope. This experience is akin to the one which Nagase had when he placed the wreath at the base of the white cross in the Allied war cemetery.

Eventually the individual realizes that she has indeed "experienced forgiveness," and that what she had earlier condemned in herself and tried to change can now be accepted, since it is part of who she is. She feels a growing "sense of ease about [her] identity and a lessening of self-recrimination and anguish over [her] relationship to the world." As one self-forgiver in Halling's study put it, forgiving meant "loving myself including my mistakes or hurting other people . . . [it] seems very peaceful and empowering."

It is not the case that the self-forgiver "*never* feels bad or wrong, but that these feelings do not pervade the entire fabric of one's life." When he has fully accepted his humanness, the self-forgiver feels more closely connected to the world and to others, more intimately involved in life, at home with "renewed trust and acceptance of one's place in the world . . . more fully integrated into the ebb and flow of day-to-day living." This sense of being at home in the world and honest with oneself and with others brings with it "peace of mind, a sense of unity, a feeling that life is fundamentally right and needs no correction."

I think that this account of the emotional journey of the self-forgiver is what troubles those, like me, who are wary of the misuses to which self-forgiveness can be put. The emphasis is more on accepting who you are with your moral warts and pimples than on trying to treat them with the ointment of repentance. Both Enright and Halling seem to be more concerned with enabling the sinner to "accept" forgiveness, whether from himself, from others, or from God, than with inducing him to change his ways. Enright's forgiveness triad includes "forgiving others," "receiving forgiveness from others," and forgiving oneself; in counseling, these are to interact with one another. I think that offenders would be better served in counseling if there were less of an emphasis on helping them "receive or accept forgiveness" than on guiding them in how to repent. I also don't think that the main motive for repenting should be to receive forgiveness, but to rectify the evil you did and to make yourself a better person. If you do that, God, in Jewish and Christian theology, will forgive you, and if you are fortunate, so might your victim. But don't repent *in order to* assuage your guilt by "receiving forgiveness," but rather in order to transform yourself.

· · ·

"I will never forgive God for allowing my innocent son to suffer so much from cancer of the brain."

"After many years of anger at God for the loss of my entire family in a horrible car accident I have finally been able to forgive him."

"I can no longer pray to God because I cannot forgive him for sitting idly by while the Nazis tortured my beloved and pious father to death in front of my younger sister's and my eyes."

Why are some people angry at God?

Does it make sense to talk about "forgiving or not forgiving God?"

These questions have to be addressed at two levels, the theological one and the personal, emotional one.

People conceive of God and relate to God in different ways. For some, God is believed to be all-powerful and totally good and just. If God is just, good, and omnipotent, why does he allow the innocent to suffer? The apparent contradiction between this conception of God and tragic human experience can generate logical and emotional quandaries, especially for people who suffer greatly or who are sensitive to the suffering of others. Since they believe God is good and just, they can't hold him responsible for the evil and suffering in the world. On the other hand, since they believe he is all-powerful, they wonder why God allows evil and suffering to exist. Religious thinkers and theologians have suggested many different resolutions to this problem of theodicy (divine justice). It is not my purpose here to assess the logical adequacy of theologies about the nature of God or of theodicies, but to consider some of the effects that religious beliefs about the nature of God and how he relates to our world can have on human emotions directed toward God, especially anger and forgiveness.

Anger and resentment are aroused when we attribute malicious intent to the person, or to the being to whom we attribute the action (or inaction) that has hurt us. And forgiveness is a meaningful concept only when there is anger to be dissipated or subdued. It would seem, therefore, that a person who believes that God is perfectly just and good would never get angry at the God in whom he believes, since he will not attribute his suffering to divine malicious intent. In fact, most religious people with this view of God do not get angry at him. They wonder why God seems to allow tragedies and suffering, but they will not hold him responsible for them. Their belief in his justice and benevolence far outweighs their puzzlement and pain. Since, however, beliefs about God, and faith in him, can be modified, and tragedy in particular can make people reconsider their beliefs and faith commitments, one of the things that religions do is try to reinforce the beliefs they uphold, especially during traumatic and stressful life experiences that might induce people to waver. So, for example, it is the Jewish custom, upon hearing of someone's death, immediately to recite the phrase "Blessed is the true judge." This utterance reminds the believer that, notwithstanding what may seem to be a "false judgment" by God, the death of a beloved, or in fact of anyone, is not really unjust. God's judgments are always just and true. They are fair and true to the "facts" of the totality of the deceased's life. God has taken into account all of the information about the person, and we must have absolute confidence that his judgment that now was the time for the person to die was true to the facts. Interestingly, this phrase is only recited on hearing of a death, but not while a person is alive and suffering. Perhaps this is because there is a danger in ascribing the specific suffering of a specific individual at a specific time to being a "judgment" by God of him—even if we believe that some suffering is a punishment for sin. To do so might make us feel less responsible than we should for alleviating his suffering—why should we interfere with God's just judgment? Once he has died, however, we can't harm him by calling his death a judgment of God, and we can reinforce our faith in God if it wavers during this time of emotional crisis. This is especially the case when the death seems undeserved, as in the case of a child, when death was particularly painful, or when it is the death of a middle-aged person known to be righteous and who, we feel, should have been given a chance to live out his years. When the deceased is being brought to the cemetery for burial, mourners recite a more elaborate prayer that serves the same purpose of reinforcing belief in God's goodness, justice, benevolence, and omniscience. Similar prayers and ideas are part of the Muslim and Christian rituals of bereavement and mourning, adapted to their specific beliefs, but sharing the belief in divine omnipotence, justice, and perfection.

A religious person facing or witnessing suffering might for a while question whether God is indeed benevolent and just, and that person can experience some disappointment in, and anger at him. These feelings, however, will be short-lived, once he reaffirms for himself his basic belief that even though he may not understand God's ways, God is good and just.

I recently had the sad privilege of speaking with a devout Catholic gentleman in his seventies just a few days after his thirty-three-year-old son, a navy pilot, was killed during a test flight of a new airplane. This man and his wife had traveled from the Midwest to the East Coast in order to visit their son, his wife, and their two young children to joyously celebrate with them his thirty-fourth birthday. When they arrived at their son's home, they were informed that he had died that very same day in the crash. This man had the deepest love, respect, and admiration for his son, who was of sterling moral character, intellectually accomplished, and highly talented. I was impressed and inspired by his spiritual fortitude. He spoke of his belief that his son is now in paradise and that he hopes that when God sees fit to take him, he will be greeted by and reunited with his son. He cast no blame on anyone for the tragedy, praising the navy effusively for the moral and other support it gave him and his family in this difficult period. Nor was there any trace of anger or bitterness at God. He spoke lovingly of Jesus' love, accepting God's taking of his son as surely an expression of that love. The very notion of his having to forgive God would have been totally alien to his understanding of God, to his way of relating to God, and to his feelings of how God relates to him.

In order for us be angry, we have to believe that the injury we suffered is indeed an injury. Whether or not something is an injury is not always a simple, objective question with a straightforward answer. Our perception and interpretation of events and experiences determines whether we consider them to be hurtful to us. The martyr in flames at the stake who believes that it is noble to die for God and that suffering purifies the soul, although she is in great physical pain, does not interpret her experience as harm to her but rather as an opportunity to serve God at the highest level possible. She will not be angry at God. In fact, she might not even be angry at her tormentors, but will thank them for giving her the chance to martyr herself.

Another way, then, that religions address the problem of theodicy is by maintaining that what might appear to us to be evil and tragic is not really so. We only see bits and pieces of experience, fragments of a greater reality. Were we to "know" the world the way God knows it, in its fullness, and view it from his perspective, we would realize that the suffering, even of the innocents, serves some ultimate good end beyond our mortal horizon. Or, the innocent sufferers in this life will enjoy eternal and incomparable bliss in an afterlife, so that in retrospect their suffering will be seen to have been inconsequential as it was experienced for a fleeting moment. Moreover, for those who are not totally free of sin, suffering is a blessing in disguise because it cleanses their souls from the stain of sin, thereby purifying it for entry into the kingdom of heaven. These and similar beliefs both console and prevent or dissipate anger directed at God. The bereaved father of the navy pilot invoked some of these views as he grieved over his loss.

Why then, and when, do some religious people—Jews, Christians, and Muslims who believe in God's benevolence and justice—become angry at God for a *sustained* period of time, such that to speak of forgiveness or non-forgiveness of him can be imagined?

We should not assume that a person's intellectual understanding of God is the only determinant of how he feels about God or experiences his relationship with the God in whom he believes. A recurring tension in the three monotheistic faiths is between a conception of God as transcendent, impersonal, and unemotional on the one hand, and as immanent, personal, and emotional on the other. The God of the philosophers tends to be the former; the God of the Bible is predominantly the latter. Much theological ink has been devoted to reconciling the two different ways of thinking and feeling about God. Whatever might be the logical adequacy or inadequacy of these resolutions of the two different views at the theological level of analysis, most religious people find the immanent, personal, emotional God to be the one to which they can best relate, even if they would intellectually affirm that God, who is perfect, cannot err or do wrong and is not subject to the transitory vagaries of emotion. Moreover, most people's religiosity is not shaped by theology but by popular and devotional teachings and prayer. One prays to a God who hears, cares, and is empathetic. One beseeches God to be loving, compassionate, merciful, and forgiving. People importune God that he not be angry at them. If, then, a religious person relates to God as a being who is person-like, who has the freedom to behave and feel in ways that can be influenced by human entreaty or human actions, he can also experience feelings toward God that he would typically experience toward humans, including anger and disappointment, or even, in extreme cases, hatred. The fact that this way of experiencing God might not make sense at an abstract theological level may indicate that theology is far less important to the experienced religious life than is psychology.

In fact, disappointment in God, anger at him, and protests to him, are important themes in the Hebrew Bible, in narratives about Moses, in the prophet Jeremiah, in "lament" Psalms, and in the book of Job. Moses challenges the Lord's decision to destroy the people of Israel after the sin of the golden calf, and God relents. Job the Just, in particular, audaciously criticizes God for his apparent unjust ways. He expresses indignation and hurt not only for God's mistreatment of him but for the suffering and oppression of other innocent people.

> They thrust the needy off the road;
> The poor of the earth all hide themselves . . .
> They lie all night naked, without clothing,
> And have no covering in the cold.
> They are wet with the rain of the mountains,
> And cling to the rock for want of shelter . . .
> From the city the dying groan,
> And the throat of the wounded cries for help;
> Yet God pays no attention to their prayer. (Job 24:4, 7, 8, 12)

Job's reproach of God is all the more powerful when contrasted with Job's accounting of the concern and compassion he himself has shown for the poor, the helpless, and the abused (Job 28:12–17).

What is remarkable about the Jewish sages was their decision to include the book of Job in the canon of sacred scriptures notwithstanding its harsh critique of God. By the end of the book, Job accepts the idea that God's ways are inscrutable, but he is praised by God for his emotional integrity in expressing his bitterness at God and resentment of him, rather than suppressing these feelings by denying the reality of suffering, his own righteousness, or the apparent injustices that God tolerates or even perpetrates. Job doesn't forgive God. However, his anger is assuaged by his realization that there are things about God's nature and governance that are beyond his understanding.[10] This Jobean response to suffering and oppression might be adequate to dissipate the feelings of anger toward God of some religious people.

In his study of *The Holy Fire,* the teachings of Rabbi Kalonymous Kalman Shapira (the Hasidic Rebbe of the Warsaw Ghetto), Nehemia Polen addresses the biblical and rabbinic tradition of protest to God.[11]

> We find then, in Esh Kodesh (The Holy Fire), two apparently different responses to catastrophe: an attitude of radical and unconditional acceptance on the one hand, and a spirit of protest, confrontation, even outrage, on the other. . . . Expressions of protest and challenge are quite proper when directed to God as part of an ongoing relationship with him. . . . For Rabbi Shapira, as for the biblical and rabbinic tradition in general, the two attitudes—submission and challenge—are in no way contradictory; they are two complementary aspects of a full and healthy relationship between human being and God. By the very nature of the parties involved, the relationship cannot be one of equality; God, after all, always has the last say. Nevertheless, the human party to the relationship has the right to question, to challenge, to resist, especially if it is on behalf of the community. . . . However, once the divine will has been expressed, there must be self-surrender and unconditional acceptance.

Not all religious people angry at God eventually respond with submission or acceptance. Some change their conception of God, from a personal God who interacts with humans to an impersonal Creator or Source of All Being, who is remote from human affairs. Not expecting him to intervene in what happens here on earth, there is no disappointment when he doesn't. Others reconceive God as being benevolent but not all-powerful. He cannot be blamed for evil, since there are demonic forces, human or otherwise, which he, as much as he might want to, cannot always subdue. And some angry and disappointed believers eventually become agnostics or atheists. These transformations of one's views and feelings about God, especially when prompted by great suffering, often involve an intense emotional struggle, characterized by ambivalent, wavering feelings and guilt. Reeve Brenner[12] interviewed Holocaust survivors to find out how their experiences affected their faith and doubt. Here are two excerpts from responses that poignantly describe the emotional struggle of pious Jews caught in the Nazi maelstrom of atrocities. The first passage is by a survivor who had been forced to work in a gas chamber of a concentration camp, washing down the corpses of the innocent with a water hose.

> As far as religious belief in God is concerned, it seems to me in the camps there were two kinds of believing Jews . . . two contradictory responses to God for the horror of the life in camp. They are, either complete submission to God, capitulation to his enormous incomprehensible inscrutable will; or blaspheming him, cursing him, not really denying him but detesting him, despising him, menacing him; threatening him, threatening to withhold faith in him: "God, if you don't do something I'm going to stop believing in you . . ."
>
> You've got to be very close to God, you have to know him very well to blaspheme him. Only a deeply religious person can despise God, shake his fist at God and abuse him. A blaspheming Jew is a believing Jew. And the camps were composed of these Jews in great numbers. There were Jews who always tried to keep their heads covered when they ate, even if they only had the palm of their hand to serve as a skull cap. And they never took a gulp or bite without mumbling a prayer over the bread, regardless of how hungry they were. Moments earlier these same Jews were threatening God with denying His existence.
>
> Being an atheist in the camp was no easy thing. (p. 100)

Another survivor wrote,

> I call myself an atheist although I know deep in my heart that God exists. It is just that I refuse to give him the satisfaction of acknowledging it.
>
> I and others of the Saved Remnant are among the few of this world who understand what the death of God really means. We Jews of the Polish Jewish community lived with God as with an ever-available, always nearby Father who guided and sustained us and upheld our faltering steps. Suddenly He was there no longer; we were utterly alone.
>
> I shared a bunk in camp with a brilliant and sarcastic man who until his own death recited the kaddish [the prayer addressed to God on behalf of the dead] nightly—for God! He often laughed at himself bitterly, sar-

donically: here I am chanting the prayer for the dead [addressed to God] to the very One whose death I've pronounced. Does my dead God hear the prayers I'm reciting over His grave? (p. 118)

After reflecting upon the responses of Holocaust survivors who declared themselves to have become atheists as a result of their experiences during the war, Brenner comments,

for many "atheist" survivors, God's nonexistence was often declaimed when it was radical abandonment being experienced. Labeling oneself an atheist is not necessarily a theological posture. It is often an expression or manifestation of a psychological need, an emotional device to "get back at God," to "hurt" him, "punishing" God for hiding His face at a time when His presence was desperately sought. (p. 101)

One way in which individuals resolve or at least attenuate this anger at God without actually becoming atheists is, as we said, by adopting a revised conception of God, usually after considerable struggle and turmoil. Thus Harold Kushner in his immensely popular book *When Bad Things Happen to Good People* suggests that a theology which conceives of God as compassionate but with limited power can help people feel close to and supported by God, while not holding him responsible for their suffering and, therefore, not becoming angry at him. Most theologians are reluctant to think of a God who is not omnipotent and are critical of such an approach. However, as much as this idea of God might go against the predominant theologies of God in Judaism and in Christianity, Jon Levenson has persuasively argued that such a static notion of God's omnipotence prevents us from understanding the nature of God's action.[13] In Levenson's analysis of the Hebrew Bible, he shows that God is often depicted as still engaged in combat against powerful forces of chaos and evil in the world, so that the full import of his omnipotence has not yet fully manifested itself.

The concern of the creation theology is not creatio ex nihilo, but the establishment of a benevolent and life-sustaining order, founded upon the demonstrated authority of the God who is triumphant over all rivals. . . . YHWH's mastery is often fragile, in continual need of reactivation and reassertion, and at times, as in the laments, painfully distant from ordinary experience, a memory and a hope rather than a current reality. It is, in short, a confession of faith. (p. 47)[14]

God hasn't yet definitively subdued the powerful forces of chaos that he subjugated at the time of creation.

> Creation itself offers no ground for the optimistic belief that the malign powers will not deprive the human community of its friendly and supportive environment. . . . We are left with the bittersweet impression that the travails of the present, indeed of all history, are owing to the fact that the present order of things stands before rather than after the triumph of God. Leviathan is still loose, and the absolute sovereignty of the absolutely just God lies ahead. (pp. 47–48)

Levenson traces the subsequent development and elaboration of this biblical motif in the rabbinic idea that "God's rule will become complete only when the human heart, upon which it partly depends, will embrace his commands with wholeness and integrity" and in the medieval mystical belief in the power of the performance of God's commandments to "enable life-enhancing divine energy to flow freely and without inhibition" (p. 46). As long as there are people in the world who choose to do evil, the innocent may suffer because God's will is thereby not yet fully realized.

One emotional implication of this theology would be to lessen or eliminate anger at God for the evil and suffering the believer experiences, since the blame has been shifted from God to man, albeit not necessarily to the specific person who is suffering.

If we think of "forgiving" rather loosely, as simply letting go of anger, then we can understand how some religious people become angry at God and then "forgive" him. By revising their expectations of him, or by not holding him responsible for their suffering, they reduce or eliminate their anger at him. This, however, is a weak, self-therapeutic sense of forgiving. If forgiving refers to forgoing one's anger at someone who really wronged you and against whom you have a legitimate moral or legal claim and, in some cases, voluntarily forfeiting your right to have them punished by you or by others, then what we have been describing here with respect to feelings toward God is not really forgiving God. Of course people often will say "I forgive," "I won't forgive," or "I can't forgive," even though their use of the term doesn't make philosophical or theological sense. Philosophers, theologians, and psychologists don't dictate the use of language or have any monopoly over it. Given the different ways in which people use the word "forgive" and the fact that even the same person can use it with several different senses, some of the empirical research on forgiveness which relies on people's self-reports about their having "forgiven" someone, are not very reliable or valid indices of "true for-giveness."[15]

In everyday discourse, people usually have the right to use words as they like and not necessarily in accordance with any authoritative definition of them. There are situations, however, in which imprecise use of a word is a breach of moral, legal, or professional norms. If we didn't have shared mean-ings of words, then no one could be accused of deception, lying, or misrep-resentation. Some theologians to whom precise definitions of words, and the concepts and values they represent, are of great importance for the religious beliefs and values they wish to convey—as is the case with "to forgive" and "forgiveness"—are critical when others, especially those addressing the same constituencies, use the terms imprecisely. L. Gregory Jones attacks Smedes's discussion of forgiving God.[16] "Smedes's therapeutic forgiveness . . . finds its reductio ad absurdum when he suggests that we not only can but indeed ought to forgive God. It does not matter that God is not culpable; what matters are my own feelings and health." (Jones, p. 52)

Jones cites Smedes, "Would it bother God too much if we found our peace by forgiving him for the wrongs we suffer? What if we found a way to forgive him without blaming him? A special sort of forgiving for a special sort of relationship. Would he mind?" (Smedes, p. 83), and comments,

> Once one makes the move to a therapeutic mind-set, it becomes mind-numbingly difficult to explain why God "would mind." It hardly needs noting, however, that this is a god very different from the God who answers Job out of the whirlwind, the God to whom Jesus appeals in Gethsemane and again on the cross, the God in whose service Bonhoeffer accepted his own tragic death. (Jones p. 52). . . . It is inappropriate to hold God "re-sponsible" as the author of particular evils. Hence, though it might be psychologically comforting to "forgive God," as Lewis Smedes proposes . . . that is a theological and ethical mistake. There are other ways to deal with such situations than to engage in the mistake of thinking that we can or should "forgive" God. (p. 231, n. 35)

Notwithstanding theological difficulty with the concept of "forgiving God," it is for some people an important emotional issue, but one which has been rarely investigated empirically by psychologists. Within the context of research on the relationships between the tendency to forgive others and emotional well-being, a recent study examined the relationship between difficulty in forgiving God and the negative emotions of depression and anxiety in undergraduate college students.[17] The study also looked at whether subjects who were high on "trait anger," that is, have relatively stronger dispositions to become angry, in general, are less forgiving of God, and whether difficulty in forgiving God was related to a sense of alienation from God. They found that people who reported having difficulty forgiving God also scored higher on measures of depression, anxiety, trait anger, and sense of alienation from God. Since the study was correlational, it cannot be definitively interpreted to prove that, for the population studied, difficulty in forgiving God *causes* depression or anxiety or that trait anger or alienation from God is what makes forgiving God difficult. However, the findings do suggest to the authors that, insofar as certain religious beliefs and attitudes serve as adaptive skills for coping with stress and traumatic events,[18] the ability to forgive God might be more emotionally adaptive, in the sense of alleviating negative emotions, than the inability to forgive God.

Finally, anger at God can be displaced anger. It has long been observed that sometimes people will displace their anger from the person toward whom one would expect it to be directed onto another. This displacement may occur because to express anger, or even to feel angry toward the person who is really responsible for the angering event, could be dangerous, yet the anger needs some outlet, so it is taken out on a scapegoat. If a young child dashes into the road and is hit by a car and killed because of his father's neglect in watching over him, the mother, who holds the father responsible for the tragedy, might be afraid of being angry at him and blaming him. She might fear his retaliation, or she might pity him because he is suffering deeply from the loss of his child and his guilt at his negligence. She may therefore direct her anger instead at God, who might be a safer target if the God in whom she believes is not one who will punish her for being angry at him. If the mother eventually learns to recognize, acknowledge, and get over her underlying anger, of which she might not even be aware, at her husband, she will no longer need to feel angry at God. She will have, so to speak, "forgiven" both her husband and God.

SIX

The Essence of Repentance

From a religious perspective, one can commit sins against God or against humans. All sins against humans, however, are also offenses against God.

Judaism, Christianity, and Islam teach that we can rectify the damage we cause by our sins through the process of repentance. The three faiths' understandings of sin and repentance share many common elements but differ in some as well.

Christianity assumes that repentance will usually precede a sinner's conversion to Christ as Savior and forgiver of sins. However, even if the sinner does not *fully* repent (for example, if he has not apologized or made restitution to his victim) before his conversion, *some* Christians believe that God will forgive his sins anyway[1] because he has accepted Jesus as the vicarious sacrifice whose suffering and death atone for human sin. They assume that, in such a case, repentance will follow as a consequence of conversion to Christ. How frequently the acceptance of Jesus as Savior and redeemer from sin and sinfulness actually produces authentic and full repentance in the believing Christian is an empirical question not yet adequately researched.

Judaism and Islam place a greater emphasis on repentance as a precondition for divine forgiveness. In both religions there is, for the most part, no substitute for repentance as a means of attaining divine forgiveness of sins, although on occasion God's mercy and forgiveness will extend even to an unrepentant sinner. For example, the prophet Ezekiel proclaims that God will redeem Israel from captivity in Babylon and return her to the Holy Land, but not because she has earned this redemption by virtue of repentance. God will invest the people of Israel with a new and pure heart because it is in his interest that Israel be reestablished in the land and renew her covenantal relationship with him. Other prophets, such as Hosea and Jeremiah, speak of God's passionate love of Israel. Though she remains wayward, he will forgive her and redeem her from her suffering, which was punishment for her sins. For the most part, however, especially with respect to the individual rather than the nation, repentance is a precondition for forgiveness.

Psalm 51 provides one of the best biblical examples of the phenomenology of repentance. It is attributed to King David, who had sinned by commiting adultery with Bathsheba and then arranging for her soldier husband, Uriah, to be killed in battle so that he could take her as a wife. When confronted and condemned by the prophet Nathan for his crimes, David confessed his sins and pleaded for divine mercy. God showed mercy to David by not punishing him with immediate death. However, the child of the adulterous union dies, and for the remainder of his life David suffers. His family disintegrates in a maelstrom of incestuous rape, fratricide, and the untimely death of beloved sons who had challenged his royal authority.

The fact that God did not kill David immediately for his adultery and murder was considered to be a reflection of divine mercy. The subsequent tragic events are reflections of divine justice. Neither of these divine approaches to dealing with David and his family conforms to our notions of mercy or justice. As influenced as we are by the Bible, and as much as we should look to it for inspiration and moral guidance in many areas of life, not all of its values are acceptable to us today.[2]

The editor of the book of Psalms wondered what David experienced when rebuked by Nathan. His answer was Psalm 51.[3] He believed that the sentiments expressed in it were more or less appropriate to David the sinner when he recognized his sins and confessed them, as described in the book of Samuel. David had said to Nathan the Prophet, "I have sinned against the Lord," and Nathan responded, "Now the Lord has put away your sin; you shall not die. Nevertheless, because by this deed you have utterly scorned the Lord, the child that is born to you shall die" (2 Sam. 12:13–14).[4]

Let us turn now to the Psalm (51:1–17).

> Have mercy on me, O God,
> According to your steadfast love;
> According to your abundant mercy
> Blot out my transgression.
> Wash me thoroughly from my iniquity,
> And cleanse me from my sin.

For I know my transgressions,
And my sin is ever before me.
Against you, you alone, have I sinned,
And done what is evil in your sight,
So that you are justified in your sentence
And blameless when you pass judgment.
Indeed, I was born guilty,
A sinner when my mother conceived me.
You desire truth in the inward being;
Therefore teach me wisdom in my secret heart.
Purge me with hyssop, and I shall be clean;
Wash me and I shall be whiter than snow.
Let me hear joy and gladness;
Let the bones that you have crushed rejoice.
Hide your face from my sins,
And blot out all my iniquities.
Create in me a clean heart, O God,
And put a new and right spirit within me.
Do not cast me away from your presence,
And do not take your holy spirit from me.
Restore to me the joy of your salvation,
And sustain in me a willing spirit.
Then I will teach transgressors your ways,
And sinners will return to you.
Deliver me from bloodshed, O God, O God of my salvation,
And my tongue will sing aloud of your deliverance.
O Lord, open my lips,
And my mouth will declare your praise.
For you have no delight in sacrifice;
If I were to give you a burnt offering, you would not be pleased.
The sacrifice acceptable to God is a broken spirit;
A broken and contrite heart, O God, you will not despise.

What does the sinner experience?

The sinner is suffering, which induces him to cry out to God in his pain, a natural response of a religious person who believes in divine providence. He is also aware of his sin and feels alienated from God. This alienation has two effects on him. A spiritual void results from disconnectedness with the source of life, joy, and happiness. Although not explicit in this particular psalm, in similar ones there is also the fear that because God has turned away from him in response to his turning away from God in his sin, he is now vulnerable to further misfortunes. In the absence of God's caring protection, the sinner is exposed to forces of man or nature that can harm him.

A person who is not religious may experience a similiar feeling. When an individual violates an important social norm, he is punished, whether corporally or by imprisonment. However, an even more distressing punishment is for him to be excluded from the community and denied its protection, left alone in fear, anxiety, and helplessness to face the unknown and unpredictable, vulnerable to sickness and enemies. The existential angst of loneliness and vulnerability can be more painful than lashes or incarceration. In ancient Athens, some criminals were forced into exile. This is the punishment that God imposed on Cain, banishing him from his homeland to be a perennial wanderer, lacking the support of a community in the face of life's dangers. In the Middle Ages, sinners were excommunicated, especially if their sins reflected a challenge to the authority of the church or state. The threat of excommunication was a most powerful deterrent and means of social control. In the psalm, the sense of loss of divine protection is the psychological equivalent of the sense of abandonement of the excommunicant. The sinner in the psalm also experiences the burden of guilt for having transgressed divine law.

Induced to repent by his suffering, guilt, sense of abandonment, and recognition of his sin, the sinner pleads for mercy, forgiveness, and atonement. Naturally he wants his suffering to cease and his punishment to be waived. But he wants much more than just that. Of greater importance to him is that God reestablish the earlier relationship of love and care that they had prior to his sin. He wants to be close to God, to know and feel that he and God are in dialogue, he a loyal servant, and God a trustworthy and compassionate master. For this to occur, it is not enough that God mercifully desist from punishing him. He wants God to cleanse him from the stains of his specific sins and from the state of sinfulness in which he finds himself. He realizes that this can only be done if he is fully aware of his sins and their effects, to which he must attest. Indeed, he not only recognizes and remembers that he has sinned, but his sin is ever before him. His plea for mercy is not a challenge to God's justice. He fully accepts that he deserves his fate. He offers no excuses or justifications for what he did, appealing only to God's steadfast love. The sinner knows that if his plea for mercy, forgiveness, and atonement are granted, he will experience a deep joy and gratitude. Joy at the cessation of suffering, joy in the feeling of having been cleansed and purified, and joy in the restoration to him of the holy spirit—his once again being allowed into the presence of God and having the presence of God enveloping him. His gratitude to God for this will be expressed in several ways. Naturally he will refrain from sinning again. Moreover, his abounding joy in God's loving forgiveness and salvation will induce him to tell other transgressors that they too can return to God, who is ready to accept them again as long as they, like the psalmist, come to him with a contrite heart, their spirit of rebellious pride shattered into gleaming fragments of humility.

The psalmist asks God to "create in me a clean heart . . . put a new and right spirit within me," which might superficially suggest that he wants God to do the work of spiritual restoration for him, rather than do it on his own. In truth, however, the entire psalm declares to us that the sinner has become fully aware of his faults and it is he who initiates the process of repentance. Having fallen into sin, he is aware that he might sin again, as much as he does not want to. The spirit is weak, temptations are strong, man is foolish. He therefore appeals to God to give him the strength and wisdom to sustain his commitment to good. He is not shirking his own responsibility but reminding God of his human limitations, hoping thereby to arouse divine empathy and sympathy as well as divine assistance.

Many of these feelings, albeit in attenuated form, may be experienced when we realize we have sinned against others, especially those whose authority we fear and whose support we cherish. These may be parents, teachers, or a just government. We know that without them we could not survive or flourish, and we know too that their authority must be maintained in order for them to be able to protect and support us. Therefore, when we violate their trust or their norms or hurt them and feel alienated from them, it behooves us to repent and return. We must honestly face up to our sins and transgressions and through change and self-transformation restore the relationship we have ruptured. When the relationship has been infused with love and concern, the rupture and alienation can be deeply depressing, but the reestablishment of it can be a source of great comfort and joy.

If you have been deeply pained by the alienating consequences of your wrongdoing against loved ones, know that joy and comfort may await you if you do what you should to encourage your estranged parent, lover, or child to reconcile. They may be waiting for you, as God waits for the sinner to return, and the father of the prodigal son waited lovingly for him to come home, humbled but renewed.

The psalmist says that he has sinned against God alone, which suggests that the psalm wasn't actually composed by David, since David sinned against Uriah and Bathsheba as well. The psalmist also says that he was born guilty,

a sinner from the very moment of his conception. Although this could suggest
the Christian notion of original sin, the fact that such an idea is rarely if ever
expressed elsewhere in the Hebrew Bible suggests that he might be referring
to the biblical assumption that intrinisic to being human is the *propensity* to
sin.[5] He asks God to take this into consideration as a mitigating factor when
judging him and when considering his plea for forgiveness.

One of the strangest books of the Bible is the book of Jonah, which I
discussed when analyzing retribution, punishment, and justice. Recall that the
inhabitants of the city of Nineveh, capital of ancient Assyria, committed grievous sins against God and man. God is planning to destroy the city, as he had
done earlier to the corrupt cities Sodom and Gomorrah. Before doing so,
however, he decides to give the Ninevites an opportunity to repent and
thereby avoid their doom. He instructs the prophet Jonah to go to Nineveh
and warn its residents that, if they do not repent of their sins, God will destroy
the city and its inhabitants.[6] Jonah unsuccessfully attempts to flee from this
mission and, after spending some time in the belly of a large fish (no mention
of a whale in the text), makes his way to Nineveh to announce God's message.
The people repent and they are forgiven, but Jonah is depressed by this turn
of events. He would have preferred that the Ninevites be destroyed, and he
is rebuked by God for his attitude.

> When God saw what they did, how they turned from their evil ways,
> God changed his mind about the calamity that he had said he would bring
> upon them; and he did not do it.
>
> But this was very displeasing to Jonah, and he became angry. He prayed
> to the Lord and said, "Oh Lord! Is this not what I said while I was still in
> my own country? That is why I fled to Tarshish at the beginning; for I
> knew that you are a gracious God and merciful, slow to anger, and abound-
> ing in steadfast love, and ready to relent from punishing.
>
> The Lord said "Is it right for you to be angry? . . . Should I not be
> concerned about Nineveh, that great city, in which there are more than a
> hundred and twenty thousand persons? (Jon. 3:10–4:11)

What is the debate between God and Jonah? Why is Jonah troubled by
God's magnanimity and compassion? What does Jonah have against the idea
of repentance?

The doctrine of repentance is radical and revolutionary. That is why Jonah
has to be forced to go to Nineveh. Jonah probably made this argument to
God. "God, it isn't fair and just that the Ninevites who have sinned so much

against you (and others) should get off so easily just by repenting." After all, in terms of strict justice, why should someone who sinned be "let off the hook?" Why shouldn't he first be punished for his sins, and after that, if he repents, he can start with a clean slate from the time of repentance. The theological doctrine of repentance, in its full development in the late prophetic books of the Bible, however, is much more liberal and gracious to the sinner, because it promises that God will ignore, wipe away, or "conceal" some of the penitent's past sins. God loves his creations and prefers that they repent and be forgiven for what they have done rather than be punished for it.

In the Book of Jonah, God takes the initiative in calling the sinners of Nineveh to repentance by informing them of their impending doom. He doesn't wait passively for them to initiate repentance of their own volition. This theme recurs in the Hebrew Bible, as for example in Isaiah 55 where God declares, through his prophet,

> Seek the Lord while he may be found,
> Call upon him while he is near;
> Let the wicked forsake their way,
> And the unrighteous their thoughts;
> Let them return to the Lord, that he may have mercy on them,
> And to our God, for he will abundantly pardon. (Is.55: 6–7)

God's love and grace for sinners is not that he forgives them when they persist in their sinfulness, but that he offers them the possibility of repentance, which is grace enough. This offer of repentance and forgiveness is a double-edged sword. While opening the door to reconciliation, the offer also means that failure to repent compounds the initial sin, because failing to repent is a sin in itself, sometimes more damning than the initial one. The initial sin might have been a single, discrete event, but ignoring the divine call to repent is a continuous sin.[7]

. . .

It is rare that those whom we hurt explicitly ask us to repent and reconcile. They may not be interested in our friendship or love. When we hurt those who love us and who assumed that we loved them, they often hope that we will apologize and make amends so that they can reconcile, but are uncomfortable articulating these feelings. We should know, though, that our repentance for the wrongs we have done to others can be emotionally and morally valuable for us and them. In our culture, and in many others, there is an expectation that if we hurt others we should apologize, whether or not we are asked to do so. Sincere apologies are stepping stones to healing and reconciliation.

Often, in conflict, both parties have offended each other, albeit not to the same degree and not to the same measure of guilt, and both have to acknowledge the wrongs they have done, apologize, and repent for healing to occur. Indeed, since none of us are morally or emotionally unblemished, when two or more imperfect beings such as we are interact, there is a high probability that offenses will be committed by both. This is often the case in reasonably healthy marriages and families, in which there are so many different and interlocking strands in the relationships and dynamics that it would be rare to find the onus of all guilt and responsibility for offenses falling on just one member of the family. However, when a parent sexually or otherwise abuses an innocent, helpless child or other family member, obviously the victim does not share in any of the blame and guilt, although she often may irrationally or neurotically believe that she does. Similarly, there are ethnic conflicts in which one party is unequivocally the aggressor against an innocent victim, whereas, in others, both groups have done wrong to each other. To say, though, that neither antagonist is fully innocent of wrongdoing is not to say that both are equally guilty. Both may have to repent, but each has to acknowledge its specific sins, its level of guilt, and the reparation that it should accordingly be responsible for.

When you commit an offense against someone, whether by an act of commission or of omission, you usually produce three deleterious effects. First, in doing evil you lessen your own moral status. You are a less worthy individual than you were before your offense. Second, you have caused pain, humiliation, or injury to your victim. Third, beyond the specific pain or suffering which you inflicted, you have breached a human relationship. As a consequence of your offense there is now a net increase in the quantity or level of bitterness, hatred, and ill will in your familial or social setting. Not only does your victim bear you a grudge or feel resentful, but usually friends and family are also affected by what you have done, so that many human relationships which, before your offense, were amicable, or neutral, have now become infected with negative affect.

Repentance is the process whereby you rectify the harms you have caused. What does repentance entail and how might it repair the deleterious consequences of interpersonal sins or offenses?

Ideally, repentance includes four elements.

First, you must recognize and acknowledge your sin, and feel guilt and remorse for having committed it.

Second, you must repair the injury you caused.

Third, you must apologize to your victim.

Fourth, you should be able to face again a situation similar in its pressures and temptations to the situation in which your offense was committed, and not succumb. For example, if you were unfaithful to your spouse, having breached your oath of fidelity because of your lust for someone you met at work, full repentance would be demonstrated if you refrained from having sexual relations with that person when tempted again to do so, because you know that it is wrong. If, however, you refrained the second time around because you no longer found the person as attractive, you would not have yet demonstrated full repentance.

Recognition and acknowledgment of your sin and remorse for it constitute guilt. Justifiable, or warranted, guilt, unlike neurotic or irrational guilt, is an emotion that is necessary and desirable as a stage in the process of repentance.

After World War II, the Jewish philosopher Martin Buber[8] addressed a group of theologians and psychologists on the theme "The Genesis of Guilt." He distinguished between *guilt,* in the sense of full acknowledgment that you did something morally wrong and feel badly afterwards, and *guilt feelings* that one may have even in the absence of actual wrongdoing. For example, a young child whose mother, when annoyed or frustrated at his misbehavior, says to him, "You are making me sick!" and then gets sick and dies, might experience terrible guilt for many years after his mother's death. This is because in his childish way of thinking, he comes to believe that it was indeed his misbehavior (which might have been nothing more than being too noisy or untidy) which brought about his mother's illness and subsequent death. Carrying this burden of guilt with him throughout his childhood and adolescence, and into adulthood, he will experience guilt feelings; but since he actually was innocent of any responsibility for his mother's fate, he bears no real moral guilt. He might need the help of a therapist to identify and explain the origin of his feelings of guilt and to help eliminate them, but there is nothing for him to repent for, because he committed no offense.

On the other hand, there are too many of us who have committed sins or offenses, and are thus objectively guilty, who do not experience the guilt feelings that we should. Sometimes we may feel an unease or a vague or repressed sense that we have done something wrong, but we need to be prodded, by our own consciences, or by others, to examine ourselves and repent. If we do not, we will be morally at fault forever, and if not totally in denial, continuously gnawed at by this sense that we have violated a moral norm. Buber had in mind, among others, the German theologians and other "respectable" Germans who remained "neutral," so to speak, during the period of Nazi atrocities against Jews and others. They did not speak up in protest, and sometimes silently or indirectly collaborated. After the war, some were in denial of their dereliction of moral responsibility, others felt an uneasy anxiety, and some experienced actual guilt feelings. Is it the responsibility of the therapist, asks Buber, to help these people assuage their anxiety and guilt feelings without pointing them to the way of remorse and repentance? No. Each one of us has to live up to our responsibilities and hold ourselves accountable for our misdeeds. Deserved guilt feelings, deserved because we are actually morally guilty, should not, and often cannot, be severed from the objective evils we did, and "therapeutically treated" independently of their source in our actions or inactions. The therapeutically and morally correct approach is to undertake repentance, either in its religious form—for those who are religious, or in a secular equivalent of it. Buber held that at times the therapist's role is to point the guilt-ridden or guilt-deserving patient in the direction of the three demands of conscience and repentance, which are:

> first, to illuminate the darkness that still weaves itself about the guilt . . . with a broad and enduring light; second . . . to persevere in that newly won humble knowledge of the identity of the present person with the person of that time;[9] and third, in his place and according to his capacity . . . to restore the order-of-being injured by him through active devotion to the world— for the wounds of the order-of-being can be healed in infinitely many other places than those at which they were inflicted. (p. 122)

In *Macbeth* Shakespeare enlightens us about our propensity to deny or avoid facing up to our guilt, and the necessary "medication" for it. At the prodding of his ambitious wife, Macbeth has murdered Duncan, king of Scotland, hoping to ascend the throne. After the deed has been done, he feels guilty. Lady Macbeth, seeing him isolating himself and ruminating on his deed and the evil he has done, tries to dissuade him from taking his guilt feelings to heart. Coldly she says to him,

> How now my lord! Why do you keep alone,
> Of sorriest fancies your companions making;
> Using those thoughts which should indeed have died
> With them they think on? Things without all remedy
> Should be without regard; what's done is done.
>
> (3.2.10–14)

Fortunately for society, most of us are not as callous as Lady Macbeth seems to be, but like Macbeth are capable of regret and remorse. Macbeth's remorse and guilt doesn't deter him from commiting more crimes, whereas guilt often does restrain people from repeating a sin after they have witnessed the pain it caused and its injustice. What Lady Macbeth does not realize is that, although Duncan cannot be brought back to life, perhaps Macbeth's soul can be. Moreover, although "what's done is done," insofar as Duncan's life is concerned, it turns out that as the play unfolds much more evil is yet to be done. Had Lady Macbeth encouraged rather than denigrated Macbeth's incipient remorse, his subsequent murders might have been prevented.

Allowing evil to go unchecked, including or especially one's own evil, allows evil to be compounded. Indeed, one sin will often lead to another, since the more one does evil the more mired in it one becomes, making it ever more difficult to extricate oneself from its web. Having cheated, stolen, or lied, I am now afraid of being caught and fear the shame and punishment that will ensue. So I may lie about having lied, or kill the witness to my original crime, or neglect again my responsibility to my loved ones since, as a result of my initial neglect, they now have even greater needs, which I feel I cannot meet. Were I to feel guilty and use that guilt as a prod to self-analysis and honest acknowledgment of where I went wrong, the chain of evil might be cut early on.

What Lady Macbeth also does not acknowledge is that, although there is no remedy for Duncan's death, there still might be remedies for the pain and injury that Macbeth's murder has caused his family and others. If Macbeth were to acknowledge his guilt at this stage and accept the consequences, or even flee rather than persist in his evil ways, civil war could be averted and there would be a peaceful accession to the throne by Duncan's heir.

Shakespeare is too astute an observer of human nature to leave Lady Macbeth devoid of all conscience or guilt. I suppose he could have chosen to portray her as a totally conscienceless psychopath or sociopath, but he chose instead to explore a more complex trajectory of a sinner's guilt. As Lady Macbeth becomes more deeply entrenched in realizing her ambition for queenly power and status by further goading and encouraging Macbeth to commit additional crimes, she eventually experiences a deep and debilitating anxiety. It is not felt or expressed consciously, but in dreams and hallucinations as she sleepwalks and tries to rub out the stains of the innocents' blood that she believes to be on her hands. On the surface, it would seem that Lady Macbeth's emotional reaction to her evil deeds is motivated not primarily by moral regret but by fear of being apprehended and punished. Her thoughts and feelings shuttle back and forth from fear of detection to self-calming. She calms her anxiety by telling herself that even if her deeds were revealed, no one in the kingdom would have the power to punish her. She doesn't realize the irony of her being self-punished by her fears and encroaching insanity. Nor does she fear the hand of God.

> Out damned spot! Out, I say! . . . What need we
> fear who knows it, when none can call our power to
> account? Yet who would have thought the old man
> To have had so much blood in him? . . .
> What, will these hands ne'er be clean? . . .
> Here's the smell of the blood still: all the
> perfumes of Arabia will not sweeten this little hand . . .
> To bed, to bed! . . . what's
> done cannot be undone: to bed, to bed, to bed!
>
> (5.1.33–66)

Her echoing to herself what she had told Macbeth, when he was plagued by incipient guilt—"What's done cannot be undone"—suggests that at her unconscious level of conflict over what she has done and become, more than simple fear of detection and punishment is at play. Escape from responsibility into the numbness of sleep, then madness, and ultimately death in or by insanity, is how Lady Macbeth "deals" with her fear, anxiety, and guilt. Shakespeare tells us, in the words of Lady Macbeth's physician, that her "sickness" is not physical but spiritual. She needs a confessor rather than a doctor.

> Foul whisperings are abroad: unnatural deeds
> Do breed unnatural troubles: infected minds
> To their deaf pillows will discharge their secrets.
> More needs she the divine than the physician.
> God, God forgive us all!
>
> (5.1.75–79)

The lady's pillows are deaf, and so even if she discharges her secrets to them it will be of no psychological or spiritual avail to her. Perhaps there will be a transitory relief, some catharsis. But deaf pillows cannot reply, offer guidance, and show her the path to repentance. Only she herself, a fellow human being, or God can do that for her. Her anxiety and guilt will consume her.

But as Buber realized, and as many people seeking therapy today may not, there is no easy medication for the guilt incurred by real sin. Neither Prozac nor any diversionary activity can ease the guilt for that majority of us who do have consciences—else why write about repentance. When Macbeth encounters his wife's doctor, he inquires of her health. Her doctor replies:

> Not so sick, my lord,
> As she is troubled with thick-coming fancies,
> That keep her from her rest.

To which Macbeth responds:

> Cure her of that:
> Canst thou not minister to a mind deceased;
> Pluck from the memory a rooted sorrow;
> Raze out the written troubles of the brain;
> And with some sweet oblivious antidote
> Cleanse the stuff'd bosom of that perilous stuff
> Which weighs upon the heart?

How convenient it would be if there were a pill to assuage our guilt and our guilt feelings for the hurts we have caused! Lady Macbeth's doctor is too psychologically and morally wise to say that avoiding responsibility is an antidote to guilt. "Therein the patient must minister to himself" (5.3.45–57).

Sometimes your guilt can be so intense that you seek punishment or suffering in order to assuage it, which may be why some people confess to crimes they did not commit in order to atone and be punished for evils they did commit. This isn't a healthy way of dealing with guilt, but it is one worth being aware of.

Once you acknowledge your guilt, you must do all that you can to repair the specific pain or damage—physical or psychological—that you have wrought by your offense. This would usually involve apologizing and making reparation to your victim for the harm or loss you caused. Sadly, too often this is impossible. There are many harms you can never undo. If you insulted or abused your wife or child, once or regularly, is there anything you can do to heal the hurt that they felt at the time, and the pain they still bear from your insensitivity or cruelty? The past cannot be undone, and it lingers. Yet there are some things you might be able to do, which though not undoing the past, can make your relationship with your emotionally estranged spouse or child more loving, affectionate, and supportive. One of these is to apologize.

Apologies are best made by the offender to his victim, face-to-face. They are psychologically more powerful and more morally significant than those offered through a mediator. If the offender is sincerely remorseful and is painfully aware of the hurt and damage he has caused, it will be difficult for him to look into the pained, and even vengeful eyes of his victim. Being ashamed of his behavior, he will naturally try to avoid the accusatory stare of the wounded one. Therefore, his willingness to look her in the face, when his guilt is authentic, testifies to his sincerity.

I once offended my niece, without realizing that I had done so, by declining her request to spend a few evenings as a guest in my home together with a friend of hers with whom she had been traveling. Whatever my reasons for turning her down, I decided, when my children told me that she was deeply hurt, that I wanted to apologize. I felt especially guilty because her parents, my brother-in-law and sister-in-law, always graciously opened their home to me and my children. I live in Boston, and my young niece lives in Israel. I could have asked my children, who were in Jerusalem, to apologize in my name and on my behalf. It would have been easier for me. But I felt that, especially as someone writing a book on repentance and forgiveness, I should be able to learn from my own preaching and do what was right. There is something in a direct personal encounter that cannot be replicated by a me-diator. An apology is not something to be offered strictly on the terms and under the control of the apologizer. Perhaps the offended party wants to express her hurt and dismay at what the offender did and elaborate on the impact it had on her and on the relationship. The offender should not pre-sume that he fully understands the ways in which his offense offended his victim. If you want your apology to be the beginning of a process of healing and reconciliation rather than a quasi-magical formula for exonerating yourself from guilt, then you have to enable it to be as effective as possible, which is facilitated by eye-to-eye contact. When I was in Israel for a brief visit, I put on my list of priorities to meet with and apologize to my niece. I met with her privately to say that I was at fault and was sorry and that she should know that she is always welcome to stay at my home and to bring friends along as well. (I knew that she was mature and sensitive enough not to abuse my offer of hospitality.) Interestingly, she told me that my children had over-estimated the degree to which she had been hurt. What had disturbed her most was that I had not trusted her judgment in friends, since my objection had not been to her staying with us but to her bringing her friend along. My niece was very receptive to my apology, and I hope the breach in the relationship for which I was responsible has been repaired.

Sometimes, though, the victim does not want to see her offender. The pain and the shame that a rapist inflicts on his victim can be intense, searing, and chronic. The violated woman may feel deep anger, depression, or hatred of the rapist and may suffer fear and anxiety in his presence, so that the last thing she wants is to face him again. In such a case, a truly remorseful offender should respect his victim's feelings and seek other ways to apologize, such as through a mediator or by writing a letter to his victim.

The Talmud heaps praise upon Aaron the High Priest for being a pursuer of peace, active in devising creative strategies for reconciliation. One of his techniques was to act as a mediator between two people in conflict, each of whom perceived himself as an innocent victim and the other as a guilty offender. Aaron would shuttle back and forth between the antagonists, informing each one of the other's sincere remorse (sometimes using white lies), thereby softening the emotional impact of the wounds each party felt had been inflicted on him by the other. Eventually both parties to the conflict were convinced by Aaron that the other was sincere in his remorse. This prepared the psychological ground for them to meet in direct encounter and reconcile.

All too often the person whom you hurt is no longer accessible to you, perhaps even no longer alive. How can you apologize to and alleviate the pain you caused to a member of your family who has gone to the grave bearing the wounds you inflicted? A major concern of religious moralists was how to deal with guilt and repentance when apology and reparation were no longer objectively possible.

For Buber, an offense against a single human being is also an offense against "the order-of-being"—analogous in religious thought to an offense against God. Since one often cannot repair the damage caused to a specific individual, does that mean that there is no hope for the truly remorseful offender to allay his guilt? Buber and the moralists suggest that there are other paths to reparation and healing.

If, for example, I embezzled money from someone and that person has now died, impoverished and without heirs, I might donate to the poor the money I should have returned to my victim. Naturally, this does not heal the actual wound I caused, but in the absence of that possibility I can at least try to lessen poverty in the order-of-being. However, not only did I cause my victim's poverty, I also caused him emotional pain, sorrow, and worry. To rectify the sadness that I injected in to the order-of being, I should think of ways to eliminate some such sadness of others. The function of this idea of substitute reparation and repair, which one finds in the religious traditions, is to provide the repentant wrongdoer with hope, constructive outlets for his guilt and sorrow, and therapeutic pathways for his soul. If he is sincerely penitent, he will always remember that there is nothing he can do to fully repair the damage and hurt he caused, but he need not therefore believe that repentance in such a circumstance can be of no value to him or to the world.

Maimonides, in his Laws of Repentance, instructs that:

> One who sins against his friend [i.e., anyone] and his friend dies before forgiveness is sought he should bring ten men and stand at his grave and say to them: "I have sinned against the God of Israel and my friend and have done this to him." If he owed money it should be returned to the inheritors; if they are not known it should be left with the court with a confession.

A public confession, when the victim is dead, serves several practical and spiritual purposes. Confession serves a cathartic, therapeutic function. The public confession is made in lieu of the private one that should have been made directly to the victim. The public confession is a way of letting the community know that you are truly remorseful and would have apologized and asked forgiveness from your victim if only he were still alive. Moreover, since many offenses against others are breaches of communal norms, the public confession is a declaration of acceptance of the community's norms. Once the sinner has announced his sin before ten men, he will not deny it later when his feelings or circumstances might change. Having become part of the public record, it cannot be easily recanted.

When I steal something, I have, from a Judaic perspective, committed at least five offenses. One against my victim, a second against his heirs, a third against God, a fourth against the community, and a fifth against myself. When the authentically repentant sinner cannot identify or locate his victim, it is not enough that he return the stolen money to the court to be kept in escrow for heirs that might later appear, or to be distributed to the poor; his repentance is far from complete insofar as the interpersonal spheres are concerned. Even though God might want to forgive, he has limited authority since he isn't the only offended party. This is an audacious religious idea—setting limits on God's jurisdiction to forgive. But if the human victim hasn't forgiven, the sinner will have to settle for less than full repentance and the reciprocal full forgiveness that he might have received from a still-living victim. The public confession increases the possibility that the victim's heirs or others adversely affected by what the offender has done will become aware that they are entitled to the money that he stole or embezzled. They can then come forth to claim it, as justice would want, and at the same time provide the sinner the opportunity to make reparations and thereby lessen his guilt.

Islam is close to Judaism in its general approach to repentance, as the following questions and answers show. However, unlike Islam, Judaism does not provide for any monetary compensation for murder, or for forgiveness of a murder in lieu of punishment. The answers provide guidance to sinners in accordance with Islamic law and thought:

Question # 1: How does a murderer repent for his sin?
Answer: A murderer has three rights [i.e., legal or moral claims] on him. That of Allah, that of the murdered person, and those of his or her immediate kin.
1) As for Allah's right it cannot be requited but with true repentance.
2) The right of the immediate kin can be requited by the murderer by handing himself over to them in order that they: a) either turn him over to the authorities for execution, b) accept monetary compensation from him, or c) forgive him.
3) The right of the person himself who was murdered cannot be compensated for in this world. Some scholars are of the opinion—and this seems to be the preferable opinion—that if the murderer is true in his repentance, Allah will clear him of his sin and compensate on his behalf by satisfying the person murdered on the Day of Judgment.

Question #2: I stole from some people. Now I have repented. But I do not know where they live. Or, another may say: I embezzled some money from a firm which has wound up its business. . . . What shall I do now?
Answer: In all these cases the requirement on you is to search for them to the extent of your means. If you find them return them their right. If the owner or owners have died, then their right should be returned to their immediate kin. However, if you cannot locate them then spend in charity equal amounts on their behalf. Allah will give them the reward of this charity.[10]

Christian moral theologians also demand of the sinner that he do what he can to rectify the injuries he caused. The official teaching of Catholicism is that a sinner who confesses should not be granted absolution of his sin by the priest if, for example, he refuses to give up its ill-gotten fruits. He must restore to their rightful owner any goods he has stolen, do what is within his power to reestablish the good reputation of someone whom he has maligned (a very difficult thing to accomplish), or, even more demanding, reconcile with his enemies. Moreover, the priest should, in general, impose sacramental "satisfaction" or penances on the sinner with the general aim of neutralizing the evil consequences of his sin to others and to his own soul.

Some Christian preachers, especially in certain Protestant denominations, are more concerned with getting the sinner to confess to Christ and put his faith and hope in Christ's saving forgiveness, than with inducing the sinner to invest time and energy in making restitution, the alleged "legalistic" preoccupation of Judaism and Islam. With this approach, God's love can offer a detour around reparation and justice, enabling the sinner to avoid facing up to their difficult demands. This position, however, is criticized by many Christian theologians.

Allen Bergin, a prominent psychotherapist and psychologist of religion, has analyzed the psychology of repentance from his Mormon perspective. The repentance process includes self-confrontation, self-control, and self-sacrifice. Included in the latter are restitution, reconciliation, restoration, and forgiveness.

> Self-sacrifice depicts the broad range of elements in the repentance process that are necessary to make repentance complete. This is not only a matter of restitution in the sense of returning a stolen item, but also of extending the necessary effort to alter the fabric of relationships, the negative consequences, or mistrust and broken covenants that need to be corrected. We often shrink from the effort required to make these corrections, but such self-sacrificing effort is an essential part of redeeming the situation. . . . Analysis of the social consequences of our actions requires the courage to face unpleasant facts about our conduct and unpleasant feelings people may have toward us. . . . What was broken should be fixed. What was lost should be restored. . . . One young man donated to a victim reparation fund. Another met with family members to make amends for afflictions produced by her abuse of one family member. Another has written letters to persons offended and others influenced by his bad example. . . . I've been pleased with the reports I've received from family members, friends, and associates, who have been encouraged by the healing effect on an individual who has sincerely attempted to make restitution. This requires going back and making amends in a way that is more profound than simply saying, "I'm sorry."

Where there are amends that cannot be made personally, individuals have the opportunity to compensate for the past by serving others in a profound and extensive way.[11]

Devout Jews, Christians, and Jesus himself draw from the same spiritual well, the Hebrew Bible. However, Jewish and Christian understandings and experiences of repentance developed along somewhat different trajectories. Christianity introduced Jesus as a mediator between man and God, and emphasized, much more than did Judaism, man's dependence upon God's grace in his quest for spiritual renewal and moral purification. In addition,

> The differences between *teshuva* and the sacrament of penance give the devout Jew and Christian their own unique experience. The Catholic who depends on the priest for confession and absolution feels less autonomous than the Jew in his ability to change his ways. Protestant denominations that deemphasize or deny the salvational efficacy of good works, eliminate the sacrament of penance or its equivalent, and focus on man's inherent depravity rather than his potential for good, produce different feelings from Judaism and Catholicism. Howard Levine compares *teshuva* with the conversion experiences of Methodists and Revivalists. In *teshuva* the individual repents of his own volition. He turns away from sin and towards God by changing his attitudes and behaviors. In the Protestant groups, conversion does not result from good works, penance, or rectification of the harm produced by past sins, but by self-surrender to God. In response, God, in His grace, miraculously, and usually suddenly, transforms the sinner. (Schimmel 1997, p. 237)

The Protestant assumption is that a truly transformed sinner will be better able to overcome temptation and live a godly life. He may at times relapse into sin, since temptation is ever present and spiritual weakness is intrinsic to human nature. But having turned to God and sustained his newfound faith in him, the penitent will, overall, be a better human being in his relationships with his fellows and with God.

Judaism, Islam, and Christianity base their teachings about repentance on their respective sacred scriptures and theological beliefs. Those who share these beliefs and are supported by communities of the like-minded take the desirability of repentance for granted. This does not mean that devout Jews, Muslims, and Christians regularly repent of their misdeeds. The fact that each of these faiths has generated a voluminous library of spiritual guides to repentance, as well as a steady flow of sermons, essays, and homilies on the subject, indicates that there is a perennial need to jar even the devout out of their complacency toward wrongdoing. But the ethos of repentance permeates their lives, always calling them to moral and spiritual self-examination and self-improvement. I assume that such an ethos has its effect and that people who take their religious commitments seriously do aspire to repent so that they can be true to their spiritual ideals and aspirations.

In my youth, I studied in a rabbinical seminary (*yeshiva*) permeated with the values of *musar*, which means edifying spiritual instruction and refers to the study and implementation in one's daily life of moral, ethical, and spiritual values. The atmosphere of the seminary was saturated with a spirit of repentance (*teshuva*). Efforts to repair deficiencies in one's character (*tikkun hamiddot*) were not reserved for the ten days of penitence from Rosh Hashana (the Jewish New Year) through Yom Kippur (the Day of Atonement), but continued throughout the year. In this heightened atmosphere of introspection, self-criticism, and efforts at self-renewal, many of my teachers and fellow students did their best to improve themselves and their relationships with God and with each other.

Can individuals who do not share the religious worldview of the devout believer be expected to repent of their evil ways insofar as they affect interpersonal relationships? I believe that to a significant degree they can, although not with the same passion of the pious man or woman of faith. However, one need not be religious in order to aspire to be kind, compassionate, and just, or to be aware of one's failure to be so. One need not be religious to be morally self-critical and to strive toward self-improvement. To the extent that the moral and psychological insights of religious teachings on repentance are sensible and inspiring they can, even when no longer anchored in theology, be applied by all who seek moral wisdom and guidance in their lives.

After the death of his wife of many years, from whom he had gradually become estranged, the English poet Thomas Hardy wrote moving poems describing his regret for what their relationship could and should have been. Revisiting their courtship and early happy years of marriage, he reflected with deep melancholy on what might have been.

In the poem, "An Upbraiding," he imagines what his dead wife Emma is thinking about him as he visits her grave.

> Now I am dead you sing to me
>   The songs we used to know,
> But while I lived you had no wish
>   Or care for doing so.

> Now I am dead you come to me
>   In the moonlight, comfortless;
> Ah, what would I have given alive
>   To win such tenderness!
> When you are dead, and stand to me
>   Not differenced, as now,
> But like again, will you be cold
>   As when we lived, or how?

Emma (in Hardy's imagination) wonders whether Hardy's nostalgia for the early years when they used to sing together, and his tender thoughts at the moonlit grave are authentic or are merely expressions of his loneliness. Emma is skeptical about his attempt to reunite with her in spirit: How and why should I trust you? Why didn't you appreciate me when I was still alive? Indeed, when you join me in the hereafter, will you really have changed from your coldhearted indifference to genuine tenderness and love? The poet uses Emma to project his own ambivalence about the feelings he is experiencing. He is not sure himself how authentic his regrets for his coldness actually are. Hardy stated that these poems that he wrote about his wife were an expiation for him. However, it is not clear that they express actual remorse, since as we see here, he himself doubts whether he is truly remorseful, even as he tries to reconnect with the happier years of his relatioship with Emma. The poem reveals the complexities of remorse, both for the remorseful person and for the one whom he has hurt.

When we hurt someone, we often feel that we were justified in doing so, at least to some extent. Therefore, our remorse is attenuated with a degree of defensiveness and self-justification. Given the realities of relationships, especially close and intimate ones—in which it is usually the case that both partners share in the burden of blame for the hurt and pain in the relationship, albeit to different degrees—the ambivalence about remorse and apology is understandable. And since the paths of repentance were always available, a repentance undertaken after the death of one's partner is indeed suspect. If Emma were still alive and Hardy had to live with her again, would he be able to overcome the coldness he had developed toward her (perhaps for reasons that do not necessarily make him totally morally at fault)? It is easier to say you are sorry to a dead person with whom you no longer have to interact than to a live one who still makes demands of you, whether of affection or resources. So, the deferral of repentance until the death of your victim makes your repentance far from full and ideal. Indeed, in such a case, perhaps the only true repentance and healing can take place via substitute activities—some action whereby you will increase love and tenderness in the order-of-being, whether in your own family or elsewhere.

Above and beyond making an apology for and reparation of the *specific* pain or injury you caused, you should do what you can to heal in your personal relationships breaches that resulted from your action or inaction. You have to work actively toward an authentic personal reconciliation with your victim and others who have been affected by what you did. It is amazing how effective being kind and caring toward someone whom you hurt can be in leading to reconciliation and the renewal of loving relationships.

Repentance, then, serves several functions. When most effective, it makes you a better person, heals you of your deserved guilt, repairs the injury you caused to the other, and can lead to your victim's willingness and ability to forgive you and to reconcile with you. Even when only some of these fruits of repentance are possible, it is a potent instrument for rectifying and minimizing evil and ill will in our individual and social lives.

.   .   .

So far I have spoken of repentance for specific sins or offenses. There is another way in which religious thinkers and moral philosophers have construed repentance. Repentance can refer to a significant and successful effort at self-transformation. If you have a morally or spiritually undesirable character trait, how can you change that trait for the better? You might be a greedy, lustful, envious, irascible, gluttonous, slothful, or arrogant person—in other words, one carrying a deadly sin in your personality structure. These traits, in turn, often result in harmful behavior toward others. Is there a way for you to modify or transform your character for the better, or at least to channel your negative tendencies toward positive rather than harmful ends? The mandate to do so and strategies for doing so are elaborated upon in many guides to moral and spiritual self-improvement, some of which I have discussed in *The Seven Deadly Sins*.

Another focus of repentance is an even deeper and broader transformation of self that goes beyond changing a specific character trait. Sometimes, for example, a heretofore incorrigible sinner or criminal undergoes a conversion experience in which he becomes a new and different person, so to speak.

Rabbi Abraham Isaac Kook, a great twentieth-century mystic, has described the experiences of such a person from a Jewish perspective. The person's repentance involves more than turning away from wrongful past actions or making attempts to remedy flawed traits. This *baal teshuva* (penitent) has become aware of his alienation from God, the source of his and all being, and of all meaning. Through the process of *teshuva* (turning away from the abyss of meaningless and nothingness and turning toward God), he experiences a spiritual cleansing, a release from guilt, a renewal of life purpose, and an ecstatic joy in worshiping God and being in His presence.[12]

In Christianity, the phenomenology of the "conversion" experience has been studied by William James. These experiences are emotionally intense and have a powerful impact on those who undergo them, although their stability over time and their positive consequences on transformation of character tend to be exaggerated by preachers and spiritual leaders. For some people, however, they do have lasting consequences, and even temporary improvement in one's spiritual or moral life is valuable. Whether such radical repentance or conversion experiences have an analogue in secular culture is doubtful.[13]

What are some of the characteristics of these radical repenters and converts?

William James devoted two chapters to conversion in his masterful psychological analysis of religious experience. People who have had conversion experiences feel that they have undergone radical transformations of the self from a state of faithlessness to one of faith, from a state of sinfulness to purification, and from a state of alienation from God to communion (or in the case of mystics, union) with him. Some experience the conversion as gradual, others as sudden; some as volitional, others as a gift of God's grace. There is often an emotional shift from despair and melancholy to joy and hope, and from existential meaninglessness to a fullness of purpose and delight in living. Adolescents and young adults are particularly prone to experience conversion.

Although the conversion often appears to be sudden and without cause, it frequently has been incubating for years, sometimes in consciousness, sometimes repressed. It is often related to conflict—whether of ideas such as faith and doubt or of emotions such as love and hate—in significant personal relationships. These conflicts are difficult to sustain, and a psychologically "successful" conversion will resolve them, at least insofar as it makes them emotionally tolerable. Of particular interest are the effects of such conversions on personality and on behavior.

William James and others who have studied the phenomenon of radical spiritual and moral transformation have seen many instances of it in alcoholics and drug addicts. Their conversion experiences resulted in a new ability to resist the temptations that had marred their lives and the lives of those affected by them. Here is one alcoholic's description of his transformation:

One Tuesday evening I sat in a saloon in Harlem, a homeless, friendless, dying drunkard. . . . I had often said "I will never be a tramp. I will never be cornered, for when that time comes, if it ever comes, I will find a home in the bottom of the river. . . ." But the Lord so ordered it that when that time did come I was not able to walk . . . to the river. As I sat there thinking, I seemed to feel some great and mighty presence. I did not know then what it was. I did learn afterwards that it was Jesus, the sinner's friend. . . . I said I would never take another drink. . . . I went [to Jerry MacAuley's Mission House]. . . . I listened to the testimony of twenty-five or thirty persons, every one of whom had been saved from rum, and I made up my mind that I would be saved or die right there. When the invitation was given, I knelt down with a crowd of drunkards. Jerry made the first prayer. . . . O what a conflict was going on for my poor soul! A blessed whisper said, "Come"; the devil said, "Be careful." I halted but a moment, and then, with a breaking heart, I said, "Dear Jesus, can you help me?" Never with mortal tongue can I describe that moment. Although up to that moment my soul had been filled with indescribable gloom, I felt the glorious brightness of the noonday sun shine into my heart. I felt I was a free man. Oh, the precious feeling of safety, of freedom, of resting on Jesus! I felt that Christ with all his brightness and power had come into my life; that indeed, old things had passed away and all things had become new.

From that moment till now I have never wanted a drink of whiskey. . . . I promised God that night that if he would take away the appetite for strong drink, I would work for him all my life. He has done his part, and I have been trying to do mine. (James, 207–9, citing Leuba)[14]

James, anticipating the skepticism that would greet such conversion experiences, preempted his audience with the following remarks:

Some of you, I feel sure, knowing that numerous backslidings and relapses take place . . . dismiss it with a pitying smile as so much "hysterics." Psychologically, as well as religiously, however, this is shallow. It misses the point of serious interest, which is not so much the duration as the nature and quality of these shiftings of character to higher levels. Men lapse from every level—we need no statistics to tell us that. Love is, for instance, well known not to be irrevocable, yet constant or inconsistent, it reveals new flights and reaches of ideality while it lasts. These revelations form its significance to men and women, whatever be its duration. So with the conversion experience: that it should for even a short time show a human being what the high-water mark of his spiritual capacity is, this is what constitutes its importance—an importance which backsliding cannot diminish, although persistence might increase it. . . . The persons who have passed through conversion, having once taken a stand for the religious life, tend to feel themselves identified with it, no matter how much their religious enthusiasm declines.[15]

The Talmud (Avodah Zara 17a) recounts the story of a repentant sexual sinner who meets a tragic end, at least from a this-worldly perspective, though not from an eternal one.

> It was told of Rabbi Elazar the son of Durdaya that there wasn't a whore in the world with whom he did not have sexual intercourse. Once he heard that there was a prostitute in a distant city of the sea who charged a bowl of denarii [an exorbitant sum] for her services. He took a bowl of denarii and traversed seven seas to reach her. As they were having intercourse she farted. She said to him, "Just as this fart will never return to its source, so too Elazar the son of Durdaya will never be accepted as a penitent."

Elazar pleaded with mountains and hills, heaven and earth, the sun, the moon, the stars, and the constellations to appeal for mercy on his behalf, but all declined to do so. Eventually Elazar came to the realization, and said, that "The matter is dependent only on me."

He lowered his head between his knees and cried out and wept until his soul departed his body. A heavenly voice then declared: "Rabbi Elazar the son of Durdaya is invited to life in the world to come."

When Rabbi Judah the Patriarch heard this story, he cried and said, "There are those who acquire their portion in the world to come only after many years, and there are those who acquire their portion in the world to come in one hour."

He also said: "Not only are repenters received [by God] but they are also referred to as Rabbi [an honorific title reserved for pious scholars]."

Let us look at several features of this moral tale.

First of all, sexual promiscuity was a grave sin in the rabbinic value system. Elazar's sexual picadillos, however, were not run-of-the-mill, periodic concessions to his lust. He was challenged by temptation to maximize the carnal pleasures and pluck all he could from the garden of earthly delights. There isn't a prostitute in the world he hasn't enjoyed. Here is a man who idolizes lust, is mired in it. I will not say that he is, in contemporary parlance, addicted to lust, because that would imply it is beyond his control, which is the very opposite of the story's message. Then, a new sexual challenge appears, far on the horizon, and he is not daunted by the cost and effort of experiencing this newly discovered erotic siren that beckons him from the sea. Elazar's very self is defined by his sexual lust.

But even a sinner as corrupt as Elazar wants in the depths of his soul, ultimate salvation. He might defer his repentance, procrastinate, say to himself: just this one more sin and then I'll repent. Why not have this world and the world to come as well? So when God's message is conveyed by his accomplice in sin that this is the end of the road and there is no hope beyond this point, Elazar is aroused from his moral slumber. At first he wants others to do his spiritual work for him. Upon his realization, however, that only Elazar can help Elazar, he accepts his personal responsibility. The flash of realization sparks sudden and dramatic change. Enmeshed in lust only moments before, Elazar is now contrite and humbled, crying out to the Lord, transformed from condemned sinner into a welcomed penitent.

How awesome the power of repentance is! It can change man or woman in an instant and draw him or her up from the abyss to the peak. He earns divine love and human honor—for is he remembered not simply as Elazar, but as Rabbi Elazar, although we know nothing of his scholarship.

Rabbi Judah the Patriarch is bewildered and amazed by this power of repentance. Most people need years of good deeds and virtue to earn eternal life, whereas the genuine penitent can earn it almost instantly.

Rabbi Judah and the narrator of this tale do not want their audience to choose Rabbi Elazar's way—sin, repent, and be saved. This goes against all of the teachings of the rabbis. Moreover, Elazar, though earning eternal life, paid dearly, since life in this world is also precious and he squandered it. Virtue and following God's Torah are of intrinsic worth, not only valuable as means to enter the world-to-come after death. Moreover, only a few of those who become mired in sin succeed in extricating themselves from it as Rabbi Elazar did.

However, even when one is mired in sin one must not utterly despair, because the gates of repentance are always open. With the proper will and commitment, one can perform spiritual surgery and reconstruction on oneself, and Rabbi Elazar's tale is told to remind us of this. Elsewhere the rabbis teach that one who says "I will sin and then repent" will not be given the opportunity to repent. They do not say, however, that if he does repent his repentance will be spurned. Perhaps the rabbis are making a psychological observation—one who is so mired in evil deeds or evil habits will find it extremely difficult to extricate himself from this way of life and from the vices that have, through practice, become his second nature. Few succeed in doing so. But the few who do are the models and exemplars that we have to hold up to ourselves and to those in our charge.

Are there, or can there be, secular analogues to these pervasive character transformations? We find them occasionally when a person in despair of her achievement or direction in life resolves to reassess and redirect her thoughts and energies to goals she had never before considered, at least consciously. I have seen successful businessmen and professionals, narcissistically preoccupied with power, status, and wealth, wake up one morning with an awareness that their life is devoid of true significance. Sometimes this realization is triggered by a traumatic experience—a grave illness, the death of a child, or a divorce. At other times it is more philosophical in nature—a sense that there must be more to life than the rise they get from a hike in the value of their investment portfolios. Their response to these "illuminations" is to rechannel their talents, resources, and skills toward social justice, the alleviation of pain and suffering, or some other beneficent contribution to humanity. Whereas before they were preoccupied with self, they now look to the needs of others. Whereas before they saw other people as "instruments" whereby to satisfy their own needs, they now see themselves as instruments to help the less fortunate. Whereas before they were apathetic and indifferent to the tragedy of the human condition as revealed in hunger, sickness, natural disaster, and war, they now hear, see, and feel the broad expanse of pain that lies beyond the confines of their secure and prosperous enclaves. These people do not necessarily change their personality traits but rather their worldview and their views of themselves. Indeed, the very same traits that brought them material and social success, such as ingenuity, relentless drive, and goal-oriented dedication, are now enlisted in the service of humanitarian goals that endow their life with the existential meaning and purpose it had sorely lacked. These new goals aren't necessarily "global" in scope. Just as the hasidic teachers taught that everyone should find at least one *mitzvah* (spiritual mission) on which to concentrate his energies, so too one can perform small missions and acts of compassion, each according to his ability, and feel good for it. Some may set up billion-dollar foundations to support international development, whereas others may work with the homeless in a local shelter. Some write books to help people cope better with misfortune; others make their contribution through the arts. What all of these indivuduals share is that they made radical moral changes in how they lead their lives, similar in many ways to those who turned from sin to God, albeit within a secular rather than a religious worldview.

.   .   .

There are many similarities between the experience of repentance and the experience of psychotherapy. In both processes, an individual feels an unease about some aspect(s) of the self. In conventional psychotherapy, the unease might be manifested as deep anger, anxiety, depression, guilt, and shame, and an inability to develop satisfying relationships or to undertake significant endeavors. Often a spiritual and moral malaise is partially responsible for these symptoms, and unless these are addressed on their own terms, no lasting healing can occur. In religious repentance, the person is primarily concerned with his inability to live up to the standards of the faith to which he is committed. Here too there is often depression, anger at oneself, guilt, shame, and frustration with one's perceived religious and spiritual failures. In both processes, the individual is expected to undertake a journey of transformation that may entail painful introspection and self-analysis, usually guided by another person or by a self-help book.

The analysis of one's feelings, thoughts, or behaviors should eventually lead to insight as to the roots of the unease and failures. Once that self-awareness and self-understanding is achieved, the patient and the penitent commit themselves to changing their ways. Beyond commitment to change, however, they have to acquire concrete tactics and strategies for change, which is what the therapist and, in religious culture, the spiritual mentor, help them do. Successful non-religious therapy, like effective repentance, brings relief and hope for the future. When moral flaws and spiritual aridity were elements in the secular malaise and therapy, the "healed" patient, like the sincere penitent, emerges from the journey not only happier, but a better human being.

Because of the similarities between psychotherapy and repentance, there can be a mutually enhancing integration of them. For example, a pastoral counselor who is attuned to the religious values and commitments of his patient can incorporate those values meaningfully into the therapeutic plan. If a devout person in therapy feels guilt because he has not lived his life with the love and charity that he believes he must demonstrate, the therapist can help him understand the impediments to his benevolence and how he can overcome them. This is not all that different from the penitent troubled by the same concerns who turns to a clergyperson for guidance.

Sometimes, however, psychologically troubled individuals can mask their problems under the guise of religion and repentance. For example, there are orthodox Jews and devout Catholics who suffer from obsessive-compulsive disorder. They will engage in overly scrupulous, punctilious, and repeated recitation of prayers or performance of rituals. These behaviors are extremely disruptive of their own lives and those of their families. They may justify their behavior as devotion to God and to his law, or as necessary correctives for some laxities in observance or prayer, as though their compulsions were genuine penitential acts. Yet, to a discerning psychiatrist and a knowledgeable clergyperson, their obsessive thoughts and compulsive behaviors are transparently pathological and unspiritual. They go beyond the demands of their religion and actually result in more, rather than fewer, violations of its moral or ritual requirements. The obsessive-compulsive penitent will spend so much time "repenting" his presumed sins of the past that he will neglect his present obligations, be they good works or Torah study. When in therapy, he might resist a diagnosis of pathology by insisting that his ritualistic performances are expressions of piety. An astute therapist will find a way to express deep respect for the patient's commitment to his religion, while sensitively guiding him to an understanding of the distinction between religiously valid penance and a pathological masquerade of it.

Since repentance can be therapeutic for the individual himself and for social relationships, a religiously sympathetic therapist can use the religious patient's appreciation of repentance to facilitate healing, reconciliation, and spiritual growth.

An interesting example of therapeutic use of repentance is provided by Frankel who finds that when a perpetrator of sexual or child abuse in a family context, repents, admitting guilt and apologizing to his victim, both he and his victim benefit.

> As one patient of mine put it, "I need my father to acknowledge and stop denying that what went on was abuse—not just 'discipline.' Until he faces the truth, I can't have a close or honest relationship with him." When I asked this patient what stopped him from confronting his father in the past, he replied: "When I tried to approach the subject in the past, my father felt so bad that I started feeling guilty and I couldn't bear to destroy him." I suggested that he try again by presenting it to his father in the context of the possibility of repentance and forgiveness. Perhaps his father would be more able to bear his painful feelings of guilt if he knew that ultimately it would lead to a healing between him and his son, whom he did love. When confronted in this fashion, the father was finally able to admit his

mistakes and express deep feelings of regret over the past. Hearing his father's sincere regret helped my patient overcome his own shame and denial over the abuse, and ultimately enabled him to rebuild a more honest relationship with his father.

On a number of occasions I have been able to arrange family therapy sessions for individual patients of mine who were victimized by another family member. These sessions have been beneficial not only to my patient, but to the perpetrator as well. By creating an opportunity for perpetrators to express remorse and ask forgiveness, they have been freed from carrying a lifelong burden of guilt and alienation from a loved one.[16]

. . .

Why is it so difficult to repent? Why is repentance such a struggle and a challenge? How recently have you acknowledged to someone that you wronged her, felt guilty about what you did (or failed to do), expressed remorse and apologized, offered to repair or restore the damage you caused—whether physical, financial, or psychological, and had an occasion to repeat your offense but did not do so?

Have you insulted your spouse or child recently? Have you humiliated an employee? Have you shirked an opportunity to help someone in need? Have you cut corners in your business dealings? Have you been lax in living up to your responsibilities at work? Have you lost your temper and lashed out at someone unjustifiably? Have you been disloyal to your spouse for no reason other than to satisfy your lust? Have you cheated on an exam? Have you lied? Have you allowed your skills and talents to be wasted when they could have been of use to others, as well as to your own growth? Have you stood by silently in the face of injustice when your voice could have been raised in protest?

For the criminals who are reading this book, have you stolen from, defamed, raped, assaulted, or murdered anyone and not yet repented of your crime?

There are many reasons that we find it hard to repent. The most obvious, perhaps trivial, one is that we do not repent, but instead repeat our sins for the same reasons that we committed them in the first place. We are arrogant, wrathful, envious, lazy, lustful, gluttonous, and greedy, and because of these traits we sin against others. It isn't easy to eliminate or significantly modify a trait, no matter if we were born with it or acquired it later. So we become repeat offenders.

We commit offenses because they are gratifying, and they remain gratifying even though we know that we were wrong for committing them. So we commit them again. Some people feel elevated when they tread upon others. Sex is so intensely pleasurable that kings have gone to war in order to acquire a woman they desire. Money buys influence, power, and goods. Having submitted once to the seduction of sex, status, or money and enjoyed them, and not having been apprehended and punished for whatever sins we committed to acquire them, it is natural that we should commit them again.

Sometimes we don't repent because we are not aware that what we did was hurtful. This is especially the case when we behave without any malicious intent, but the person affected by our behavior suffers.

Because of my particular cultural upbringing, I have a tendency to talk in a loud, argumentative tone, even about trivial matters. Most of the time I am unaware of this and will talk that way to friends and family members, indeed, even to mere acquaintances. My wife and children are more delicate in their sensitivities and have been frequently hurt by what they perceive and experience as a critical, hostile tone of voice. Why are you talking so angrily, why are you mad, why can't you speak softly and gently, they have often remonstrated. Yet unless they call my offensive manner of speech to my attention, I am not aware of it. Even when they do point it out to me, my usual response is, don't you know by now that my "angry" way of talking is innocuous and that there is no malevolence? Although I realize that, notwithstanding my innocent state of mind, I do hurt them, it is still a struggle for me to change. This is not only because of ingrained cultural habits, but because I say to myself that since I intend no harm, the problem lies not in me but in their exaggerated emotional response. Perhaps there is some truth in my self-defense, but if I really were concerned about their feelings, I would make a concerted effort to become more aware of how I talk. It is not enough that I don't carry a big stick, I should speak softly as well.

So the first obstacle to repentance is our lack of awareness of what we do and how it might be hurting others.

Sometimes we feel that it will be so difficult for us to change our behaviors that it doesn't pay to try to repent, since we doubt that we will succeed in any case. This reaction is like that of the person who has dieted many times but always relapses into his gluttonous behavior. Eventually he decides that dieting is a waste of time. The same may be said of the person who easily loses his temper and lashes out in violence against loved ones or even strangers. He gives up trying to control himself. If you are like this, what you need to know is that there are techniques, many of which I have described in *The Seven Deadly Sins*, that you can learn that will teach you how to control your impulses.

Another obstacle to repentance is our tendency to justify and rationalize the evil that we do even though it is transparent to any objective observer that we have done wrong. Baumeister and his colleagues devised a series of experiments to examine this phenomenon. They asked college students to write accounts of actual incidents in their lives—one in which they did something to offend others and another in which they were victims of someone else. Their perspectives as perpetrators were compared with their perspectives as victims, in terms of how they explained the offenses, and what they did after the offense. The study found that perpetrators are more likely to ascribe an offense to causes that tend to excuse or justify the behavior, such as mitigating circumstances or provocations, than are victims. Julia Exline, using a similar method, found that perpetrators' descriptions of their own behaviors, when compared with victims' descriptions of hurtful behaviors, characterized them as less harmful, less frequent, less malicious, more justifiable, and more reparable. These experiments corroborate what numerous religious moralists who have written guides to self-scrutiny and repentance have observed about human nature.[17] Jeremy Taylor, for example, who analyzed the vice of pride or arrogance,

> develops the argument for honesty in appraising our own faults by reminding us of how ready we are to see the faults of others. If we would apply the same standards of criticism to ourselves as we do to our neighbors, our pride would be deflated. . . . When the tendency to accentuate our neighbor's evil is combined with our opposite tendency to give greater weight to the good in our selves while ignoring our own evils, we have a formula for sinful pride. . . . The proud person rationalizes his faults, since to acknowledge them would threaten his sense of superiority. The humble person, on the other hand, readily admits guilt and patiently listens to the reproofs and anger even of his enemies. Our enemies do not seek to protect our self-image with falsehoods and often monitor our behavior more accurately than does many a friend. Therefore, our enemies' admonishments are often of greater value to us in exposing our faults than are the kind and soothing words of a friend. (Schimmel 1997, *The Seven Deadly Sins,* pp. 43, 46)

Even when the perpetrators in these psychological experiments acknowledged that they had hurt others, they perceived themselves, more than did victims, as being repentant. (Exline and Baumeister, 2000, p. 140)

So deleterious to moral rehabilitation is this tendency to deny and rationalize our faults that it is a major theme in the first account of human sinfulness in the Bible. God commands Adam and Eve not to eat of the fruit of the tree of knowledge of good and evil. The serpent tempts Eve to violate the Lord's command and she does. She offers Adam the fruit and he eats of it as well. The Lord confronts Adam in the Garden of Eden with his disobedience.

"Have you eaten from the tree of which I commanded you not to eat?"

How does he respond?

"The woman whom you gave to be with me, she gave me the fruit from the tree, and I ate."

The Lord confronts Eve.

"What is this that you have done?"

How does she respond?

"The serpent tricked me, and I ate."

Neither Adam nor Eve accepts responsibility for what they did. Eve blames the serpent and Adam audaciously blames not only Eve, but God himself, "the woman whom *you* gave to be with me." Instead of being grateful to the Lord for having given him a woman as a companion, and being contrite for his sin, Adam is ungrateful and shifts the blame. Had Adam repented then and there, perhaps he would not have been cast out of the garden and things would have been better for all of us, at least from the biblical perspective.[18]

Rabbinic commentators condemn Adam's refusal to accept personal responsibility for his sin. In an ingenious midrash, the rabbis note that Adam lived for 930 years and King David for seventy years. Both had committed grave sins and were confronted by God. David immediately said, "I have sinned against the Lord," and repented, whereas Adam shifted blame. Juxtaposing the two similar episodes and the life spans of the two sinners, the rabbis, who were always looking for a moral or religious message encrypted in Scripture, said that Adam had originally been destined to live for one thousand years and David to die stillborn. But God, in his omniscience, saw that if David were to live, he would model repentance and extol its virtues in Psalm 51, whereas Adam would model refusal to acknowledge guilt and repent. So God decided that for the sake of repentance and its benefits to humankind, he would take seventy years off of Adam's life and give them to David instead.

Many biblical commentators see Adam's disobedience, his resistance to repentance, and his audacity, as rooted in his pride. Aaron Lazare, a psychiatrist who has studied the psychology of shame and humiliation, highlights the connection between pride and shame and people's refusal to apologize for wrongs they have committed.

To apologize you have to acknowledge that you made a mistake. You have to admit that you failed to live up to values like sensitivity, thoughtfulness, fairness, and honesty. This is an admission that our own self-concept, our story about ourself, is flawed. To honestly admit what you did and show regret may stir an experience of profound shame, a public exposure of weakness. Such an admission is especially difficult to bear when there was some degree of intention behind the wrongdoing.[19]

A particularly distressing experience for me was the first time that my self-image as a caring person was challenged by my wife and children (who are much readier to go out of their way to help others than I am). They would often point out to me my selfishness. My usual response to these criticisms was to challenge their assertions, or to come up with excuses to convince myself (and to try to convince them) that they were wrong in their moral assessment of me. It has taken me a long time finally to admit to myself that I am indeed much more selfish than I ever believed myself to be. If it is so difficult to admit your own faults to yourself, how much more difficult is it to admit them to others—which is what a confession and apology requires. We don't like to be ashamed of ourselves, even in the privacy of our self-knowledge. We surely don't want to admit our faults to others, because making it public makes it more painful.

In many family conflicts, pride and fear of shame are major obstacles to apology and reconciliation. Parents in particular find it difficult to admit guilt and apologize to their children for their wrongdoing. I am talking about well-meaning parents who with good intentions engaged in misguided behaviors. Some parents force their children to take music lessons and disparage them if they show no interest or skill. Some parents believe that criticism of a child is necessary to getting the child to do better in school or sports. They forget that praise and encouragement are no less important and that excessive or humiliating (rather than constructive and gentle) criticism can produce deep emotional scars. The child who hears a constant barrage of negative comments can have his self-esteem destroyed and develop an inferiority complex that will haunt him throughout his life. In later years, when the parent is angrily accused by the now-adult child of having been harsh and insensitive, the parent finds it extremely painful to acknowledge fault since he or she may have behaved that way toward the child out of a sincere and deep love and concern for him. The parent's self-concept of having been a good parent may have given meaning to his life. To admit to yourself or, more painfully, to admit to your adult child, for whom you labored and sacrificed so much, that you wronged her by making disparaging comments and criticizing her as a child might shatter your self-image as a good and loving parent of many years. This hurts deeply. Yet such an admission and apology on your part may be essential if your adult child is to get over his or her deep resentment, heal, and become emotionally mature enough to realize and appreciate that indeed, behind the painful parental putdowns, there was (and still is) a reservoir of love.

As Exline and Baumeister (2000) point out,

> In cases of mutual transgression, such as marital argument that degenerates to the level of caustic remarks and name-calling by both parties, people are especially likely to disagree with charges against them. They are likely to focus on their victim status while overlooking their roles as perpetrators. Perpetrators are also more likely to protest when they are placed on the defensive by a victim who angrily confronts them in a blaming manner (Kubany et al. 1995). Persons who tend to externalize blame and have difficulty empathizing with others should also be more likely to view themselves as innocent. (p. 141)

It is often in anger that we offend others and others offend us. We lose our temper and do or say things that we later come to regret. The victim of wrath who rebukes gently can encourage expressions of remorse and sincere apology. Rebuke, however, can be a double-edged sword.

> Frank but tactful criticism of the individual who has offended us is an important instrument for preventing anger. By approaching the person who has injured you and asking him why he did such and such, he may be induced to apologize. . . . Since the objective of our rebuke is to prevent our hostility from festering and to provide the offender with an opportunity to explain or excuse himself, we must be extremely cautious in the manner in which we rebuke and criticize. When confrontation of the alleged offender is performed improperly, it may be ineffective in inducing apology and in dissipating wrath. Even worse, it may, on the contrary, incite further anger and generate a vicious cycle of attack and counterattack. (Schimmel 1997, *The Seven Deadly Sins,* 107–8)

Sometimes we don't repent because we fear the consequences of doing so. If I have committed a punishable offense, but no one knows that I did, then repenting, which includes confessing, can be costly. So even though I might want to repent, I don't. This issue does not come up with sins against God alone if the sinner believes that nothing can be concealed from God. On the contrary, fear of God will induce rather than inhibit confession to God. Religious people believe that God also knows of their sins against fellow humans. The sinner, however, may prefer to leave it to God, rather than to religious or civil authorities, to punish him, and so he might confess his sins against man to God, but not to man.

Judaism, as we have seen, considers this confession inadequate, since it doesn't result in reparation of the damage done, when reparation is feasible.

Even in cases in which confession and repentance will not result in punishment, it might result in social opprobrium or in the disappointment of loved ones. There are people whose children, spouse, or parents look up to them as moral and ethical models. If such a person committed a serious moral offense of which his family is not aware, confessing it might shatter their illusions about him and be very painful to them. I tell my children that, were they aware of my sins, they wouldn't think so highly of me (assuming that they do). I thus prepare them for the eventuality that my sins might be revealed, or that I might decide to repent and confess them.

Some people's professional and economic standing may depend upon their public image as honest, faithful, or compassionate. A preacher is expected to practice what he preaches. If he doesn't, he won't want to confess publicly, lest he be accused of hypocrisy (and lose his job). This can inhibit rabbis, ministers, priests, and public officials who preach from openly confessing their sins and repenting. One way that some preachers, sincere as well as duplicitous, deal with the quandary in which the role of moral beacon places them is to frequently point out that everyone, pious or moral preachers and leaders included, sins sometimes. This stance gives them the option of confessing and repenting without being denounced as hypocrites. Unfortunately, we have seen too many preachers and politicians who sin or commit crimes, confess and apologize, and then claim that this suffices as penance and repentance, so they needn't be punished for their misdeeds or repair the damage they caused.

David Hartman suggests that one function of the period of the Jewish Ten Days of Repentance is to help the individual overcome a social barrier to repentance.

> The individual is often inhibited from altering habits and styles of life by the image of himself or herself which has become entrenched in his or her social environment. Change requires heroic efforts when one must defy

the expectations to which one's "significant others" have become accustomed. . . . When change is collectively initiated, however, there are greater chances of success.

In accordance with this reasoning, the Halakhah sought to create collective structures that would place the individual in a collective context conducive to individual *teshuvah*. By institutionalizing a period of time expressly dedicated to *teshuvah*, Halakhah supported the individual's quest for change; the period of "ten days of *teshuvah*" bridging Rosh Ha-Shanah and Yom Kippur attempts to confer social legitimization on the individual's struggle to change the course of his or her life.[20]

During this period of time *halakhah* mandates that every person not only confess before God and go through the various stages of repentance but that they make whatever restitution they owe for what they acquired dishonestly and that they try to reconcile with those whom they offended. The fact that this is a formal requirement incumbent upon everyone induces people who consider the *halakhah* to be binding upon them to do what they would have been ashamed or afraid to do voluntarily—personally approach another person, admit wrongdoing, apologize, and ask for forgiveness. The *teshuva* requirement of this period includes saying special penitential prayers, reading devotional guides, and listening to sermons and homilies on repentance. These requirements are designed to arouse one emotionally so that the repentance will not be hollow, a ritualistic formula devoid of spiritual–psychological substance.

Given the fact that during this penitential period many people pray and fast more than usual, make it a point to perform deeds of charity and other *mitzvot,* and become especially fastidious in their performance of religious rites and rituals, they may delude themselves into believing that these suffice to assure atonement for all of their sins, including those against their neighbor. To prevent this misconception, the exhortations to *teshuva* in the legal and devotional texts emphasize that all the prayers, sacrifices, penances, and good deeds that one may offer do not and cannot atone for the offenses that have been committed against another person if the sinner does not first apologize, make restitution, and repair, to the best of his ability, the emotional, social, economic, or physical, injury that he has caused. Sins of the "evil tongue" are among the most common ones and are especially difficult to repair and so are especially dangerous.

Another obstacle to repentance is the potential loss of power and status in a relationship. A spouse who admits to having done something wrong to a wife or husband might fear that the hurt partner can use this admission to control their future interactions. "How can you deny me the vacation that I want, given that you spent several thousand dollars on prostitutes?" "Don't expect me to be responsive to your sexual needs. Did you think about mine when you were having an affair with your boss and neglecting me?" Admission of guilt and repentance isn't always rewarded with forgiveness. Even if the victim is willing to forgive, he or she may not forget, and the knowledge provided by the confession can be used to the victim's advantage. When the victim knows of the offense from another source, the offender may feel that apologizing and admitting guilt can still be humiliating and a sign of vulnerability, and he or she might fear that the victim will take advantage of this "lowering of the guard."[21]

Finally, repentance involves an intensive expenditure of emotional resources, and some people may simply lack the psychic energy to undertake the process.

· · ·

Given all of these obstacles to repentance, how might we induce ourselves and others to overcome them and repent?

First and foremost we, as a society, have to reintroduce the concept and language of repentance into our moral vocabulary and compass. I refer here to moral or secular repentance, since religiously motivated repentance is already an integral part of the worldview of those committed to Judaism, Christianity, and Islam, even if more in theory than in actual practice. Etzioni coined the phrase "moral megalogue" to refer to "moral dialogue projected onto a larger scale" and argues for a moral megalogue on repentance.[22] How might a megalogue on repentance occur?

Members of the print and electronic media who are convinced of the value of inculcating an ethos conducive to repentance would play a major role in calling attention to moral conversations on repentance and developing thoughtful programs for widespread discussion and analysis of its social utility. Something analogous is taking place with respect to the related values of forgiveness and character education, which have received impetus from foundations and other private organizations. The Templeton Foundation, for example, has funded research projects, conferences, and books on forgiveness and on character education; what a decade or two ago was tangential both to broad public interest and to scholars is gradually receiving greater attention. A similar infusion of financial support and the development of thoughtful projects and programs devoted to repentance might accord it a more central place in our social and cultural awareness and afford it a larger role in relevant governmental policies, such as those concerning reform of the penal justice system. Some television programs are regularly viewed by tens of millions of Americans. If a few episodes of a popular TV series were to approach the subject of repentance with intelligence and in an interesting way, it could contribute substantially to a repentance megalogue. Documentaries on repentance on public television stations would do so as well. It would be important that these media productions not be seen as promoting religion, but as reflections on a value that can be shared by all Americans, non-religious and religious, and that can enhance the lives of all.

If the value of repentance is to take hold in society, it has to be inculcated in our children at home and in school. Conscientious parents and teachers already do teach the values of taking responsibility for one's misdeeds and apologizing, if not always to the degree required by full repentance. These values have to be reinforced through children's literature and incorporated into textbooks and curricula. Biblical literature that imparts values of universal import such as moral accountability and the human capacity for self-purification and renewal, and other literary works that plumb the depths of these psychological and moral potentialities of men and women should be studied.[23]

What can you, as an individual who is aware that you hurt another, do to help facilitate your own repentance?

The first thing to do is to reflect upon why you should repent and the benefits it will bring. It will truly make you a better person. It will benefit you emotionally, alleviating guilt and anxiety. It will help you sustain and enhance cherished relationships with parents, siblings, children, and your spouse. It will infuse your home with greater love and harmony. Your entire family is hurt and harmed by unresolved resentments for wrongs done to them, directly or indirectly. If, for example, you have insulted or abused your wife, do not think that she alone suffers; your children suffer as well. If you refuse to acknowledge your wrongdoing and repair it, not only will your wife resent you, but so will your children. They will see or sense her resentment and feel the pall of anger and injustice that permeates the household, poisoning its atmosphere. Repentance can rectify the injustices, heal the resentments, and cleanse the home of its spiritually polluted environment. When you think about these things, you will be more inclined to try to repent and make amends, without, one hopes, undue delay.

For many years a husband, whom I was seeing in therapy, had taken his wife for granted, rarely praising her for her devotion to their children and to the household. She worked long and difficult hours feeding, nurturing, and cleaning, and he barely lifted a finger to help her. Over time whatever feelings of affection she had for him dissipated. Sadly she even came to dislike him, so that after decades of marriage hurt and anger replaced love. When he finally realized the wrongs he had done to his wife and wanted to repair them, what could he do? The companionate love he had hoped for could not be magically created as they approached old age; the wife's years of feeling herself taken advantage of could not be undone. They had made their indelible and corrosive imprint, and there was no undoing the past.

This man wanted desperately to repair and rebuild a loving relationship. At best all he was capable of doing in the remaining years of their marriage was to admit to his wife that he had been insensitive and wrong, and to try to be as helpful and appreciative as possible. He also made it a point to be more attuned to his wife's hopes and dreams for a better future. He tried to compensate for the irreparable harm he had caused by providing her with some substitute joys, in lieu of those he had deprived her of during those many years of emotional neglect, indifference, and ingratitude. He could only hope that these measures might make her feel better and perhaps eventually change her feelings toward him. From the wife's perspective, the issue was whether she could forgive and reconcile so late in life. If, however, the husband had been schooled in self-examination and repentance, and had repented earlier, this sad situation might have been avoided.

One of the most important skills and attitudes for you to cultivate in order to repent is empathy. You must try to imagine the thoughts and feelings experienced by the person you hurt. If you do not feel ready or able to fully repent, at least initiate the process with some sign or signal that you feel bad for what you did and would like to apologize, make amends, and be forgiven, even if you cannot get yourself to explicitly articulate these feelings. When the relationship is at its core a loving one, the person whom you hurt has probably been longing for such a gesture and may respond with some appreciation that will enable you to proceed to the next stage of repentance. If you hurt someone with whom your relationship is not emotionally intense, such as a colleague, employee, or stranger, your repentance will dissipate resentment. If you have committed grievous offenses, such as serious crimes, your repentance may bring you back into the good graces of the community that you alienated. Sometimes, out of shame or out of fear that your sincere apology and desire to make amends will be spurned and rebuffed, you will find it difficult to repent. In such a case, seek out someone who can mediate on your behalf, a mutual friend or a relative who has both your and your victim's interests at heart. These, then, are some of the thoughts and strategies you can use when you know you should repent but find yourself resisting your better inclination.

So much for the essence of repentance and its role in our individual lives. I turn now to the role that repentance can play in the criminal justice system and in the resolution of ethnic, religious, and political conflicts. I will also discuss whether we bear any responsibility to repent for evil deeds perpetrated by groups or institutions with which we identify even though we were not personally involved in committing those deeds.

SEVEN

Repentance & Reconciliation

Criminals are sent to *penitent*-iaries, suggesting that they are expected to become penitent and repent for their crimes during their stay in prison. Prisons are also called correctional institutions, implying that the prisoner is to correct his deviant ways while imprisoned. Why this expectation? After all, prisons are not churches, wardens are not priests, and security guards are not altar boys. Aren't criminals locked up in cells and deprived of their freedom as punishment for crimes they committed, rather than as opportunities for spiritual retreat in civic monasteries? Our society imprisons people who commit crimes because justice demands retribution or because society wishes to deter them or others from committing crimes in the future, not to induce repentance.

Perhaps retribution and deterrence are the main or exclusive motives for our putting people in prison today. However, in the nineteenth century, many people who administered the criminal justice system believed that *penitent*-iaries were meant to educate prisoners as to why what they did was wrong and to rehabilitate them morally, as well as to dispense "just desserts" and deter further crime. Today few legislators, judges, lawyers, or prison wardens see themselves as primarily responsible for the moral or spiritual rehabilitation of criminals. Even if they would like to see the criminal justice system function in such a way, they do not believe that it is a realistic objective, for several reasons. For one, we simply do not know how to reliably rehabilitate criminals morally. Moreover, the prison environment as presently constructed is not conducive to moral rehabilitation. Housing criminals with one another is not an effective means of getting them to regret what they have done and to learn new ways of behaving. If anything, imprisonment hardens many inmates rather than induces them to be penitent.

Moral rehabilitation can mean two things. Some people accept the values of society even though they violate them. Rehabilitation means learning how to avoid violating them again. However, some people do not accept the validity of the social norms that they violate. Rehabilitation in this case means coming to accept a value system that you once rejected. This second kind of rehabilitation is probably more difficult and rare than the first. Many prisoners do not accept the values of the society that has convicted and sentenced them. They feel that society has been unfair to them and they justify their crimes with arguments or elaborate theories. The Unabomber, who murdered three people and wounded many others, believes that he was morally justified, or even obligated, to kill scientists and engineers because, for him, science and technology are evil. Incarceration or any other punishment—in the absence of re-education and re-socialization—will seldom change one's value system.

In addition, many prisons do not have the resources to teach inmates useful skills that will make it more probable that, when released from prison, they will be able to support themselves and their families without resorting to crime once again. Also, most criminals who are incarcerated for violent crimes, such as rape or murder, are not taught during their stay in prison how to control their sexual or violent impulses. Given the realities of incarceration today, prisons are not *penitent*-iaries, and maybe not even correctional institutions.

Notwithstanding this reality, there are some thoughtful students of our criminal justice system who argue that a major function of punishment should be to induce moral improvement in prisoners. They would like to reintroduce repentance into the system, albeit in civic rather than religious garb.

Are there ways in which our criminal justice system can encourage a criminal to repent? What would civic or secular repentance entail? How can we know that the criminal has sincerely repented? What should be the legal implications of his repentance? And, if a criminal does morally rehabilitate himself, how should he be treated by society once he is released from prison?

. . .

Questions similar to these have been discussed by rabbinical scholars over two millennia. It is interesting to see how they were approached by *halakha,* Jewish law, which expresses the religious values of Judaism.

Judaism took it for granted that society should do what it can to encourage sinners to repent, and that if they did sincerely repent they should be reintegrated into the community. The communitarian ethos is strong in Judaism, making every member of society responsible for one another's moral and spiritual state. Judaism also places a great emphasis on justice. Sometimes these two values can be in conflict and a decision has to be made as to which prevails. This issue comes to the fore in the intriguing talmudic rulings known as *takanat ha'shavim*, an ordinance for the sake of those who want to repent. This ruling refers to a robber who wants to repent of his crime.

The biblical law (Lev. 5:23) about a robber who want to make amends states, "When one has thus sinned and, realizing his guilt, would restore that which he got through robbery."

This verse was interpreted to mean that a robber was obligated to restore to its rightful owner the actual item that he stole, as long as it was still available and in its original state. He could not opt to pay the owner its monetary value and retain the stolen object for himself.

In general, this is an eminently reasonable and just law. However, if applied strictly, there are times when it could be severe in its moral implications. What is the law, for example, if I stole a beam, and then, without making any change in the beam itself, incorporated it into a building that I constructed? Technically, I am under an obligation to remove the beam from the building, even if that means destroying the entire building in order to retrieve it so that I can return the actual beam to its rightful owner. This indeed is what, according to the Talmud, the biblical law requires.

The rabbis of the talmudic period were concerned that the severity of the biblical law with respect to returning stolen items might deter a robber who would like to repent from actually doing so. He knew that in order for his repentance to be valid he would have to return the stolen object itself, because both the law and spiritual repentance require proper restitution. To encourage him to repent, the rabbis legislated *takanat ha'shavim*—that in situations where strict application of the law of Leviticus would entail too severe a financial burden on the robber, he was permitted to retain the stolen object and pay its owner a cash equivalent (Mishnah Gittin 5:5).

More radical than this ordinance was a subsequent one recorded in the Talmud, which states that if a robber or someone who had lent money on interest (which was forbidden) and who wants to repent offers repayment to the victim, the victim should not accept the payment, and if he does, "the spirit of the wise does not look with favor upon him." This expression means that the victim cannot be legally prevented from accepting his due, but that it would be magnanimous and spiritually sensitive of him to forgive the debt. The Talmud records an anecdote that explains the origin of this teaching at the end of the second century.

It happened that a man wanted to repent. His wife said to him: "Empty one, if you repent you will not be left with even your belt." This deterred him and he did not repent. At once they [the rabbis] said "One should not accept payment from robbers and money-lenders, and he who does, the spirit of the wise does not look with favor upon him."[1]

Maimonides makes it clear that this teaching applied only to robbers and money lenders who on their own initiative stepped forth to return what they had illegally taken. Having demonstrated that they sincerely wanted to repent and were willing to make restitution as required, presumably even at great hardship to themselves and even to the point of impoverishment (as the anecdote suggests), the response of the victim and of the community should be supportive and forgiving.[2] If, however, the robber, though now not required to pay, insisted on doing so in order that he might fully repent, the victim could accept the money.

This radical innovation of the rabbis is difficult to understand without some qualification. As important as repentance is, and despite every individual's responsibility to support one another's spiritual growth, it does not, practically speaking, seem plausible that all victims should sustain substantial monetary losses in order to encourage criminals who want to repent to actually do so. From the talmudic anecdote, it seems that the robber is totally dependent on his illegal trade for his income. Moreover, he may steal small sums from a large number of individuals. He probably steals in order to ensure his family's survival. If so, the ruling seems more realistic. For the robber to return what he stole would be a great sacrifice, albeit one that strict justice demands. His offer to repay testifies to the authenticity of his repentance. On the other hand, the losses to each of his victims may be relatively minimal (even though to steal even a penny is a grave sin in Jewish law). The rabbis decided that, in such a case, forgiving the debt and encouraging repentance takes priority over demanding just restitution.

Whatever the actual origins of this ruling and the circumstances in which it was applied, it demonstrates the great importance that Jewish tradition placed on helping criminals to repent. Of course, one problem it raises is that once an unrepentant robber learns of this ruling, he has an incentive to come forth and feign repentance in order to have the debt abrogated. In cases in which this was a reasonable suspicion, the robber would have to prove in some other way that his repentance was sincere.[3]

Can a criminal or sinner who has repented and who has paid whatever penalty the law requires be trusted and be restored to his pre-criminal social status and rights? The question is debated by the Jewish jurists. Maimonides states that various sinners, including thieves and others who take money illegally, are disqualifed to be witnesses. The thief is barred from testifying in any judicial proceeding even if he returned that which he stole. Some jurists maintain that if he returns the money on his own initiative, rather than because he is compelled to do so by a court, he is assumed to have repented and can now serve as a witness. Others maintain that, even in the latter case, he remains disqualified from being a witness. Perhaps this stricter view reflects a deep suspicion of the sincerity of an ostensible penitent's repentance, or a gnawing suspicion that even a sincere penitent is in danger of relapsing. Since testimony in court affects the fate and fortune of others, it is necessary to be especially careful with respect to who is permitted to testify.

Is there anything a repentant sinner can or must do to convince society that he is sincere and deserves to be restored to full and trusted membership in it? Since only God "knows the thoughts of man," mortals have to rely on the behaviors that they observe in others when they want to assess whether apparent repentance is feigned or authentic. Addressing this issue, the Talmud tells of a *shohet*, a ritual slaughterer and butcher, who sold to a Jew meat that the *shohet* knew to be non-kosher, because the *shohet* did not want to sustain the financial loss of discarding the meat. The *shohet* had, for the sake of money, committed the sin of causing a fellow Jew to unknowingly eat forbidden food. When the communal leader, Rabbi Nahman found out about this, he declared that the *shohet* could no longer be trusted, thereby depriving him of his occupation and income. The *shohet* let his hair and nails grow long, making himself disgusting, traditional acts of self-humiliation that penitents were accustomed to perform as signs of their repentance. Rabbi Nahman was prepared to reinstate him in his position. However, Rava objected on the grounds that he might simply be feigning repentance in order to get his job back. Was there anything, then, that he could do to convince Rava that he was sincere, and that he could now be trusted to be willing to sustain a financial loss rather than sell to an unknowing public non-kosher meat as if it were kosher? Yes, says the Talmud, as Rabbi Idi the son of Avin taught:

> One who is suspected of selling non-kosher food as kosher has no remedy [that will restore his trustworthiness] until he goes to a place where no one knows who he is and having found a valuable lost object returns it to its rightful owner, or who having slaughtered an expensive animal of his own

and then found it [by examining its innards] to be non-kosher, declares it to be so. [4]

In other words the litmus test has to be some behavior that unambiguously suggests that the sinner, having faced a situation of temptation similar to the one in which he initially succumbed [tempted by money, he violated God's law], will not repeat the offense. In both of these "test" situations, the slaughterer could get away with violating the law, without detection, for the sake of monetary gain or to prevent monetary loss, and yet he chooses to follow the law and sustain a loss. The reason he must do this in a locale where he is not known is that that lessens the probability that he is doing what he does in order to regain his original job as slaughterer. In this new locale, he would have no such motive.

A similar question is discussed in a responsum by Rabbi Asher, a late twelfth-century rabbi. In this case, a communally appointed *shohet* and cantor committed perjury for a bribe, not related to the sale of non-kosher meat, but with respect to the marital status of a certain woman, a very serious sin since his false testimony enabled the woman to commit adultery. He was punished with flogging, a substantial monetary fine, and public shaming by having his hair cut. In addition to these punishments, it was decreed that he could not serve as a *shohet* or a leader of the prayer service for a five-year period, unless before then he repented a "superior" repentance, one which was sincere and profound.

After about a year, the *shohet* came and said that ever since that event he had fasted twice a week for a full year and requested that the ban be lifted. Rabbi Asher ruled that his penitential acts did not suffice to assure us that he was sincere, since they might have been deceitful, given that he did not voluntarily initiate repentance but was ordered by the court to repent. The only repentance that would be acceptable would be one that was undertaken voluntarily and that provided an opportunity, as we saw in the talmudic text cited above, to demonstrate that, under circumstances more or less identical to those in which he sinned, he would refrain from doing so again.

Rabbi Asher cites another rabbinic text that states that in order for money lenders or gamblers to regain their trustworthiness, they must destroy their IOU documents or their dice, and not take interest on a loan or play with dice even in situations in which the law would permit it. In other words, they must not only abide by the strict letter of the law that they violated but must go beyond its formal requirements. [5] These acts also demonstrate that the repentant sinner abhors any activity or object that is associated with his sin, even if not sinful itself. Floggings and fasts do not meet these criteria, and so he is not to be reinstated as a publicly approved ritual slaughterer, whose probity must be beyond reproach.[6]

Although this test of probity and sincerity is very demanding, it does enable a sincere penitent to regain his good reputation and reclaim his social status and rights.

A responsum, by the tenth-century jurist Rabbenu Gershom, deals with the restoration of ritual privileges to a *kohen,* a member of the priestly family. After the destruction of the Temple in Jerusalem in 70 C.E., priests retained a few vestigial ritual obligations and privileges. One of these is to bless publicly the congregants in the synagogue in a special ceremony conducted on certain festivals. All the priests in the congregation stand in the front of the synagogue where the Ark and its Torah Scroll are kept and chant the blessings. Priests are also called up to recite the first of the blessings recited when the Torah is read in public during a service. These honors are accorded to priests in recognition of their lineage, and as signs that the priests have maintained their sanctity notwithstanding the loss of the Temple and its worship service.

A certain priest had committed one of the gravest sins imaginable to a medieval Jew. He had converted to Christianity. The priest now repented of this sin and wanted once again to participate in the privileged priestly blessings. Rabbenu Gershom ruled that since he had repented he could do so. In supporting his ruling he cited several biblical and rabbinic texts that testify to the great concern, as well as respect, for the repentant sinner, which permeates the Jewish ethos.

For example, the rabbis expand the meaning of the biblical prohibition against monetarily oppressing one's fellow to refer to verbal oppression as well. They give as an example that it is forbidden to say to a repentant sinner "remember your previous [sinful] deeds." There is no greater oppression of this repentant priest, says Rabbenu Gershom, than to deny him his original privileges. Since these privileges are manisfested in public settings, the very fact that the priest would be publicly denied the right to perform them would be a recurring public reminder to him, in the presence of the congregation, that he had once been a sinner.

Moreover, says Rabbenu Gershom, consonant with the rationale of *takanat hashavim*—if you do not allow the priest to begin his life anew as a purified penitent, you will discourage him (and others) from repenting in the first place.

These rabbinic teachings and rulings are sensitive to the fact that repentance does not take place in a social vacuum. Repentance is not exclusively a personal experience between man and God, or between man and his conscience, uninfluenced by social forces.

As further support for his ruling, Rabbenu Gershom cites the talmudic statement that "anyone who asserts that [King] Manasseh has no share in the world to come is weakening the hands of penitents" (Babylonian Talmud, Tractate Sanhedrin, 103 a). What were Manasseh's sins? We read in II Chronicles 33 that Manasseh, who assumed the throne after the death of his God-fearing father Hezekiah, "did what was evil in the sight of the Lord . . . erected altars to the Baals . . . worshipped the host of heaven and served them. He built altars [to foreign deities] in the house of the Lord."

The list of Manasseh's abominations goes on and on. His sins were not personal, but corrupted the entire nation.

In the rabbinic worldview, a leader who causes others to sin typically forfeits any right to the rewards of the hereafter, notwithstanding positive deeds he may have done. But Manasseh had a saving grace. Eventually he was bound in fetters and brought to Babylon where, we are told,

> while he was in distress he entreated the favor of the Lord his God and humbled himself greatly before the God of his ancestors. He prayed to him, and God received his entreaty, heard his plea, and restored him again to Jerusalem, and to his kingdom. Then Manasseh knew that the Lord indeed was God. (vv. 12–13)

The rabbis saw the profound psychological and theological implications of this story. Here was a man who had committed a catalogue of sins so evil that one would expect no mercy or forgiveness for him. Yet because he repented, he was reinstated. It seems that there were people in talmudic times who, quite understandably, found it difficult to imagine that such a sinner could ever merit reward in the eternal hereafter. They might have felt that his reward for his repentance was given him in this world, with his reinstatement as king, but surely such an ex-sinner cannot have a share in the world to come. To this, the rabbis responded that even Manasseh can rehabilitate himself to the point of eternal reward.

If Manasseh can be purified, then almost any sinner can. Those who would deny this possibility, by denying Manasseh his share in the world to come, are sending a message to sinners that repentance doesn't pay. There is no hope for you. This is not the message the rabbis wanted to convey to sinners, even to the worst among them. On the contrary, repent sincerely and you will be accepted no matter how far you have deviated from the path of righteousness.

Rabbenu Gershom teaches that it is not only God who accepts the repentant sinner. We, as individuals and as a community, have to reintegrate him as well. If we do not do so, we will have lost an opportunity to save a soul that is groping for redemption and needs helping hands to draw him back into the sphere of virtue. The rabbis and Rabbenu Gershom want us to overcome our natural inclination to shun the sinner even after he has repented. We are required to embrace him.

· · ·

How might repentance be reintroduced into our criminal justice system, and into society's attitude toward criminals? Advocates of this idea do not want our prisons turned into religious communities, although some of them draw upon and are inspired by religious teachings about repentance. They appreciate what many religious traditions take for granted, that a criminal's repentance is to be encouraged and that the penitent criminal is to be reintegrated into the community.[7] What is of interest here are notions about civic, moral, or secular repentance, as they have been called, and restorative justice. These concepts do not depend upon theological assumptions or religious commitments.

The stigma of being an ex-convict is very powerful and often results in what is, in effect, the indefinite extension of punishment beyond what the law demands and imposes. After the offender has completed the punishment imposed by the court and is released from prison, he has, from a legal perspective, paid his debt to society. Yet, he will find it difficult to get a job. In addition, some federal and state laws deprive former convicts of certain civic rights or bar them from practicing certain professions.

There are several rationales for these post-release "punishments." For example, like any other penalty, they might deter prospective wrongdoers. More probably, they reflect the feeling of many people that the law is too lenient on criminals and more punishment is warranted after their release. Even if the offender received a very stiff sentence, such that justice may have been satisfied from the state's perspective, the punishment usually hasn't compensated the victim for his pain or loss, and often never can. The rapist who spends twenty years in jail doesn't, and can never, undo the rape and its effect. The murderer cannot resurrect his victim. Therefore, people feel that such a criminal should suffer until the day of his death because the injury he wrought was forever. Although the law need not inflict this continuous punishment on the criminal, individual members of society can, and they do so by stigmatizing and ostracizing him.

In addition, many people quite reasonably believe that imprisonment doesn't change the character of most prisoners. The former embezzler or thief who is applying for a job that would give him access to money or goods cannot be trusted, even after he has paid for his crime. Why risk hiring him when someone honest can be hired instead? Can we trust a lawyer who committed perjury to uphold the law just because he served his time in jail?

All of these are reasonable arguments and appeals to moral emotions that should not be lightly dismissed. The problem with the attitude they generate, however, is that it is too harsh, rigid, and pessimistic. It looks at human nature as static and incapable of moral progress. It does not provide for second chances. It has more than a whiff of self-righteousness, as if only criminals are weak of character while "we" are immune to sin and crime. Even if the criminal's offense caused irrevocable and irreparable pain and suffering, justice cannot be the exclusive principle by which we deal with one another.

A fellow human being stumbled or was maliciously evil. Now he wants to improve himself. Is he to be chained forever to the mistakes of his past? Surely such rigidity is not good for the individual or for society as a whole. If "once a sinner forever a sinner," "once a criminal forever a criminal," we remove any hope and incentive for repairing individuals and the world. I think that upon serious reflection most people would agree that moral self-improvement is possible, even though they would argue, correctly, that it is difficult to accomplish. It simply isn't true that people never change, that criminals are never rehabilitated. There are many instances of people who while in prison, or after their release, devoted themselves to worthy causes that earned them great respect. One well-known example is Chuck Colson, who was imprisoned for his crimes in the Watergate scandal. As a result of his prison experience, he eventually established a prison faith ministry to help rehabilitate prisoners through conversion to Christ.[8] It is more socially useful to develop strategies for encouraging offenders to change for the better than to punish them forever by stigmatizing them.[9]

Everyone including people who violate laws and social mores, needs and seeks the approval of others. On the basis of this sound assumption, Etzioni points out that offenders

> at some time receive approval from other offenders, such as members of a
> gang, fellow inmates, and companion drug abusers. But what of the offender
> who wants to reform his deviant behavior? Once he departs from a life of

crime, he loses the affirmation of other miscreants. If he then finds that the doors to acceptance by law-abiding members of the community, those who uphold mores, are, in effect, locked, his rehabilitation is paralyzed. This "locked door" is one reason that offenders are pushed back, as indeed they often seem to be in our society, into their previous, deviant, social circles. By contrast, if offenders could complete the steps of repentance, and then be fully accepted by the upright community, this would serve as a significant incentive for offenders to embark on the road to repentance, see it through, and become and remain productive members of the community.[10]

But what about our suspicion that an offender hasn't sincerely repented and so can't be trusted? Are there ways to plausibly overcome this legitimate concern? It is difficult to know when an offender feels true remorse, although there can be some indicators, such as its duration or the ways and the contexts in which it is expressed. Psychologists have developed sophisticated instruments that reliably measure many complex human emotions and personality traits, and they should be able to devise one that measures remorse. Judges are regularly expected to assess the sincerity and depth of the remorse of defendants when they sentence them. Parole boards try to take remorse into consideration. Often these people will err, but the legal system does not shy away from attempting to assess remorse and other mental and emotional states of mind. The fact that these assessments are not always reliable does not mean that they are useless. The argument against taking professions of remorse seriously in sentencing or in determinations of eligibility for parole, on the grounds that God alone can know what is truly in people's hearts, is inconsistent with fundamental assumptions of the law and of our ability to assess the attitudes of others.[11]

A distinguished jurist, Haim Cohn, discusses the role that shame and guilt should play in determining the punishment of criminals, and the difficulty of determining the sincerity of the outward manifestations of these emotions. He finds that some judges are so offended by what appears to them to be sham remorse or sham guilt that they give a harsher sentence than they would have had the offender simply remained silent. Yet when guilt or remorse are sincere, he believes that judges should consider them a mitigating factor in sentencing.

There is one unmistakable test of true remorse—and that is the attempt of restitution or compensation. . . . Due consideration of restitution or compensation efforts of the offender in mitigation of his punishment, may operate as a general encouragement of offenders to make amends for their crimes—and it is surely the function and duty of courts of justice to see to it that (some) justice is also done to the victim. Looking at criminal law and penology from an educational vista, their purposes are surely better met by restitution or compensation than by imprisonment, and looking at guilt-consciousness in the moral and ethical context, guilt-feelings towards the victim, especially when activated, surely take preference over a bad conscience towards oneself. It is here that guilt-consciousness attains its self-fulfilment and celebrates its advancement from mental pain to active well-doing, and it is here that it should always be recognized and rewarded by judicial cognizance.[12]

More important then than expressions of remorse in assessing the sincerity of repentance are the actions undertaken by the offender to undo, amend, or substitute for the harm he caused. However, most criminal offenders, either because of the nature of their crime, such as rape, assault, or murder, or because of their lack of financial resources, cannot amend or repair the harm they caused. A poor person who steals and sells a rich man's Jaguar and spends the money on crack has little chance of reimbursing his victim for the stolen car. Is there anything they can do in lieu of restitution and repair?

What if the offender imposed upon himself some undertaking that could be reliably monitored, that would involve a high degree of self-sacrifice and that would also make a useful social contribution? If, for example, the offender, while still in prison, and on his own initiative, volunteered to undertake some such task or project, and let it be known that he was doing so out of remorse for his crime, might this not be a reliable indicator of authentic repentance?

Catholicism, in particular, and the Jewish Pietist school of thirteenth century Ashkenaz (northern France and Germany), developed systems of penances that a sinner intent on repenting could perform as one aspect of his repentance. Most of the sins atoned for were between man and God, such as failing to pray or to perform religious rituals, or violations of religious taboos, such as engaging in prohibited sexual acts or eating forbidden food. The penances were to correspond in some way with the sin. If you committed fornication, you might be required to abstain from sex with your spouse for a specified period of time. If a Catholic ate meat during Lent, or if a Jew ate pork, he might have to fast for a set number of days. Books were written to help guide penitents in determining the appropriate penance, but the choice of whether to accept and implement the penance was often the penitent's to make. This was especially so in Judaism, where there was a much less hier-archical structure of authority and more limited power of coercion than in the Catholic Church. Where the sin was a violation of the social order, such as a crime or a public flouting of the authority of the Church or of the Jewish religious leaders, the penance could be imposed on the sinner without his consent, as both a punishment and a condition for reacceptance into the good graces of the community of the faithful. Penances often involved giving alms, caring for the sick, or other benevolent actions (above and beyond what would be expected of any Jew or Christian to regularly do), rather than mere self-denial or, in Catholicism, self-mortification.

Can there be a secular or civic analogue to the medieval penitential system that helped the repenter? Would we want someone who stole food to fast, or for a rapist to abstain from sex? Perhaps some would think that these would be appropriate penalties, but that is not the official view of the legal system.[13]

There are some prison programs that do provide opportunities for inmates to volunteer their services to others in need. Sometimes the inmate partici-pates out of an altruistic motive and sometimes for the pragmatic purpose of earning early release. Even when an inmate participates in such a program out of self-interest, it can still be morally beneficial. Some criminals never had the opportunity to learn that they have something valuable to contribute to society, and this experience can be edifying. Judaism teaches that one should engage in virtuous behavior even out of selfish motives, since in the course of such involvement one may come to appreciate the inherent worth of the behavior, and will ultimately do it for its own sake.

Some psychologists maintain that criminals have low self-esteem, which is a factor in their criminal behavior. To the extent that this is so, any program that enhances a criminal's self-esteem could be morally beneficial, and helping others who then express their gratitude and appreciation for that help is esteem building.[14]

Sometimes prisoners earn reduced time by volunteering to participate in medical experiments. This is ethically problematic because medical (and other) research on humans requires free and informed consent. Given the control over a prisoner that can be exercised by prison staff, and the psychological pressure that can be applied to a prisoner, it is difficult to assure that his consent is indeed free and informed. However, if procedures can be developed to protect against coercion, inmates volunteer at signficant pain and risk to participate in such experiments because they want to counterbalance the evil they have done with some good, and there is no external reward being prom-ised, we might consider this as a significant indicator of sincere repentance.

Even if prisoners are highly motivated to do good deeds as a penance, because of the limitation on their freedom of movement, they cannot go on their own initiative to the locations at which they could be of service. Given the sophistication of modern communications technology, it is possible to engage in benevolent activities from a distance. Prisons should encourage inmates who would like to help others, by providing them with the tools and time to engage in such endeavors from within the prison confines.

Some judges have imposed sentences that include a community-service requirement. This service may be in lieu of incarceration or as a supplement to a reduced stay in prison. Compulsory community service may not induce remorse, but it gives the criminal an opportunity to perform acts of restitution, at least to society, if not to his victim. In order for community service to serve the needs of justice and restitution, it should be sufficiently demanding and meaningful that it is not perceived by the criminal or by society as an avoidance of punishment due.

In religious, and in some legal, theories of punishment and penance there is the notion that penalties should be demeaning. By his actions the offender has demeaned his victim and has demeaned the community, since his violation of the law implies that he is above his victim and the law. His crime sends the message that he feels no obligation to respect the rights of the other and that society has no authority over him. This implicit hubris needs to be squelched, and one way of doing this is by making the offender do things that will both teach him, and demonstrate to the community, that he is not above the law. This is why religious penitents and criminals who flouted the authority of the church or state had to publicly humiliate themselves or be publicly humiliated. It wasn't the severity of the punishment or penance that was so important but its symbolic significance as a ritual for reestablishing the right order of things. This was a major function of public flogging, probably even more than its deterrent effect. To the extent that this is the aim of a penalty, once the offender has acknowledged that he is subject to, rather than above, the laws of the church or state, he can be readmitted to the community. Should community service be primarily an act of restitution, or should it also include an element of humiliation and penance, as incarceration usually does? Robert Wuthnow points out that

> another potential weakness of community service is that the deeds themselves overshadow the idea of repentance to such an extent that criminal behavior is in effect excused by the possibility that offenders may still make a positive contribution to society. . . . It is for this reason that the courts

have often required doctors, lawyers, politicians, and others who might easily be able to serve the community through their work, to perform menial tasks as punishment for wrongdoing. In such instances the symbolic meaning of menial service is assumed to be more important than the sheer contribution to the community itself.[15]

Perhaps community service sentences should include ritual humbling as well as constructive activities. The haughty offender will be reminded that he is not above the law and above his victims as he cleans toilets in a homeless shelter, and he will feel that he is atoning for his misdeeds and making restitution when he uses his professional or other skills to help the shelter's residents, as a doctor, lawyer, or craftsman.

In his discussion of repentance, legal philosopher Jeffrie Murphy[16] distinguishes between grievance retributivism and character retributivism. In grievance retributivism, an offender is punished for specific wrongs he did. In character retributivism, the purpose of punishment is to change the offender's character.

Religions and their institutions take it for granted that they are in the business of molding character. In our culturally and religiously diverse society, there are differences of opinion about the extent to which public schools should be involved in character education, and the specific values that they should be trying to inculcate. At a minimum, though, the state and its lawful government is not only empowered to pass laws, enforce them, and punish violators, but has the right to expect that citizens will be socialized to accept basic moral and legal norms that are essential to a stable civil order. It also has a role in ensuring the socialization of these values. If all this is true, then government might use its authority to punish offenders as an instrument of character retributivism, to morally improve their character so that they will have respect for the law and for the rights of others. It also has a right to take into account changes in their character. In this case, the state should encourage, support, and reward civic or moral repentance, at least insofar as it is relevant to respecting the law.

Murphy draws upon the theory of punishment developed by R. A. Duff,[17] who claims that punishment is, among other things, a means whereby the community communicates a message to the criminal who has violated its norms, and it should be understood in communitarian terms. What is the message and how is it communicated? Murphy, summarizing Duff, writes:

> The suffering [of imprisonment] endured is that of separation from a valued community—a community that the criminal values (perhaps without

realizing it until he experiences its loss) and to which he would like to return—and communicates to the wrongdoer the judgment that his actions have made him, at least temporarily, unworthy of full participation in the life of the community. It requires that he experience the pain and separation so that he can come to see, in his heart, the appropriateness of that separation and thus seek, with the appropriate humility, reconciliation with the community that he has wronged. In other words, the hope is that a kind of compulsory penance will be replaced by a voluntary penance. Voluntary penance is a sincere act of reattachment or allegiance to community values[18]—an act that will allow the wrongdoer to be welcomed again and reintegrated into community life. (Murphy, pp. 154–55)

How might our penal and justice system incorporate practices that reflect this view of punishment and penance? For one,

according to Duff, the right sort of prison may help the wrongdoer to achieve the good of reintegration because "it removes the criminal from his corrupting peers, and provides the opportunity for and stimulus to reflective self-examination which will [ideally] induce repentance and self-reform." Also worth considering are such alternatives to prison as community service and restitution. (Murphy, p. 155)

Murphy points to a number of problems in applying Duff's theory. American society might not share a community of values, and not all criminals want to be "reintegrated" into a community whose values they consider to be unjust, and in which they never felt integrated in the first place. Moreover, our presently constituted prisons may corrupt inmates rather than provide an environment for moral rehabilitation.

Notwithstanding these and other reservations, Murphy suggests that there are areas in which it would pay to give Duff's approach a try, particularly with juvenile offenders, who are probably more amenable to character transformation than adults. Experiments in cultivating empathy for his victims in the young offender by having him meet with (willing) victims and their families, being exposed directly to their pain and sorrow (and perhaps forgiveness as well), might be effective in inducing moral change. He cites the sentence that a state court in Washington meted out to two native American juveniles guilty of robbery and assault. It authorized the tribal court to determine the punishment and that court sentenced each youth to eighteen months of solitary "exile" on an uninhabited Alaskan island "in the hope that the necessity of surviving on their own, with only traditional tools and folkways to guide them, would build their characters and allow them reintegration into the community."

Murphy feels that, realistically, the primary role that a notion of repentance might play in the judicial system in the near future, barring a radical transformation of our penal system and its dominant value of retribution,[19] would be in sentencing, pardoning, and restoring rights, rather than in determining the nature of the punishment or the prison environment. Thus where judges are given discretion in determining the length of a prison sentence, they can use evidence of sincere repentance and be merciful, as long as they feel confident that a lesser sentence will not compromise the legitimate retributive and deterrent functions of punishment. From the "character retributivist" perspective on punishment, "the repentant person has a better character than the unrepentant person, and thus the repentant person . . . deserves less punishment than the unrepentant person" (Murphy, p. 157).

Moreover, even from the "grievance retributivism" perspective, which is concerned with righting wrongs and with the victim's right to see the offender punished, it may be possible to justify taking into account an offender's repentance as grounds for leniency in sentencing. One element of authentic repentance is emotionally painful guilt. The suffering of guilt can be taken into consideration in determining the overall amount of suffering that the offender should be subjected to as retribution for his specific wrongdoing. Finally, the sincerely repentant offender, having been punished and having transformed his character appropriately, is entitled to reintegration into the community. Therefore, individuals and the law should restore to him the rights he lost when he committed his crimes. On this latter point, Murphy recounts a bitter controversy in which

> the admissions committee of the College of Law at my [public] university admitted a paroled murderer into the first-year class. The outcry from alumni and legislators was enormous—including a . . . threat to withdraw funding from the college and shut it down. Both the parole board and the admissions committee believed that the individual, who had served a very long prison term, was sincerely repentant and fully rehabilitated, and desired to make the rest of his life of some use to society. Critics regarded this argument as irrelevant either because they doubted the sincerity of the repentance, or more commonly, because they believed that even fully repentant murderers owed a lifetime of debt to their victims and to the community that could not be overcome by any change of character. (p. 160)

Murphy supported the admissions committee's decision to admit the applicant, but he recognizes that there can be reasonable arguments for and against it, especially in this particular case where scarce public funds were at issue. If this applicant were admitted, that would mean that another applicant, who had never committed murder, would not be, because admission was very selective.

This raises an interesting question. Who has higher moral status, the person who never sinned, or the person who sinned but repented? At first glance it would seem that the person who never sinned has the moral advantage. But the matter is not so clear-cut. In fact, there is a strange rabbinic teaching that repentant sinners are even closer to God's presence than those who were always righteous. Several explanations have been offered for this teaching. The righteous person may have been righteous because he was never subjected to the external temptations that faced the sinner. Or perhaps, those natural inclinations to sin, which we all have to some degree, such as lust, greed, and envy, were constitutionally less intense in the person who was always righteous than they were in the sinner. Another interpretation is that the sinner, who experienced the sensual or emotional pleasures and gratifications of sin, some of which can be very intense, and was able to repent and overcome further temptation, demonstrates a level of character or piety that is greater than that of someone who never tasted forbidden fruits or experienced the cathartic release of tension and psychic gratification that violence may produce.

There is in this rabbinic teaching not only an obvious incentive to the prospective penitent sinner to go forward with the process, assuring him that he can come close to God, but a psychological observation on the difficulty and challenge of abandoning sin and vice and adopting good deeds and virtue. The rabbis were awed by and admired the repentant sinner's struggle and courage, and the elevated moral and spiritual ground that he reached. Perhaps we too need to cultivate an awareness of and an appreciation for the repentant and rehabilitated former criminal, and accord him the honor, or at least respect and acceptance, that are his due.

The restorative justice movement is more ambitious in its objectives than the call for civic repentance, and it is closer to, while not crossing over into, the domain of explicit Christianity. Moreover, it is concerned not only with the criminal justice system, but with ethnic and political conflicts in which violations of justice have occurred and attempts at conflict resolution and reconciliation are being made. What are some of the basic tenets of the restorative justice movement?

> The dominant paradigm of our present system of law—retributive justice—looks to the past, determines guilt and assesses punishment. It is not conducive to forgiveness . . .

Restorative justice understands crime and legal harm as a violation of people and relationships. Its goal is making things right and creating right relations. . . . The first priority is to work toward the healing and restoration of victims . . . responding to their needs, including restitution. . . . The second priority is to hold the offender accountable for his actions, involving the offender in the decision as to how to make things right for the victim and the community which has also been harmed, with the goal of reintegrating the victim and the offender back into community. . . . A restorative justice system creates opportunities for dialogue, direct or indirect, between victims and offenders. . . . Its focus is not on establishing guilt and punishing, but on identifying needs and obligations so that things can be made right. . . . Restorative justice opens up the possibility of talking about forgiveness in political and personal relationships, but . . . in a way that is defined by healing, right relations, and a reconciliation that requires mutuality. Finally, restorative justice redefines justice in a way that looks to the future and creates community and new relationships.[20]

Insofar as repentance is concerned, the restorative justice movement and the programs it sponsors try to educate offenders as to why what they did was wrong, to make them aware of the pain and suffering sustained by their victims, to have them acknowledge and assume responsibility for their crimes, and to provide them with opportunities to make restitution and/or to undergo rehabilitation. Elsewhere in its mission statement, it emphasizes mercy, compassion, forgiveness, and healing, focusing more on the victim's attitude toward the offender.

One may disagree with the way in which the restorative justice movement includes under its rubric of justice an obligation or expectation that the victim should work toward healing and reconciliation. This is often, though not always, desirable, as we have seen. Even when it is desirable, however, to call it "justice" blurs important distinctions between justice on the one hand, and healing, forgiveness, and reconciliation on the other. In any case, this movement's concern with, among other processes, the encouragement of repentance by offenders is a welcome advance beyond an exclusive focus on punishment as retribution or deterrence.

· · ·

Are repentance and forgiveness relevant to violent injustices perpetrated by one group against another? Since groups are aggregates of individuals, group injustices are ultimately perpetrated by individuals from one group against individuals from the other. The fact that individuals act in groups, and against groups, does not absolve the individual perpetrator from his individual responsibility for what he has done. In determining the degree of his responsibility for his crime, we consider the effects of social, military, or governmental pressures on the individual. In principle, however, we do the same when we ascertain the degree of guilt of an individual acting alone, although we might emphasize other, more personal factors that influenced his behavior. If group injustice is simply shorthand for the injustices perpetrated by many people acting in concert against many others, then there is no reason to say that repentance and forgiveness are not applicable. The specific member of a white supremacist group who beat, raped, and tortured an innocent black woman could, in principle, repent by expressing remorse to her and giving restitution, and she in turn could choose to forgive him if she wanted to. The fact that the beatings occurred during one of the racist group's rampages against a group of blacks, or that the supremacist group is a social movement and the black population is an oppressed minority group has many social, economic, and political implications, but these do not change the fact that it was a particular man who violated this particular woman on this particular day, at this particular hour. Therefore, he can repent and she can forgive.

Yet there is usually a greater moral and practical complexity to group injustices perpetrated against a group of victims sharing a common identity. Group crimes, especially when committed under state auspices, are often committed indirectly, via unjust legislation, for example, rather than by way of direct violence. Moreover, many people are involved in the chain of injustice so that it is difficult to specify which particular individual or individuals bear the guilt, or to what degree. Governmental oppression is carried out by large bureaucracies in which there is a diffusion of responsibility for the crimes committed. Is the conductor of the train packed with innocents headed for the gas chambers of Auschwitz as guilty as the officer who ordered the roundup in the ghetto of the Jews who were forced into the train's cattle cars? Is the officer as guilty as the Nazi leader who formulated the policy of the "final solution"—that all Jews be exterminated—and ordered the construction of Auschwitz and gave the directives as to what was to be done there?

Ascertaining degrees of guilt is an important concern of the judicial system and of moral theory. What is of particular interest here is that the determination of the degree of responsibility of one person for his participation in an injustice that required the cooperation and coordination of many people is relevant to the repentance and forgiveness of that person. If he doesn't consider himself guilty, he won't repent, and if he is considered guilty by the victim, but doesn't repent, the victim—unless he believes in "radical" Christian forgiveness—will not forgive him. In addition, when there are numerous victims, as is often the case in group and governmental oppression, the victims are nameless, or at least unknown to individual perpetrators such as a Nazi pilot who bombed the Warsaw ghetto. Since the perpetrator did not know his victims, he would not be able to repent fully, since he couldn't apologize and make reparation to them. And no one victim (and surely no non-victim) would be authorized to forgive him on behalf of anyone but himself. Of course, these complexities can also exist when a single individual unaffiliated with any group commits a crime in which many are injured, but these difficulties are more common features of "collective" injustices perpetrated by ethnic, national, or religious groups against others. Notwithstanding these complexities in ascertaining the degree of individual responsibility, each person acting as part of an offending group is morally accountable for his or her own actions.

Is it, however, meaningful or useful to apply the concepts of repentance and forgiveness to a group or a collective? In recent years, there have been calls for the introduction into the political and the economic spheres, of the concepts (and more importantly, of the practices) of repentance and forgiveness at a group level. Supporters maintain that the practices of repentance and forgiveness are useful, or even necessary, for effecting reconciliation between groups in cases in which injustice has been perpetrated by one group against another, or by two groups against each other. When two national groups are locked in long and painful conflict, in which both suffer and hurt, the practice of "individual" repentance and forgiveness and "group" or "political" repentance and forgiveness should nurture and reinforce each other.

One of the difficulties of any conflict resolution process, whether between two individuals or two nations, is that often both parties tend to see themselves as the victims and their antagonists as the perpetrators. Sometimes there is an element of truth to these perceptions, as both have been victims and both have been perpetrators. Sometimes, however, the real perpetrator develops a theory or rationalization to "justify" his crimes and often comes to believe in his self-justifications. Many Nazis probably did not really believe the Nazi ideology about the Jews being subhumans, but used it as a cynical tool to satisfy their evil ambitions and lusts. Many others probably did believe in their racial ideology and transmitted it devoutly to their children. Likewise white Afrikaaners who supported apartheid in South Africa and slave owners who promoted the idea of "Negro inferiority" in the United States taught their children these ideas. In these three cases, the perpetrators were clearly (to dispassionate outside observers) the Nazis, the Afrikaaners, and the white slave owners, and the victims were innocent Jews and blacks.

If repentance and forgiveness are to play constructive roles in group conflict resolution, the question of the degree of moral blame of the antagonists cannot be shunted aside for the sake of peace. This does not, however, mean that reconciliation between groups should always be made contingent upon both parties eventually adopting a shared interpretation of their painful interactions, since that will rarely happen. Reconciliation also cannot be made contingent upon full repentance and full forgiveness, or on the rectification of all the injustices perpetrated during the protracted conflict, because that too can rarely happen. However, if each side comes to better understand and empathize with the other side, and some elements of repentance and forgiveness are employed at the individual, "political," and economic levels, there is a chance to end the conflict and establish peaceful coexistence. In some cases, a deeper reconciliation, with the development of positive attitudes and feelings between the antagonists, may emerge over time. Conflict resolution and reconciliation do not require that the antagonists deny or ignore the terrible wrongs of the past. On the contrary, the more honest an acceptance of the past, acknowledgment of wrongs committed, expressions of regret, efforts at reparation, and forgiveness in response to these, the greater the probability of an enduring peaceful relationship between the two groups in the future.

. . .

In order to illustrate some of these processes, I will focus on one conflict, the Israeli–Palestinian (and Israeli–Arab) one. While suggesting the roles that repentance and forgiveness can play in contributing to the peaceful resolution of this and other group conflicts, I do not assume that they are the most important processes in peacemaking. They can, however, play useful and crucial roles in supporting and shaping the contours of diplomatic, economic, and political measures that are being employed in recent years' efforts to resolve the Israeli–Palestinian conflict.

Group reconciliation and conflict resolution can take place directly between small groups of individuals who are members of the groups in conflict as well as at the level of national, political leadership. At the grassroots level, there are several groups of Israeli Jews and Palestinians of all ages who meet each other for the purpose of working toward peaceful reconciliation.[21] When the individuals who meet to reconcile have themselves suffered directly from the actions of their antagonists, the attempt has greater legitimacy and credibility in the eyes of the group than when the conciliators haven't suffered directly from the conflict. If Jews who were injured by Palestinian bombs and Palestinians who were injured by Israeli soldiers, or parents of Jews and of Palestinians who died in the conflict, can meet in a serious endeavor to overcome antagonisms and hatreds, other Jews and Palestinians, whose sufferings have been less direct, will find it easier to accept the possibility of reconciliation. Parents Circle, a group of parents and relatives of Israelis and Palestinians killed in the conflict, has been meeting to see if steps toward reconciliation can be taken. Since both groups believe that right is on their side, it is difficult to think of reconciliation in terms of repentance, which implies admission of guilt, or of forgiveness, since there is disagreement as to who should be forgiving whom. The focus is more on the pragmatic and mutually beneficial goal of overcoming the enmity on the person-to-person level in the hopes that this will reinforce the political attempts to negotiate a peace. As one participant put it, "I am not here for forgiveness or revenge but to stop the hatred and the bloodshed. I am a realist. I think Palestinians and Israelis may never agree on what is justice. So what we need is not necessarily a just peace but a wise peace. We all have to be realists."[22]

However, to be willing to make peace with an enemy when under no duress to do so suggests a measure of empathy for him and perhaps a willingness to concede that there is some justification for his animosity if not for his behavior. It may also suggest a willingness to be sufficiently self-critical of one's own position, to concede that what one's own group has done hasn't always been justifiable. These are early stages of repentance.[23]

Ami Isseroff, active in the PEACE dialogue group writes:

> The biggest job of dialogue is changing basic perceptions. The two "sides" have nurtured their belief-systems, self-image, and image of the other in total isolation, each in the conviction that they are right, of course, and that all "decent people" believe as they do.
>
> To a large extent, each side views [its members] as "innocent victims" and the other side as "perpetrators." Palestinians see themselves as dispossessed and disenfranchised. Israelis see Palestinians as terrorists and aggressors. Palestinians see Israelis as all-powerful conquerors, and themselves as helpless victims. Israelis look at Israeli soldiers and see in them their precious little children. Palestinians look at the same soldiers and see instruments of occupation and oppression.
>
> As people learn to listen to each other, they begin to understand also that they must shed the national historical myths that portray their own

side as blameless and insist that only their own cause has justice on its side.[24]

Group reconciliation and conflict resolution can also occur at the level of group leadership, whether political or religious. The acknowledged leaders of the groups in conflict can have a powerful influence on the groups they lead when the leaders take the initiative to work toward reconciliation, whether by way of apology and repentance, or forgiveness. Gestures and actions by leaders are important in *modeling* peaceful approaches to conflict resolution for their own constituencies. Moreover, they can have a powerful impact on the opposing group by suggesting to it that its adversary, or at least its adversary's leader(s), might be reevaluating its role and responsibility in the conflict and hence be a possible party to reconciliation.

The psychological significance of symbolic actions on inflaming or defusing hatred should not be underestimated. I was in Israel in 1977 and personally recall experiencing the profound and dramatic effect that Anwar Sadat's 1977 visit to Jerusalem and the Israeli Knesset (Parliament) had on many Israeli Jews. They had longed for acknowledgment on the part of Arab nations of their suffering and persecution by the Germans and others, and for recognition of their right to a sovereign Jewish state in part of the historic homeland of the Jews. Sadat's actions, and the dignified way in which he related to and spoke of Israel and its citizens, pierced layers of fear and resentment toward Egypt and paved the way for Israeli willingness to withdraw from the Sinai Peninsula as part of its peace treaty with Egypt. After a visit to Yad Vashem, the Israeli museum that memorializes the six million Jewish victims of the Holocaust, Sadat said, with regard to Hitler's war against the Jews,

> I had always thought it was exaggerated for mere propaganda. But seeing the portrayals and exhibits strengthened my determination to achieve peace for those who suffered the tragedy. I saw with my own eyes how Israelis, and Jews the world over, must feel. They are victims not of war alone but also of politics and hatred.[25]

Sadat did not apologize or repent, nor did Israelis forgive him and Egypt, for the wars that these two nations fought. Yet elements of repentance were implicit in these interactions, or were perceived as such by many Israelis. Sadat's visit of a few days softened decades of accrued animosity.

In Israel many remember with reverence and deep appreciation the speech that then Chief of Staff Yitzhak Rabin delivered after the Israeli victory in the 1967 Six Day War. Rather than gloating in the triumph of the Israeli army and in the defeat of the Arab armies, Rabin spoke of the sadness he felt at having to fight a war and kill human beings. Although most Arabs at the time were too pained and humiliated by the war's outcome to react favorably to Rabin's sentiments, many Israelis felt that he was articulating their genuine feelings. The ability and willingness to see one's antagonist empathetically is at the core of reconciliation.

When Jordan's King Hussein visited the grieving families of several young Israeli girls who were killed by a Jordanian soldier and expressed his pain and sorrow for their suffering, the gesture was received with wide appreciation in Israel and reinforced the feelings of many Israelis that reconciliation with Jordan and Jordanians was a realistic possibility.

"I Feel I've Lost a Child," King Says

Kneeling beside the bereaved families of seven schoolgirls shot dead on Thursday by one of his soldiers, King Hussein of Jordan touched this town [Beit Shemesh] today with a gesture of condolence that was at once personal and grand. . . .

The King made the grim rounds from one grief-stricken home to the next, shaking the hands of relatives, embracing and kissing some, and offering words of sympathy in Arabic and English. . . .

On the streets of Beit Shemesh, a working-class town known for its rightist political tendencies, the King's extraordinary act of conciliation seemed to strike a deep emotional chord. . . . "It gave us a feeling that he cares about us." . . .

"I admire him, because no other king would come like that to express his sorrow. It's exceptional, and it shows that he really cares. You see that he wants peace." . . .

The King's visit was seen here as an act of simple compassion that transcended political differences.[26]

Marc Gopin,[27] a pioneer in conceptualizing how religion can contribute to peace and reconciliation rather than fan the flames of hatred, as it too often does, suggests that repentance and forgiveness are two religious values that can be incorporated into conflict resolution strategies "*if* the challenge is presented equally to both sides of a conflict, and if it speaks to profound cultural and religious metaphors of both adversaries" (pp. 19–20).

There are many similarities between Judaic, Islamic, and Christian understandings of repentance, as a religious value and as a psychological process. To the extent that the antagonists in the Israeli–Palestinian conflict identify with the religious values of Judaism, Islam, and Christianity (some Palestinians are Christian), respectively, calls for repentance can be meaningful to both sides. Appeals to religious values are most effective when made by recognized spiritual leaders to their own adherents, rather than when made by the antagonist. For a rabbi to preach repentance to a Muslim or for an imam to preach repentance to Jews may engender indignation, resistance, and hostility rather than a move toward the difficult, emotionally wrenching process of repentance that, as we have seen, includes self-criticism, overcoming the denial of one's wrongdoing, remorse, empathy for the "other," apology, and restitution.[28]

Perhaps the most effective approach to harnessing religious values such as remorse, repentance, and forgiveness to resolve group conflicts would be for clergy of the different faiths that are in conflict to try to better understand how their own religious traditions can enhance peacemaking. If they can arrive at a consensus, for example, that members of their group have engaged in sinful behaviors in the context of the conflict, for which they need to repent, they can work toward educating their followers about the process of self-transformation that is repentance. Rabbis and imams have to vociferously condemn murderers as sinners. They have to condemn as well those who support the murderers. To condemn means to call upon supporters of the murderers to reassess and change their attitudes and behaviors in light of religious teachings. In other words, it means they must call them to repentance. Religious leaders regularly admonish their flock to repent for personal sins. They have to be willing to do the same for sins committed under the aegis of political acts.

For several years at the Yakar synagogue in Jerusalem, Jews and Muslims have together studied texts from Judaism and Islam in a grassroots attempt to effect reconciliation. The purpose of the study is to help Jews and Muslims come to a deeper understanding of each other's traditions. Teachers who participate in the study sessions acquire knowledge of specific texts and learn skills for thinking about and discussing, with a positive attitude, ideas from the two faiths. They can use their knowledge and skills to teach their own students about Judaism and Islam. I recently attended a session at Yakar that brought together Jews and Muslims to study the meditation practices of Sufi mystics, and that was taught by a Muslim cleric. By the end of the session, I found myself chanting along with the other participants, "In Ilaha Ila Allah"—"there is no god but God" (the same one God worshiped by devout

Jews and Muslims). My instinctual response upon hearing such a chant in
Arabic by a Muslim would be to associate it with a fanatical suicide bomber.
Yet here I was, a Jewish Zionist, experiencing how those words and that chant
were bonding Jews and Arabs in a shared vision of the divine presence and
peace, rather than being the battle cry of a terrorist.

In a workshop on the roles of repentance and forgiveness in conflict resolution, small groups can study Jewish and Islamic texts on repentance, forgiveness, and reconciliation. The participants might be asked to address four
questions as they study and reflect upon the texts together.

1) What are the assumptions about human nature in each text?

2) What are the assumptions about the consequences of repentance for the
repenter and for the person whom he injured or hurt?

3) What does the text expect of the injured partner after the offender has
repented?

4) Compare and contrast the texts in their approach to repentance, forgiveness, and reconciliation.

One of the texts from the Jewish tradition might be from Maimonides'
Laws of Repentance.[29]

9. Repentance on the Day of Atonement atones only for those sins that
are between man and the Most High, for example, eating forbidden food.
. . . But sins which are between man and his fellow men, such as injuring
or cursing, or robbing him . . . are never pardoned until he makes restitution
and appeases his fellow. Even if he returns money which is owed, he must
appease and ask for pardon. Even if he has only provoked his neighbor in
words, he must make peace and entreat him until he forgives. If his friend
is not willing to forgive him, he must bring a group of three neighbors to
appease him. If he still refuses, a second or third group should be brought
and, if they are refused, he should be left. For then the sin of refusing to
forgive rests on him . . .

10. A man is forbidden to be cruel and must be conciliatory; he should be
easily appeased, hard to make angry, and when a wrongdoer begs his forgiveness, he ought to forgive with a whole heart and willing spirit. Even if
he was persecuted and much wronged, he ought not to be vengeful and
bear a grudge, because such is the way of the upright hearts of the children
of Israel.

From the Islamic tradition we might use, for example, Koranic texts that
deal with the concept of *hilm*.[30] Muhammed referred to people who practiced

forgiveness and leniency in their dealings with others as possessing this virtue. Texts that deal with reconciliation in Islam would be included. Most Westerners have a distorted view of Islam, associating it primarily with violence and religious fanaticism. However, as Abdul Hadi Palazzi, a leader in Israeli-Muslim dialogue and reconciliation efforts teaches (as do many other Muslim scholars and clerics), tolerance, peace, and reconciliation are important Islamic values.[31]

The Judaic and the Islamic texts deal for the most part with individual rather than group repentance and forgiveness. However, their underlying assumptions and values can be extended to group contexts, with the appropriate modifications. What joint study and comparison of these texts can demonstrate to the participants is how important repentance and forgiveness are to both traditions.

Of course, Judaism, Islam, and Christianity have their share of texts of intolerance and hatred, especially of heretics or non-believers. However, the three religions have values that emphasize pro-social attitudes, not only toward the "faithful," but toward "others" as well. It is these values, along with repentance and forgiveness, that can contribute to an Israeli–Palestinian rapprochement.[32]

. . .

The focus of my discussion so far has been on repentance of one individual for offenses that he or she personally committed against another person (which often adversely affect third parties, such as family members of the victims, as well). I have also considered repentance by (and reconciliation with or forgiveness of) groups that are actively involved in violent conflicts. I turn now to the question of whether it is meaningful to use the concept of repentance (and forgiveness) when an individual who did not commit an offense wants to repent for offenses committed by his ancestors, or by a member of a community with which he identifies. Similarly, can a group repent for crimes that it did not commit, but that were committed by others with whom it identifies? Can a person or a group be guilty of a sin or crime committed by others? Is personal guilt a prerequisite for meaningful repentance?[33]

These questions have been thoughtfully analyzed by Elliot Dorff[34] and by Donald Shriver Jr.[35] Dorff is primarily interested in Jewish–Christian, especially Jewish–Catholic, relations, and the role that the contemporary Church's repentance for the historical misdeeds of its leaders and of its members might play in enhancing cooperation and reconciliation between the Church and the Jewish people. Shriver's outstanding and groundbreaking book is rich in sophisticated analyses of the difficult moral issues of repentance and forgiveness that arise in political contexts. He deals with German and Japanese aggression in World War II and American responses to it, German anti-Semitism and the Holocaust, and the legacy of slavery and racism in the United States and of apartheid in South Africa. Shriver strikes an admirable balance between the claims of justice and strategies for ethnic, religious, and national repentance, forgiveness, and reconciliation.

In our discussion of revenge, especially across generations, we saw in the Hebrew Bible two mutually exclusive ideas. One maintains that God punishes children, or more remote descendants, for the transgressions of their fathers. This does not necessarily mean that the children are considered to be guilty of or responsible for their ancestors sins, but that children (and families) are extensions of another person, and not totally independent entities.[36]

Although our moral values object to such an idea in principle, our legal system, in practice, regularly causes pain and suffering to the children and families of criminals. It considers this to be an unavoidable, unfortunate consequence of society's need and right to punish criminals. We don't view ourselves as "punishing" children for the sins of their fathers, even though that is, in effect, what usually happens. When a person who provided financial and emotional support for his children is imprisoned for a crime, society is causing great hardship and suffering to the children by depriving them of his continued support. Sometimes in sentencing a criminal, the judge will take this into consideration, but for the most part we haven't yet figured out a way of preventing such "collateral damage."

The other biblical view was expressed most emphatically by the sixth-century B.C.E. prophet Ezekiel (Chapter 18), who denied that God punishes children for the sins of their fathers: "It is only the person who sins that shall die." He maintained that only the sinner who is guilty deserves to be punished, and only the sinner is obligated to repent.

If we accept the view that only a guilty person need repent, which is the view of most modern moral theories, then we may ask whether it makes any sense for Pope John Paul II or other Catholics, whether leaders or private individuals, to repent (and ask forgiveness) for the sins of Catholics who persecuted, tortured, and murdered thousands of Jews in the name of Christianity over the centuries. The Pope himself is not a Jew-hater, indeed, he has been a leader in condemning all manifestations of anti-Semitism and denigrations of Judaism as a religion. The persecutors themselves are dead, so they can no longer repent. The victims are dead, so the Pope cannot apologize or make any restitution or reparation to them. For these and other reasons, the very idea of a papal apology on behalf of the sins of "members of the

Church" who are no longer alive has been criticized by some Catholics and non-Catholics. One objection of some Catholics is that

> contrition on the part of the Church involves the concept of collective guilt, which is theoretically questionable and practically dangerous. According to the general teaching of Catholic theologians, sin in the proper sense of the word is always the choice of an individual, personal will, and therefore cannot be imputed to the Church or any other collective subject. In the words of John Paul II, "There is nothing so personal and untransferrable in each individual as merit for virtue or responsibility for sin."[37]

One Catholic response to this objection is that all Catholics, past, present, and future, are connected in "mystical solidarity." "As fellow members of the one Body of Christ, we are bound together in a single organic whole. We benefit from one another's merits and suffer from one another's faults" (Dulles, p. 39).

The principle of exclusive individual responsibility for sin is qualified by this idea, which has its roots in the Hebrew Bible and in the rabbinic notion that all members of the community of Israel are morally and spiritually responsible for one another.

Dorff uses this concept, as applied by Catholics and Jews to their respective communities, to argue in favor of the logical possibility of Christian repentance and requests for forgiveness from Jews for sins of the past.

> What makes the request for forgiveness on the part of contemporary Catholics meaningful is that they see themselves as the current embodiment of the Church which extends back to the Apostle Peter, and they see us [Jews]—as we see ourselves—as the current embodiment of the people of Israel which extends back to the Exodus. . . . Therefore, it is the same party who committed the wrong that is now seeking forgiveness, and it is the same party who suffered the wrong who is being asked to forgive. . . . Even secular Jews in our postmodern age, I would argue, feel much of the same thing. They may not accept the religious underpinnings of Jewish identity, but few would deny their Jewishness, and many would take umbrage at any offense against Jews. (p. 205)

Not wanting, however, to blur the distinction between actual perpetrators and their contemporary "extensions," and actual victims and their contemporary "extensions," Dorff develops the notion of a

secondary sense of regret and forgiveness, one which we might call "reconciliation" or "acceptance." In this form, the regret and forgiveness are not
extended by the parties in themselves. . . . It is rather the extensions of the
parties who are now called upon to decide whether to engage in the process
of forgiveness, and that, it seems to me, is a meaningful extension of our
primary notions of regret and forgiveness. As such it is logically appropriate
for the contemporary Church to seek forgiveness and for the current Jewish
community to consider whether to grant it. (p. 204)

Another defense of the papal call for collective repentance of Catholics is that
Catholic sins of the past continue to have their effects, such as in anti-
Semitism, today. To the extent that contemporary Catholics commit or are
indifferent to these ongoing sins, they bear a measure of culpability for them.

In defense of the logic of papal and Church repentance for past sins, Avery
Dulles argues that this repentance is construed within the framework of Catholic theology and as such it is directed not only—perhaps not even primarily—toward the victims, but toward the goal of purifying Catholics of their
sins, and securing the forgiveness of God. Victims who do not subscribe to
Catholic theology may find this meaningless and even offensive, especially if
the repentance will not include reparation and radical change in the behavior
of the Church and of Catholics who will heed the call for repentance.

The papal call for Catholics to repent does refer to the making of amends,
or at least amendment regarding the future. In other words, Catholics are
henceforth to avoid the sin of anti-Semitism, as in theological retrospect they
should have avoided it in the past, since it is now perceived to have been
contrary to the true teachings of the Gospel as interpreted by the Church,
and to the true teachings of the Church itself.

Many Jews (myself included), while respecting and appreciating the Pope's
expressed regret for and forceful condemnation of persecution of Jews, feel
that the Church's repentance falls far short of what true repentance—even of
a secondary nature—should entail. There are several reasons for this unease.
Full repentance, as understood in Jewish tradition, and as I have tried to use
it as a non-theological construct, entails not only verbal confession and apology, but also an honest acknowledgment of the offenses committed, restitution, a commitment not to repeat the sin, and when an occasion to repeat
the sin presents itself, resisting temptation. Moreover, it would seem that the
true penitent would feel so guilty about what he did and so morally culpable
for it, that although he seeks or pleads for mercy and forgiveness, he would
not feel that his repentance alone *entitles* him to it.

I cannot expect the Church, which is only an *extension* of the original perpetrators, to feel the same measure of remorse and guilt that I would expect of the perpetrators themselves, if they had wanted to repent. However, I would expect that, to the extent that Catholics see themselves as extensions of their ancestors, they would feel some obligation to make concrete amends for those past misdeeds. If the papal apology included some practical reparations for past offenses, the repentance could be taken more seriously. Even if we were to invoke the talmudic concept of *takanat hashavim*—that to encourage repentance the victim should not accept reparations offered by the offender— it would at least be worthwhile for the Church to specify in similar detail as is expected of the Catholic in the confessional, the sins for which it is repenting, and to devise some "calculus" for estimating the degree of physical, emotional, and financial injury that these offenses caused over the centuries.[38] This document should then be incorporated into the weekly mass and the curricula of Catholic schools.

Lest I sound too self-righteous, I would apply the same criteria to a Jewish group or community that expressed its desire and intent to repent for offenses it committed against another group. For example, in the Israeli–Palestinian conflict, the Palestinians want the state of Israel to acknowledge that it was guilty of crimes against Palestinians, and to pay reparations for those alleged crimes and, among other actions, to allow all Palestinian refugees to return to their original homes and reclaim them. If the Israeli Jews were to accept the claim that they were primarily responsible for the suffering of the Palestinians, then sincere repentance on their part would have to directly address these claims for justice and restitution, and the Israelis would have to make significant sacrifices as restitution and amends short of self-destruction, for their sins.[39] The majority of the Jews of Israel do not accept the Palestinian interpretation of the Israeli–Palestinian conflict (and neither do I), and while admitting to some injustices on their part, hold the Palestinians (and the Arab states) to be the ones who bear the primary guilt for wars with Israel and for the refugees and their suffering. The point I am making, however, is that when someone repents, if the repentance is authentic, the penitent must be willing to acknowledge the full measure of his guilt and what that guilt would require of him in restitution. If the Church repents, it should do that as well.

The Church's repentance falls short in many other ways as well. It is presently considering the beatification and granting of sainthood to Catholics who committed grave sins against Jews, such as Pope Pius IX who, after the forced baptism and abduction of the Jewish youngster Edgardo Mortara, refused to return him to his family.[40] Pope Pius IX, and many other Catholics who sinned against Jews, no doubt were pious in many other ways and made substantial contributions to the Church. From a Jewish perspective, however, the Church cannot claim repentance for anti-Semitism when it honors, glorifies, or even fails to criticize anti-Semites. When a pope shows respect to the former Nazi Kurt Waldheim, it is difficult for a Jew to consider the Church's repentance vis-à-vis the sin of anti-Semitism to be adequate. Moreover, the Church has not and probably cannot—if it is to maintain its essential identity—change the vitriolic anti-Jewish teachings of some sections of the New Testament, and it cannot consider Jews and Judaism (or any non-Catholic faith, for that matter) to be equal in spiritual status to Catholicism. It has no choice, if it remains faithful to its own theology, but to retain elements in its teachings that nurture anti-Jewish sentiments, even though it has significantly attenuated many of them.

Peter Steinfels, the thoughtful *New York Times* commentator on religion, reflecting upon the Vatican's treatise *Memory and Reconciliation: The Church and the Faults of the Past* instigated at the initiative of Pope John Paul II, writes:

> The pope expressed contrition for sins Christians had committed in the church's name without ascribing sin to the church itself. To critics, this was a bit of an evasion. To the Vatican theologians it was crucial. . . .
>
> From New Testament times, Christians have recognized sinfulness in their ranks, even among their leaders . . . But Christians have also believed that the church is more than a purely human institution used for individual religious purposes; it is somehow a body infused with the very spirit of God, a corporate extension of Christ on earth. . . . This . . . can . . . distract it from exposing some important sources of that sinfulness . . . such as "the art, the lore, the customs, the texts, the preaching themes and catechism answers, the structures of authority and decision making" . . . what a group of French bishops [who] issued their own *Declaration of Repentance* [referred to as] an "underlying basic religious culture which shaped and deformed people's attitudes."[41]

The fact that the repentance of Pope John Paul II and the Church is not complete by the standards of Judaism or of civic repentance does not mean that it is of no value at all. On the contrary, to the extent that it induces Catholics to reflect upon the evils of anti-Semitism and the historical sins of the Church or of Catholics, it is a moral and spiritual advance over previous stances of the Church, and is to be welcomed.

Jews and Catholics can take many steps toward reconciliation, even in the absence of full repentance. Full repentance facilitates reconciliation, but reconciliation between adversaries, or between perpetrators and victims, should not have to depend on it.

· · ·

Am I in any way morally responsible for the historical evil of slavery in the United States? Should I apologize for the sins of my white countrymen of two or three hundred years ago? Am I under any obligation to make restitution to contemporary African-American descendants of slaves?

Who am I? My grandparents immigrated to the United States early in the twentieth century, fleeing European anti-Semitism manifested in discrimination and oppression. They and their ancestors did not in any way participate in the evil of slavery in America. By the time they arrived at Ellis Island, slavery was American history, not American practice. Born in 1941, I was never a participant or silent collaborator in, or an apathetic bystander to, slavery.

It would seem, therefore, self-evident that I have no responsibility for slavery and am under no moral obligation to make restitution to the descendants of slaves, who still suffer from its legacy, since I have no personal or familial connection to it. Perhaps other contemporary Americans descended from slaveowners might have a greater moral obligation to make restitution to the descendants of slaves than I do, although they can argue, with the prophet Ezekiel, that children are not responsible for the sins of their fathers.

Is that the end of the discussion?

Perhaps not.

Upon further reflection, perhaps it can be argued that although neither I nor my ancestors were in any way involved in the sin of slavery, I nevertheless have indirectly benefited materially from that crime of several centuries. I am not an economist, but I assume that some of the prosperity and luxury that the white population of America enjoys is historically due to slavery and to the low wages paid today to descendants of slaves. Although I am not legally or morally culpable for the crime, I might be morally obligated to make some restitution to African Americans from whose oppression I ultimately benefited, albeit unwittingly and unintentionally.

And who are my ancestors? Are they only my biological ones, the ones who had no connection with slavery, or do I have political ancestors as well? I am proud and grateful to be an American. I cherish the values of democracy and the freedoms that I enjoy in this land, and I appreciate these more every time I remember how my biological ancestors in Europe and elsewhere were oppressed. Indeed they immigrated to this country not only for the economic hope it offered them, but for its civic and political values and institutions. In a certain sense, I have been adopted by and have consented to be adopted by the "fathers" of this country. Thomas Jefferson and Abraham Lincoln are my political ancestors. I imbibed their values from childhood and passed them on to my own children.

But my political ancestors are not only Jefferson (a slaveowner himself) and Lincoln, but all those who helped shape this country, among them individuals who defended and practiced slavery. To the extent that I see myself as a member of the American family, I cannot dissociate myself from the history of my family. I cannot only extol its virtues while overlooking its vices. I am ashamed of what some of my American family did to African Americans (and to Native Americans and other groups as well). Although I am not personally responsible for their evils, I do want to acknowledge and decry them, precisely because I feel so deeply connected to my Americanism. It is difficult and painful to acknowledge that the American ideals of justice and equality that I learned, at home and in school, were not practiced with respect to a major segment of the inhabitants of this land. If I cannot face this truth and consider what its present implications might be, then I am in effect being disloyal to the very ideals that I claim to have inherited and to cherish.

Maimonides was asked whether a convert to Judaism, when reciting a blessing of thanks to God for the bounty of the land of Israel, can use the phrase "the land which you bequested to 'my fathers',", since the convert's biological fathers were not members of the Israelite tribes who inhabited the land of Israel. Maimonides replied that the convert, having chosen the spiritual path of Abraham, is more of a child of Abraham than is a non-believing Jew, who though a biological descendant of Abraham, is not his spiritual heir. Once the convert has accepted Judaism, he becomes fully entitled to the benefits it bestows and to the merits of his spiritual fathers. However, he also becomes responsible for the obligations it incurs, and that may mean being held accountable to some degree for the sins of his adopted fathers as well. The situation, with respect to my moral relationship with my American political and cultural heritage, is similar.

I am not arguing that I have any primary personal responsibilty, or moral guilt, for the evils perpetrated by Americans of generations ago. I do not identify with slaveowners, and consider slavery abhorrent. I am suggesting, though, that my identification with America, its past, present, and future, imposes upon me some measure of responsibility to remedy the ills that the past bequeathed to the present, and to heal the wounds from that past that continue to fester in the present.

Moreover, even though I abhor slavery, am I really free of racism? In principle, I think it is an egregious moral sin to discriminate against, oppress, or in any way act unjustly toward another human being because of the color of his or her skin. I don't think, however, that my actual feelings and behaviors always conform to the abstract moral principle in which I believe. In some sense, then, I participate, not in slavery itself, but in the values and attitudes that nurtured it. In this case I have a personal responsibility to acknowledge this evil within me and to try to overcome it—in short, to repent of it. I should try to amend the injuries that it causes to contemporary African Americans.

Of course, it is not only I who have to examine my conscience and my relationship to the historical evils of the past, but all Americans. Moreover, some African Americans are guilty of crimes against me as a Jew. Just as it is incumbent upon me to extirpate whatever conscious or unconscious racism I may harbor towards African Americans, it is incumbent upon African Americans (and anyone else) who harbor anti-Semitic attitudes to repent as well. No one should feel that one racist attitude cancels out or justifies the other, but rather that both are evil and we both need to repent of our respective racist attitudes.

So, if white Americans, non-racist as well as racist ones, have some measure of responsibility to acknowledge and rectify the evils of a racist past that live on in the present, what might be some ways for this repentance to be realized in practice?

Of course, the obligation to behave justly, to support justice, and to help alleviate the pain, suffering, and misery of others does not derive from and is not dependent upon guilt or responsibility for having caused the injustice or suffering, or for having benefited from it. So even someone who could plausibly argue that he has neither primary nor secondary responsibility for the unhappy plight of many African Americans would be under a moral obligation (at least from the perspectives of Judaism and Christianity) to actively intervene to prevent injustice, and to assist poor and vulnerable African Americans. However, his obligation is amplified to the degree that he is responsible for the injustice and the suffering, or that he benefits from it.

Shriver[42] makes the plausible claim that the legacy of slavery and segregation and the continuing social prejudice and discrimination against African Americans have been and continue to be substantial factors in the social and economic plight of a significant segment of this group. Moreover, the social and economic injustices this subgroup has experienced have no doubt contributed to the high level of crime in its communities, its poor health relative to whites, its inadequate health care, and its deep frustration, anger, despair, and hopelessness. He also maintains that notwithstanding its justified grievances, the African-American community overall has had a patient, forgiving, and reconciliation-oriented attitude toward white society, as it waits for white society to rectify the evils it inflicted and inflicts. Shriver has a deep respect and admiration for this African American ethos of patience and reconciliation and believes that white America can learn an important moral lesson from it.[43] African Americans have a right to expect from white society, at the governmental, organizational, corporate, and individual levels, repentance for historical sins and their ongoing effects. America has a long-standing, outstanding moral debt that must be paid if it is to actualize its professed ideals of justice and equality.

How might white America pay its debt? How might white America "repent"? It is not enough that white society express national remorse for the atrocities of slavery and the sin of racism. Repentance has to include restitution and repair. It may involve real economic sacrifices on the part of many Americans, if that is what is necessary. There may be more than one way in which repair and restitution can be implemented. There may be honest disagreement as to the fairest and most just way to distribute the inevitable social costs of restitution, as in the debate over affirmative action in employment or in admissions to universities and professional schools. These are complex moral questions—to do justice to one group may require doing an injustice to another, and one has to weigh the moral costs of morality. The fundamental acknowledgment, however, that there is a collective wrong that needs to be righted, a collective sin that needs to be atoned for, is critical to repairing and healing the black-white rift in America.

> [M]oral clarity . . . might move the majority of us to confess that the problem of poverty resides not alone in the poor but in the minds, the policies, and the budget priorities that link the rest of us to the life and death of the poor. Many of us are the problem; and in nothing do so many Americans participate more in that problem than in the ease with which we exempt ourselves from the accusation of racism just because we celebrate the civil rights movement and its very real political improvements in the lives of African Americans. The minds, the customs, and the institutions of this country are still enough laced with the scars and inertias of racism to keep even the most liberal and moral American in a posture of humility and repentance. . . . It is time for us to set out for ourselves an agenda of repentance in economics, one not to be accomplished overnight but one

no longer subject to indefinite delay. . . . The United States of America has been blessed by the leadership of a black community that has often expressed its willingness to forgive a nation for its crimes against black people on the condition that the nation acknowledge the crimes and make specific restitutions for their damages. Because those damages persist in the lives of so many African Americans, because those who have substantially recovered from the legacies of slavery are a minority, the agenda of restorative justice has to be heavy for this and the upcoming generation of Americans. Whether we call it justice or rehabilitation or reparation is less important than that we call it the first order of our domestic national business.[44]

These are strong demands and strong claims. Perhaps the economic costs of restitution will force Americans to "sacrifice" some of the luxuries to which they have become accustomed. There may be painful emotional costs. The recognition of one's own sin—whether as active racism or as apathy to the racism of others—has to overcome the barriers of pride and shame that always wait in ambush to suppress moral criticism as it tries to emerge from denial and repression. However, the costs of not "facing history and ourselves" with honesty and integrity are, in the long run, more exacting. They perpetuate a society in which justifiable hostility and resentment fester. They perpetuate a society whose rhetoric of justice for all is belied by justice denied. They perpetuate poverty and alienation, sickness and suffering, loveless childhoods in broken homes, the stifling of human potential in the absence of education and opportunity, and humiliation and indignity. On any scale of measurement, moral, spiritual, and even economic, these costs far outweigh the cost of repentance and repair.

· · ·

Where there is repentance there is renewed hope, for offender and for victim. Repentance prepares the ground for healing, forgiveness, and reconciliation, between individuals and between groups.

The South African Experience

We have looked at justice, forgiveness, repentance, and reconciliation in interpersonal and in intergroup relations. In the past decade, many people in South Africa have grappled with these concepts and values, intellectually and emotionally, with great sensitivity and insight. As a conclusion to this book, it is worthwhile to consider how these concepts and values have been interwoven in South Africa's ongoing journey from conflict to reconciliation.

In the 1990s South Africa was politically transformed from a white-dominated oppressive apartheid regime to a democracy for all of its citizens, in which black Africans constituted the overwhelming majority. The apartheid regime, led by the Nationalist Party that for the most part represented white Afrikaaner South Africans, had from 1960 inflicted physical, economic, and psychological abuse and violence on the majority black and other non-white populations. Millions of blacks and "coloreds" were forcibly removed from their homes and lands to make room for whites. They were deprived of the right to vote, restricted in their movements, given inferior education and health care, constrained in their freedom of expression, and imprisoned for protesting the regime's policies. Many opponents of the regime were killed, kidnapped, or tortured, either in response to their opposition to apartheid or in order to instill fear in the oppressed population.

For many decades, the victims of apartheid, with the support of some whites, had resisted the regime, sometimes using non-violent means, but with increasing resort to violence in the 1980s and early 1990s. The African National Congress (ANC), led by Nelson Mandela, even as he was imprisoned for decades, was the most prominent of the political and military organizations in the struggle against apartheid. In the course of its struggle, the ANC also killed (sometimes indiscriminately) and tortured (sometimes to death) people whom it believed were collaborating with the white regime. The opponents of apartheid also succeeded in convincing many countries to impose economic sanctions on South Africa, which had very adverse effects on its economy.

In the early 1990s both the Nationalist Party leadership and the ANC leadership came to the realization that they were heading for economic disaster, for whites and blacks alike, and to a bloody civil war. Unlike many other countries with intense internal conflicts, the leaders, Prime Minister De Klerk and Nelson Mandela, and their advisers, chose a path of negotiation and compromise rather than civil war. The white regime agreed to a gradual transition to democracy, which culminated with a democratic election with universal suffrage in 1994.

Knowing that it would become a minority party after the election, the Nationalist Party demanded in advance that a general amnesty be granted for its crimes and violations of human rights while it had been in power. This demand was rejected by the ANC, but a modified form of it was eventually agreed to unofficially. After the democratic election, in which the ANC was chosen as the majority party and Nelson Mandela was elected president, a Truth and Reconciliation Commission (TRC) was established. This commission consisted of three committees, one of which was an Amnesty Committee. Individuals could apply to this committee for amnesty for a politically motivated crime or violation of human rights to which he or she confessed. To be eligible for amnesty, the applicant had to provide full details about the nature, time, and place of the crime, its victim(s), and information about others who were accomplices to it or responsible for ordering it. If the applicant did this to the committee's satisfaction, he was granted full criminal and civil amnesty, meaning that he could neither be punished for the crime nor sued for damages.

The Human Rights Committee provided a forum for victims of the apartheid regime to publicly testify about the suffering they endured. The Reparations Committee recommended to the government (and other sectors of South African society) measures that should be taken to provide reparations to the victims of apartheid.

The commission was established in the belief that exposure of the truths about the sufferings that had been endured during the years of apartheid was a necessary process in moving forward toward national healing and reconciliation, and that revenge or legal justice were not the best avenues to those goals. The amnesty provisions of the TRC were primarily the result of a necessary political compromise with the white regime, which controlled powerful military and police forces. However, they also reflected the visionary statesmanship of Nelson Mandela, and a Christian religious ideology that promoted forgiveness and reconciliation over punishment, for those who confess their sins. The TRC was chaired by Bishop Desmond Tutu, a leader in the struggle against apartheid, and its vice chair was Alex Boraine, another leading clergyman who had been a vocal opponent of the white regime. Its membership and tone was infused, albeit unofficially, with religious, and, more specifically, Christian values and emphases. Although South Africa does not have an official state religion and church, religion plays a prominent role in the country's ethos and culture, for both blacks and whites.

In this Christian vein, victims who testified were discouraged from expressing desires for revenge and were encouraged to be forgiving and reconciling toward their oppressors. It was also hoped that perpetrators applying for amnesty would repent of their crimes/sins and express remorse. The South African Council of Churches, for example, perceived the TRC as turning its back "on any desire for revenge. It represents an extraordinary act of generosity by a people who only insist that the truth, the whole truth and nothing but the truth be told. The space is thereby created where the deeper processes of forgiveness, confession, repentance, reparation and reconciliation can take place."[1]

There was a certain irony in this appeal to Christian values as a resource for healing and reconciliation. The Dutch Reformed Church, to which most white Afrikaaners belonged, had supported the apartheid regime and developed a biblical and theological rationale for apartheid. Although a few South African churches and white Christians challenged the apartheid regime, most did not, or did so only with mild and innocuous protests. Carl Niehaus, who had been a vocal opponent of the regime, and a believing Christian, harshly indicts religious leaders and institutions on this score. "Faced with the question of whether religion is a decisive factor in the transformation of South Africa, I am afraid that I must answer, with a certain embarrassment, in the negative." Even as the regime was preparing itself for political compromise, and the Nationalist Party and the ANC were negotiating the morally difficult issue of amnesty for those who had committed grave abuses of human rights, "no significant contribution was made from the religious angle with regard to matters that address so clearly the essential questions of confession, reconciliation and forgiveness. The church was confused and silent" (pp. 81, 87).[2]

In my introduction I recounted the episode of a rabbi who objected to the tearful response of acceptance and reconciliation granted by an audience of South Africans to a white police officer who had confessed to a horrible crime he had committed. The rabbi was not the only one who objected to such forgiveness. Many in South Africa were critical of the amnesty provisions of the TRC, on the grounds that they were incompatible with justice, and that justice and accountability were more important values than forgiveness. It is one thing to acknowledge that amnesty was a necessary compromise made in an effort to reach a peaceful political accommodation in a situation wherein continued conflict might result in civil war. It is something else, however, to claim that amnesty of perpetrators of gross violations of human rights, who confess their crimes, often out of fear of prosecution rather than out of sincere remorse, and who in so doing are rewarded by being exempted from all legal obligations to make any restitution to their victims, is intrinsically more moral than bringing them before the bar of justice. Supporters of the amnesty provisions claim that public confession, which often entailed shame and humiliation, was in itself a severe punishment. Moreover, they argue that many of the perpetrators could not have been formally prosecuted because without their confession there was insufficient evidence of their crimes to convict them in a court of law.

Among those who objected to the amnesty provisions was the family of Steven Biko. Biko had been a prominent black activist leader of the anti-apartheid movement during the 1970s. He was arrested by the government and died in custody, presumably murdered by the police. Biko's family challenged the amnesty provisions of the TRC in court. In explaining their position, one family member wrote, "We noted that some South Africans were content with the granting of amnesty to those who maimed or killed their family members, but we also knew that there were a significant number who were adamant that they would like to have their day in court in order to confront the perpetrators of evil deeds" (p. 194).[3]

The family argued that the state has no right to deprive a citizen of his recourse to a court of law when his rights have been violated. The South African Constitutional Court ruled against the Biko family, and the constitutionality of the amnesty law was upheld.

Another criticism of the TRC was that it only dealt with gross human rights abuses, such as murder and torture, but not with the inherent injustices of the apartheid policies that affected millions of black and "colored" South Africans. Nor did it deal with the passive complicity of millions of South African whites who benefited economically, directly or indirectly, from the system. In its defense the ANC-led government and the TRC claimed that there had to be realistic limits on what could be expected of it in addressing past crimes and injustices, and the best way to rectify the evils of the past was to construct a new society in which democracy, respect for human dignity, and social harmony will prevail. Harping on the past would prevent the forging of a new and better future, and the forging of that future required the cooperation of all segments of society, including the white South Africans who had imposed and enforced apartheid. The ANC also maintained that the new government they led would make concerted efforts to redress the economic injustices and their deleterious effects that had resulted from apartheid. Among the measures it has been taking are affirmative action in hiring and in access to university education, and the investment of substantial funds in housing, education, and health care for the formerly oppressed population.

On the other hand, the opposing view was expressed, that if apartheid's history of injustice (and injustices perpetrated by its opponents as well) was denied or forgotten after the granting of amnesty, deep-seated resentments and desires for revenge that were suppressed would eventually erupt. Moreover, a healthy and just society cannot be built upon superficial expressions of remorse by perpetrators and upon a culturally mandated suppression of genuine and justifiable emotions of anger, hurt, and resentment.

> We remain, therefore, with questions, the question of remains. Our concern is that the discourse of reconciliation, expressed in forums such as the TRC faith communities hearings, can be used to displace precisely the trauma that this discourse seeks to ameliorate. What is displaced is the acknowledgment that survivors and victims of trauma very often do not heal, or that healing involves processes that exclude the possibilities of reconciliation. . . . The remains of the past must be borne into the present before they can be laid to rest in the service of a still deferred future.[4]

What have been some of the psychological effects of the TRC on the victims and the perpetrators who have appeared before it? The TRC maintained that recalling and publicly recounting hurts and humiliations endured have a therapeutic effect on victims and facilitate reconciliation between them and those who inflicted the injuries. The TRC completed most of its work in 1999, and although empirical studies are in progress, it is too early to know what its long-term effects will be in terms of healing and reconciliation. Anecdotal evidence suggests that some victims have found the opportunity to testify about their pain and suffering to have been therapeutic. It was very important for them to make the white population aware of the injustice and suffering that had been perpetrated by the regime which they openly or tacitly supported, or which they failed to oppose. Unfortunately, although the hearings were aired on radio and television and reported at length in other media, most whites did not tune in to them for long.

Other victims had testified before the Human Rights Committee with the expectation that they would receive restitution for their pain and loss. Although some payments were made to individuals, they were meager, and these victims were bitter and disillusioned with the process.

Some perpetrators who applied for and received amnesty expressed remorse for their deeds, but many did not. As much as the religious aura of the TRC encouraged confession, expression of remorse (sincere or otherwise) was not a condition for receiving amnesty.

One study which investigated the psychological dynamics and impact of the TRC concludes that it served as a buffer against pain, a defense mechanism against honestly confronting the reality of South Africa's past. The TRC process served conscious and unconscious needs of its own staff and of victims, perpetrators, and the general public. "All may have unconsciously required the process of the TRC to create optimism and hope for the future. Thus perhaps the success of the TRC does not lie solely within the reconciliations or reparations made, but whether the symbolism of the process itself was sufficient to foster hope within a damaged country, and a belief that its future will in no way mirror its past."[5]

In August 2001, I spent three weeks in Capetown, South Africa. I met with and heard from individuals who had been involved with the TRC or had critiqued it. I spoke to whites, blacks, and "coloreds," Christians, Muslims, and Jews. I met with academics and students, lawyers and cab drivers, rich and poor. I visited Robben Island, where Nelson Mandela and other political prisoners had been imprisoned, and participated in the government-operated educational tour of the facility. I saw a moving dramatic rendition of the history of apartheid and its demise, by a young theater troupe in Capetown. I visited townships and shanty towns where hundreds of thousands of blacks and "coloreds" live in tiny shacks of corrugated metal and plastic sheeting, where unemployment, disease, and poverty are rampant, in part, a legacy of apartheid. The message that the Robben Island Museum, the troupe, my tour guide to the townships, and many people with whom I met conveyed was that South Africans need to know and remember their past, not for the purpose of exacting revenge or retribution, but in order to prevent human rights abuses from being repeated.

Some of the people I talked with spoke very highly of the TRC and of its mission of national healing and reconciliation. Others mocked it or accentuated its flaws and deficiencies. A young black musician spoke bitterly of it, and of what he perceived to be its inappropriate equation of the violence used by the ANC in its struggle against apartheid with the violence and repression of the Nationalist Party, which had stolen the land of the blacks and relegated so many to distant, arid "homelands." However, notwithstanding the differences of opinion in South Africa with respect to the TRC, what most impressed me overall was the remarkable lack of overt rancor and hatred between blacks and whites, and the concerted effort to create a society in which racial harmony and economic justice will prevail.[6] Given that the injustices and wounds of apartheid are so recent, its effects starkly evident and still affecting so many, and that the black and "colored" populations are the majority in government and could now freely express themselves, I had expected to see and hear blatant and intense manifestations of hatred and revenge against whites. Whatever the factors that have enabled South African society to be relatively pacific in its response to its troubled past of oppression and injustice, it provides an intriguing model for individuals and groups to study as they seek to integrate justice, repentance, and forgiveness into their personal and communal lives.[7]

INTRODUCTION

1. Many also praised the attack, and among those who condemned the attacks of September 11 on the United States, many had, for decades, tacitly or openly supported Arab terrorists who targeted innocent civilians and children in many other countries, such as Israel. Notorious but not unique, for example, was the Holy Land Foundation, a United States–based Islamic "charity," which after the World Trade Center massacre was placed on the United States government's list of groups that support terror.

2. Few of those making this argument suggested that Muslim clerics and authorities have a responsibility to encourage the haters to examine whether their hatred of us is justified, and to repent.

3. Wiesenthal 1997.

4. Boteach 2000, 42–43.

CHAPTER 1: REVENGE & JUSTICE

1. See, e.g., Jordan 1997.

2. See, e.g., Pinker 1995, 413–14, 510–11.

3. Mackie 1982, 3–10.

4. Jacoby, 1983, 361–62.

5. Our Constitution and most civilized societies forbid the torture and cruel and unusual punishment of criminals. Many in our society look upon certain Islamic countries' practice of amputating the limb of a thief or meting out analogous punishments for other crimes as savage, brutal, and primitive (while ignoring the brutality that occurs in many of our not-so-enlightened prisons).

There are several valid reasons for prohibiting the mutilation and torture of convicted criminals. Torturing demeans the torturer. It can become addictive to the point that those in charge of administering it on behalf of the state come to enjoy it for sadistic pleasure, just as some soldiers who in the course of killing in wartime develop a liking for killing, divorced from the moral justification of it that a wartime context may provide (Baumeister, 1997, 235–37).

Torture dehumanizes the criminal. The Talmud teaches that when executing a criminal, care should be taken to minimize the unnecessary pain that is inflicted, since the criminal is a human being to whom the principle of "love thy neighbor" applies. The command to love functions within the context of the command to administer justice. It may be that this consideration of the humanity of the person applies on the assumption that he has repented in anticipation of his death. Other rabbinic texts are less compassionate toward evildoers who show no signs of remorse or repentance.

Another reason for outlawing torture as a form of legal punishment is the fear that the government might abuse its power and unjustly condemn innocent people. It would be bad enough if innocent people were to be punished, even humanely, let alone with torture. By outlawing cruel and unusual punishment, the danger of abuse of state authority is lessened. It is also feared that torture or the threat of torture can be used to induce unreliable confessions.

6. The "Hebrew Bible" is the way many Jewish scholars (and increasingly Christian ones as well), prefer to refer to the "Old Testament," because "Old Testament" has a Christian theological valence. Since, except for a few chapters, the "Old Testament" was originally written in Hebrew, "Hebrew Bible" has become an increasingly accepted way of referring to the sacred scriptures of Judaism (i.e., the "Old Testament").

7. If "eye for an eye" was meant to be taken literally rather than as a metaphor for proportionality in monetary compensation, then mutilation as punishment for damages might have been applied more widely in biblical times.

8. This severe punishment may have been used because damaging the sexual organ, the source of fertility, was considered an especially severe crime (New RSV note to Deut. 25:11–12). The Hebrew Bible also mandates capital punishment for several sins and crimes, including murder, adultery, idolatry, and violation of the prohibitions of working on the Sabbath.

9. See Walker 1991, for a discussion of different theories of punishment and for a critique of retributive punishment.

10. Kant 1965, 331.

11. See Murphy 1988, 88–110.

12. Determinists do not deny our ability to change our emotional responses to events by using our reason or other strategies for influencing our feelings. On the contrary, they maintain that we can learn or be taught how to do so. Even if one's innate reaction to injury may be to desire revenge, when social or cultural forces that can alter this feeling, including rational analysis, are brought into play, they can overcome the feelings of revenge and generate other emotions, such as pity, compassion, or resignation to one's fate. This does not mean, for the determinist, that we

have free will in the theological or philosophical sense of the term, but that we are capable of learning psychological techniques of self-control. For a more detailed discussion of this issue, see the chapter "Sin and Responsibility" in my *The Seven Deadly Sins* (1997) and my article "Free-will and Determinism in Jewish Law and Theology: A Psychological Analysis" (1996).

One may ask, If the perpetrator really had no choice, then why expect him to repent for what he did? Why should he feel guilty, morally responsible, and accountable? It is doubtful that a society could survive without cultivating in its members a sense of personal responsibility for their behavior. Is it possible to nurture a sense of personal responsibility without assuming free will? We will return to the implications of determinism for forgiveness and repentance later in the book.

13. The Hebrew Bible and the New Testament are rich in depicting human nature and in making attempts to shape it. Their teachings about revenge, retribution, justice, forgiveness, and repentance have had a profound influence on the values and attitudes of Western civilization and continue to be a force in the lives of many people.

14. Opposition to capital punishment by some rabbis developed in late–first century Judaism, as reflected in the views of Rabbis Tarfon and Akiba in a passage from the Mishnah, a second-century collection of Jewish law. "The Sanhedrin (a court) that puts to death one person in seven years is termed tyrannical. Rabbi Elazar ben Azariah says, One person in seventy years. Rabbi Tarfon and Rabbi Akiba say, If we had been in the Sanhedrin, no one would ever have been put to death. Rabbi Simon ben Gamliel says, They would have [thereby] increased the shedders of blood in Israel" (Mishnah Makkot 1:10).

15. One of the ethical challenges we face today is to expand our concept of who our group is beyond the narrow confines of family, fellow citizen, ethnic kin, or co-religionist to humankind in general, at least with respect to basic human rights and ethical imperatives. This is not to say that we can or should abjure specific group affiliations and identities, which in many ways are necessary for developing ethical sensitivities. Nor is it reasonable to expect that we are capable of viewing ourselves exclusively as members of only one group, universal humanity, and that we should feel the same level of affection, caring, and concern for all people, irrespective of specific relationships we have with some individuals. However, as in the movement toward a universal declaration of human rights, we can attempt to apply certain shared ethical, legal, and moral norms (and expectations and responsibilities as well) to all people. Because of contemporary technological and communication abilities, we are, in this new millennium, more of a single "family" than we have ever been in history.

Most biblical teaching is directed at the Israelites and seeks to guide them in their relationships with one another, with other nations, and with God. The Ten Commandments were addressed to the Israelites gathered around Mount Sinai, not to mankind in general, although most of the ten, including murder, theft, and adultery, were considered to be universally applicable. The commandment to love the stranger in your midst (which refers primarily not to the emotion of love but to righteous and just behavior), extends the demand to love a brother or neighbor to resident aliens who lived among Israelites though they were not members of the nation. Many biblical laws, however, apply only to the people of Israel, such as ritual command-ments like the prohibition against eating certain animals. It is not strange that the Hebrew Bible is concerned primarily with the Israelites, just as the laws of the United States are concerned primarily with the obligations and rights of citizens and residents of the United States. Christianity, which extended the concept of "brother" beyond ethnicity or nation, substituted confessional group markers. Your "brother" was often interpreted to mean one who believed in Jesus Christ as you do. This left out of the Christian orbit of brotherhood and neighborly love those of other faiths, such as Jews, Muslims, Hindus (who were considered pagans), and heretics, which included Protestants for Catholics, and Catholics for Protestants, when these Christian denom-inations were locked in fierce religious conflict.

16. Several factors, in addition to Joseph's piety, might have facilitated his forgiving his brothers rather than punishing them. In his powerful and respected position relative to their weak one, the brothers were no longer a threat to him. Thus, to the extent that revenge serves to deter future threats or to restore a victim's self-esteem before the perpetrator and others, Joseph did not need to act on any impulse for revenge, if in fact he felt any. Moreover, the brothers had apologized and humbled themselves before him, acts which assuage a victim's desire for revenge. Fear of guilt can also inhibit one from acting on an impulse to avenge, and it played a role in Joseph's benevolence. The brothers, in appealing to him for mercy and forgiveness, reminded him of the paternal concern that their recently deceased father, Jacob, had for them. If Joseph had violated his beloved father's will by harming them, he would have been distressed by guilt. These three factors—removal of the offender as a future threat, the offender's expressions of remorse, and the victim's fear of guilt were he to act upon his impulse for revenge—are among the inhibitors of vengeful behavior. See Baumeister 1997, 156–68. In the biblical account, the explicit motive ascribed to Joseph's magnanimity is that he interpreted his brothers's evil toward him as part of a divine plan. His brothers were actors in a play directed by God. By shifting the burden of responsibility from the evildoer to another force, the victim can more easily forgive.

17. See Babylonian Talmud, Bava Metzia 32b. Another view is that the law's con-cern is not really for my relationship with my enemy but for the pain of a stray or falling animal. I am not allowed to let my animosity toward my enemy prevent me from being compassionate toward his animal.

18. McKane 1990, 592.

19. Although many Christian theologians have interpreted it that way, many Christian individuals and institutions have not acted in accordance with this universal, timeless interpretation of Paul's teaching and have committed numerous evils against those whom they considered to be enemies.

20. Another interpretation is that the offender will become ashamed of, and angry at, himself when he is unexpectedly forgiven by his victim, which in turn may bring him to change his ways for the better. This was one of the pragmatic justifications

that Martin Luther King Jr. invoked to defend his ethic of nonviolent resistance to bigotry and discrimination.

21. Paul does instruct his community to obey governmental authorities (not all of whom persecuted Christians), rather than resist them, because God has given the government the temporal power that it exercises. Given the precarious position of Christians in first-century Rome, Paul's advice was prudent.

22. In the chapter "Anger" in my book *The Seven Deadly Sins* (1997), I discuss in detail specific strategies for overcoming anger.

23. Gen. 34.

24. The motto on the letterhead of John Cardinal O'Connor, Archbishop of New York, reads, "There can be no love without justice." I am not sure if this means that forgiveness of offenders cannot be at the expense of justice, or that true love of our fellow human beings requires that they be treated with social, legal, and economic justice.

25. Baumeister 1997.

26. It is possible that the texts attributing to God the command that the Amalekites be slaughtered were composed after the slaughter took place as ex post facto justifications of it.

27. Since devout Jews and Christians considered the Hebrew Bible/Old Testament to be the revealed word of God, they could not challenge its morality and had to resort to ingenious, apologetic interpretations of what to them were morally problematic texts. These often tell us more about their moral struggles with the Bible than about the original intent of the biblical passages themselves.

28. This lengthy Talmudic passage is analyzed by the French Jewish philosopher Levinas (1990, 12–29). Parts of my analysis are based upon his. Yebamot 78b–79a.

29. Dershowitz 1999.

30. Exod. 34:6–7; the full episode is in Exod. 32–34.

31. Milgrom 1990, 392–96.

32. See Fishbane 1985, 325–50, for an analysis of the relationships between the various biblical texts that deal with the divine attributes, and changes in theologies of divine justice, forgiveness, and individual vs. transgenerational punishment.

33. The emotions and behaviors we have been discussing—revenge, retribution, and punishment—are usually connected with either anger or the related, more "ethical" emotion of righteous indignation. There are many admonitions against anger in the Bible, yet God is frequently described as angry. If people are to imitate God, when is anger a virtue rather than a vice? What differentiates divine anger from human anger, as depicted in the Bible?

Baloian (1992) compares and contrasts biblical descriptions of and attitudes toward human and divine anger, from theological and psychological perspectives. According to Baloian, unlike human anger, divine anger is always "operating on the axes of justice and love"—it is rational and controlled. Divine anger is a response either to rebellion against God or to human oppression. The functions of anger are to warn, to induce repentance (and thereby blessings), or to punish. Since God is not subject to human limitations, such as subjectivity and biased self-interest when judging what is an offense, lack of information, the inability to know for certain what was the intention of the perpetrator of an offensive act, or loss of self-control, his anger need not be subject to delay, an admonition frequently given in the Bible to humans when they are aroused to anger. When God does delay the punishment that follows from his anger, it is because of his patience, mercy, and love.

> The passionate nature of Yahweh is always wedded to His rationality . . . Perhaps the most significant difference [between human and divine anger] entails the irrationality that can often accompany human anger. Human anger has been shown to usually produce negative results that the Old Testament terms as sinful. Divine anger has been shown to be most rational, and indeed conspicuously justifiable to human beings through the motive clauses found in its expression. Human anger is often shown to be illogical if it obtains the upper hand in an individual, whereas the divine wrath is in the service of Yahweh's rational intentions. . . . God is shown to act in passion without conflict with reason. . . . All of Yahweh's anger was operating in the service of His justice and love. (pp. 157, 163–4)

34. Heschel 1962, 297–98. Heschel based his analysis of divine wrath primarily on prophetic texts but claimed that it characterized divine wrath in the Hebrew Bible as a whole. Although his generalization about divine anger being fundamentally rational is for the most part correct, as Baloian demonstrates in his more wide-ranging analysis of biblical texts, there are instances where the divine anger appears, at least on the surface, to be sudden and spontaneous rather than following upon compassion. This does not preclude its basic rationality and justification within biblical covenant theology.

35. Genesis Rabbah, Section 55.

36. Himmelfarb 1983; Bernstein, 1993.

37. Delumeau 1990.

38. Ibid., 373–82.

39. See Walls 1992.

40. Loyola 1964, 59.

41. This analysis of grudges is based primarily on Baumeister et. al., 1998, 79–104.

CHAPTER 2: THE ESSENCE OF FORGIVENESS

1. Butler 1897, 137.

2. Baumeister et al. 1998, 86–87.

3. E.g., McCullough and Worthington Jr., 1994; Enright 1996; Worthington Jr., 1998.

4. They often also conduct research, develop therapeutic approaches, and write theoretical articles from an explicitly Christian perspective, directing them at Christian audiences, such as Christian counselors, clergy, or devout laypersons.

5. Worthington Jr., 1999(b); Worthington Jr., 1999(c)

6. McCullough, Worthington, and Rachal 1997.

7. The contribution of Christian psychologists to broadening and deepening the general psychological interest in and research on forgiveness is an excellent example of how secular psychology can benefit from greater attention to the psychological concerns of religion. This does not mean that religious assumptions about human nature and human psychology are necessarily valid, but only that we should give serious attention to what religions have to say, since they have thought long and hard about these questions for thousands of years.

8. Worthington Jr., 1999(a). Review of *Exploring Forgiveness*, edited by Enright and North.

9. See Kolnai 1978; North 1987, 499–508; Murphy and Hampton 1988; Lang 1994; Enright and Coyle 1998, 139–61.

10. Roberts 1995.

11. See Schimmel 1977; 1997.

12. *The Rule and Exercises of Holy Living* 1857, 333.

13. I would suggest, however, that giving up the emotion of anger while still maintaining that the offender is culpable doesn't address the concern of Aristotle and other critics of radical forgiveness that, in the absence of anger, and in the cultivation of compassion toward the culpable offender, accountability and justice will be sacrificed.

14. Tolstoy, *War and Peace*. Book Three, Part Two, Chapter 3.

15. Ward 1975, 117.

16. Murphy 1992, 74–75, writes:

According to this argument [condemning *all* hatred as immoral] (often appealed to by Christians), all human beings are of equal moral worth—perhaps even absolute moral worth—and are to be equally loved, because it is both irrational and immoral for any one of these creatures to rule any of his equals outside the domain of benevolent concern—as hatred certainly does. (In religious terms, this Kantian point might be made by saying that we are all children of God, are equally beloved in His sight; that God's perspective should then be adopted in our own dealings with our fellow human beings.) To this argument I have the following response: that all human beings (no matter how morally vile) are to be loved strikes me as a claim whose *intrinsic implausibility* is staggering. Thus I can imagine no reason for taking such a claim seriously unless one views it as a command of God—i.e., one therefore has an *extrinsic* reason for taking it seriously. Here, then, we have a good example of an ethical issue where a secular worldview leads us in one direction and the Christian worldview leads in quite another.

17. Arnold 1997.

18. Murphy and Hampton 1988, 101–3.

19. In a discussion of repentance, Murphy (Etzioni, 1997, 160–62) makes a similar point.

> When one thinks of repentance in connection with criminal punishment, one tends to think that all demands for repentance must be addressed to the criminal. But surely the community—through its patterns of abuse, neglect, and discrimination—sometimes creates a social environment that undermines the development of virtuous character and makes the temptations to crime very great, greater than many of us might have been able to resist if similarly situated.
>
> The important idea here is not that criminals, if they are from social groups that are poor or despised or abused or discriminated against, are not to any degree responsible for their criminality. They are. As a part of their dignity as human beings, they must be seen as responsible agents and not merely as helpless victims. But their responsibility is, in my view, sometimes *shared* with those of us in the larger community. In these cases, we too may be legitimately called upon for repentance and atonement—attitudes of mind that should prevent us from thinking of criminals as totally other, and should thus moderate our tendencies to respond to them with nothing but malice . . . Even though we cannot always grant mercy, we should always be open to it—even disposed towards it—because at some level, we all require it and should hope that our repentance might be seen as grounds for it. . . . As we demand repentance of the criminal, [we should] demand it also of ourselves. If we find that we are unwilling or unable to demand it of ourselves, perhaps we should conclude that we have forfeited our right to demand it from the criminal.

Roberts uses philosophical analysis to formulate a conception of forgivingness as a virtuous personality trait. His analysis, like that of most philosophical, theological, and devotional analyses of what forgiving is and entails, includes psychological assumptions and concepts, given the roles that emotions and attitudes play in the process of forgiving. However, like most philosophers who enrich our understanding by their sophisticated methods of conceptual analysis, his approach is not itself experimental, empirical, or quantitative.

20. Tangney et al. 1999. I am summarizing only a part of their study, which examined more variables than the ones I include here.

21. This distinction between guilt and shame used by Tangney is not the only way of differentiating the two emotions.

22. Even if our objective is not to inculcate a trait of "forgivingness," it would be advisable to nurture in our children the quality of empathy, which has value in many other spheres of life and human relationships.

CHAPTER 3: WHY & WHEN TO FORGIVE

1. Jacoby 1983, 304–5.

2. The Mishnah is an authoritative compendium of Jewish law edited under the auspices of Rabbi Judah the Prince (or Patriarch), the spiritual and political leader of the Jews in the land of Israel at the end of the second century.

3. Mishnah, Sanhedrin 4:5; Neusner 1988.

4. Jones 1995, 265–66.

5. I would not expect a Palestinian mother or father to forgive and forget the Israeli soldier who killed their child in a bomb raid, even though I do not consider the terrorist and the soldier to be morally equivalent.

6. See, for example, responses by Goldstein, A. Heschel, S. Heschel, Prager, and Levinas in Wiesenthal's *The Sunflower.* See also Amery 1980, 62–81. For one Christian analysis and critique of Jewish approaches in *The Sunflower,* see Jones 1995, 281–90.

7. Jones is aware of most of these criticisms and tries to address them from his particular Christian theological perspective. Since I don't subscribe to his triune theology, the theology alone is not, for me and others like me, a *rational* argument in favor of radical forgiveness. When Jones defends radical forgiveness on nontheological, psychological, moral, or philosophical grounds, I can engage in intellectual dialogue with him. Although Jones provides many valuable insights into forgiveness and addresses in a sophisticated way some of the most difficult issues and challenges it poses for us, in the final analysis I find the rational and empirical objections to *radical* forgiveness to be more convincing than his defense of it.

8. The theological corollary to this process is that when the sinner sees that he has been forgiven by his victim who is motivated by Christian faith, he will not only repent of the harm he has caused his victim, but may also be converted to faith in the forgiving god of Christianity. Moreover, the forgiving victim will be forgiven his or her own sins, as Jesus said, "Do not judge, so that you may not be judged" (Matt. 7:1) and "If you forgive others their trespasses, your heavenly Father will also forgive you; but if you do not forgive others, neither will your father forgive your trespasses" (Matt. 6:14–15).

9. Murphy and Hampton 1988, 79–87.

10. It is doubtful that the original biblical expression had the range and depth of meaning ascribed to it by postbiblical Jews and Christians.

11. Cf. Murphy and Hampton 1988, 32.

12. See my chapter on anger in *The Seven Deadly Sins.*

13. See Jones 1985, 251–53, for a discussion of Hell and God's vengeance.

14. Personal communication.

15. For the record, I think that my children and I have, overall, mutually respectful and loving relationships. That doesn't mean that we don't hurt one another once in a while.

16. Murphy and Hampton 1988, 24–29.

17. Reimer 1966, 266.

18. The Greek original, which is translated in the New RSV as "member of the church," literally means "your brother." The context of the passage suggests that the reference is to a member of the church.

19. A tax collector here probably means someone who is not a Christian. He needn't be treated with the same love and forgiving attitude as a fellow Christian. Or the passage might mean only that you should not associate with the repeat offender.

20. Murphy and Hampton 1988, 122.

21. For the relationship between Purgatory and Hell, see Le Goff 1984; Bernstein 1993, 320–26.

22. See, e.g., Sanders 1992.

23. In the Jewish–Christian polemic of the first few centuries C.E., some Jews also persecuted Christians and consigned them, and other sinners, to Hell. The harsh words of Jews and Christians toward those with whom they were in ideological conflict are somewhat softened when one considers the context of ancient traditions of polemical rhetoric. These words should not be read and interpreted as theological pronouncements from which dangerous and harsh doctrines should be developed.

24. See Schimmel 1988, 60–65.

25. However, on his death bed, David instructs Solomon to exact revenge on Joab and on Shimei, son of Gera (1 Kings 2:5–9).

26. The books known as the Apocrypha are not included in the Jewish biblical canon although they are included in the Roman Catholic and Greek Orthodox Bibles.

27. Kee, Testament of Gad 6:3, 6–7 in Charlesworth (editor) 1983, 775–828. Reimer concludes:

> In the world of early [postbiblical] Judaism and nascent Christianity, notions of interpersonal forgiveness overlap almost entirely. Despite the claims that have been made for the radical nature of Jesus' teaching on this subject, he was heir to an interpretive tradition which had already linked the love command to the idea of forgiveness. . . . The command to love one's neighbor . . . comes to be understood more in terms of a divine and universal love and forbearance. And in both early Jewish and nascent Christian communities, this meant that hostility or an unwillingness to forgive impeded the operation of divine forgiveness. This being the case, the need *both* for the offended party to forgive *and* for the offending party to seek forgiveness becomes paramount. In the centuries around the turn of the era, both of these have their obligations to the other: one to offer forgiveness, one to seek it. In other words, there is a complementary movement of repentance and forgiveness. (281–82)

28. *Summa Theologiae*, 2a2ae, 21, 2; 2a2ae 25, 6.

29. The victim, if he or she so chooses, may forgive the offender, as long as there will not be any adverse consequences for others as a result of this voluntary forgiveness.

30. Mishnah, Bava Kamma 8:7.

31. Tosefta, Bava Kamma 9:1. The Tosefta is either a commentary and a supplement to the late-second-century c.e. Mishnah, or else it might have preceded the Mishnah.

32. E.g., Midrash Tanhuma Buber. Vayera.

33. Jacobs 1960.

34. The book, meant as a spiritual guide for the Jews and the Jewish community, focuses on intrapersonal Jewish behaviors, alluding only briefly to mankind in general. It is possible that the ethos that Cordovero advocates might not be expected by him to apply in all contexts, since the demands he makes, as we shall see, are emotionally and ethically daunting.

35. For brevity's sake, I will not cite his mystical, theosophical explanations of how God behaves, which are the underpinning of his teachings on human forgiveness.

CHAPTER 4: HOW TO FORGIVE

1. One of the problems with the loose use of forgiveness is that few people have really thought through all of the moral issues it raises and the negative as well as positive consequences it can have. If people have a more sophisticated understanding of what forgiveness entails, they will be able to forgive intelligently rather than indiscriminately. Therapists, clergy, and pastoral counselors need to familiarize themselves with the philosophical, theological, and psychological literature on forgiveness if they intend to incorporate it into their practices constructively.

2. In my presentation and explication of three models of forgiveness, Enright's, Worthington's, and McCullough's, I include my own examples of how they can be applied to concrete situations and my critiques of some aspects of them with which I take issue or qualify.

3. Enright and Coyle 1998, 139–61. The Phase and Unit chart to which I refer in my summary, analysis, and amplification of Enright's process model in the following pages is from Enright and Coyle, 144–45. I have omitted their references to articles that provide examples of or discuss the ideas of each unit.

4. *Summa Theologiae*, 2a2ae, 25, articles 6, 8, 9.

5. See, e.g., Sternberg 1988.

6. Enright and his colleagues (1992) have been sensitive to the arguments about the possible adverse effects of forgiveness when used in therapy and counseling, which have been raised by some critics. In response, they have made the following recommendations:

1) A client should never be cajoled into forgiving. Because forgiveness is a supererogatory act it must be freely given; some may not wish to give it at all. This is their prerogative.

2) A counselor must be particularly sensitive to the client's level of anger. All legitimate programs that incorporate forgiveness as a goal must allow

for a distinct period of anger in the client. As long as the client's goal is to cast off the anger rather than derive a certain pleasure from harboring it, the person may be on a forgiveness path even if the anger is prolonged. A too ready willingness to abandon anger may signal pseudo-forgiveness in the client, where anger is suppressed. It is the counselor's task to distinguish genuine and pseudo forms of forgiveness.

3) Distinguish between forgiveness and reconciliation. Reconciliation is an ideal following forgiveness, but it should be reached only if the other's potentially destructive behavior and intentions change. The client who truly forgives (and now has cultivated empathy and compassion toward the other) certainly has the obligation to avoid placing himself or herself in danger.

4) Realize that forgiveness is interpersonal. Even though the forgiveness transformations are primarily internal, the fruition of forgiveness is entering into loving community with others (with the exception discussed above). A counselor, therefore, should resist interpreting forgiveness as exclusively or even primarily a self-help approach.

5) Realize that forgiveness is sometimes a long journey. . . . On the other hand, a counselor must be open to those individual differences where forgiveness may occur more quickly than expected. (pp. 98–99)

7. Exline and Baumeister 2000, 133–55.

8. Worthington, 1998, 107–37.

9. Worthington, 1999(b).

10. Worthington, 1999(c). It is with trepidation that I will critique aspects of Worthington's account. I have had the pleasure of meeting Worthington, a wonderful person, who in his personal and professional life has for many years been devoted to nurturing forgiveness, reconciliation, and love between people and groups. I have benefited much from his writings. I have never experienced the kind of hurt and pain he has. Were it not for the fact that in writing this book I am trying to help myself and others gain better insight into matters of profound importance in human relations, I would avoid any critical comment.

11. McCullough, Sandage, and Worthington, 1995, 355–64.

12. See Schimmel, *The Seven Deadly Sins*, 1–26.

13. Worthington 1998, 59–76.

14. McCullough 1996. The workshop can be conducted in a variety of settings, such as businesses, workplaces and churches. The manual contains useful summaries, charts, and diagrams.

15. McCullough 1997, 81–96.

16. Gottman and Krokoff 1989, 47–52; Gottman 1993(a), 57–75; Gottman 1993(b), 6–15.

17. One response to this suggested strategy for eliciting sincere apologies was that "it seem[s] potentially very manipulative. It gives me the creeps. I once received a phone call from someone I knew slightly who felt that it was important that I know

that she had found something I had said hurtful. It elicited a highly insincere apology from me and made me angry." (Personal communication)

Regarding the proper way to rebuke see chapter 6 of this book (p. 175) and *The Seven Deadly Sins,* 108–9.

18. Christensen, Jacobson, and Babcock 1995, 31–64.

19. I discussed this notion earlier when I suggested that the best way to overcome anger against an offender is to convince yourself that he could not have willed to do otherwise because of factors, whether internal or external, that were beyond his voluntary control. I also pointed out the moral dangers of such an approach. McCullough is sensitive to this issue and grapples with it, which doesn't mean that he has resolved it satisfactorily, as almost no one has. He writes:

> Helping clients to widen their attributional repertoire may seem to enable offending spouses to build excuses for their behavior. However, identifying the situational and historical factors that might condition a person to act a certain way does not have to be identical with excusing the behavior. It is not the goal of attribution-focused interventions to relieve an offending spouse of his or her moral responsibility. Rather, their goal is to promote empathy, and thus forgiveness, to prevent the hurts caused by the offending spouse's hurtful behavior from leading to an increased probability of flooding [of negative emotion]. While there is certainly a place in marriage (and marital therapy) for assigning moral responsibility for the hurtful behavior of one's spouse, I think spouses should learn to ask themselves, "Do I want to make things bitter or better?" Their attributional activity plays a role in whether their relationship becomes bitter or better after hurtful events have occurred. Nevertheless, issues of guilt, responsibility, repentance and the restoration of trust following hurtful marital events should certainly be discussed as complements to forgiving. (p. 89)

20. My reservations about McCullough's approach are the same as the ones I have with Worthington's, for example, the overemphasis on the similarity between actual perpetrators of atrocities and those who haven't perpetrated any but presumably have the capacity to do so. Overall, however, McCullough's sympathetic approach to forgiveness is characterized by conceptual depth, clinical creativity and ingenuity, intellectual honesty, scientific rigor, and compassion.

21. Lomax 1995.

22. Lomax's ability and decision to forgive Nagase were possible because of Nagase's genuine and full—indeed, his overflowing—repentance. Moreover, it seems to me that Lomax could forgive Nagase when he learned that Nagase was an unwilling and unsympathetic participant in his interrogation and torture. Furthermore, Nagase hadn't tortured Lomax himself, but had been the translator/interpreter for the torturers. He became the focal point of Lomax's hatred and desire for revenge because their shared language enabled Lomax to better remember him than the others involved.

What would have been Lomax's reaction if he had discovered not Nagase but one of the actual torturers, who did not feel any guilt or remorse about what they had done to him, and who continued to espouse Japanese militarism? It seems to me that Lomax would not have forgiven him.

CHAPTER 5: FORGIVING ONESELF & FORGIVING GOD

1. Marino 1995, 9.

2. Enright 1996, 116.

3. Since "the God of the philosophers," unlike the God of the Bible, can't actually be angry or be injured, the philosophers' emotionless, omnipotent God who "forgives" is also not forgiving in the sense that humans are.

4. Enright, 116–18.

5. A religious Jew, Christian, or Muslim who has fully and sincerely repented of sins that have not harmed other human beings but have only been "against God," can "forgive himself," or be comforted in the knowledge that God has forgiven him. Some such sins require penances in Judaism, Catholicism, and Islam, as integral elements of the process of repentance. For example, the Christian who "lusted in his heart," or the Jew who ate non-kosher food, are required, in some theologies of repentance, to deprive themselves of legitimate pleasure that corresponds to the sinful pleasure they enjoyed when they sinned. Having met the requirements of penitence and atonement, the repentant sinner is guaranteed divine forgiveness, and can therefore feel "forgiven," and accept this forgiveness. If you believe and internalize the idea that you have now been forgiven, you no longer need to linger on your past. There may be some sins against God, however, which are considered so serious that even repentance will not induce God to forgive them. In Luke 12:10 for example, there is reference to an unforgivable sin, "Whoever blasphemes against the Holy Spirit will not be forgiven." There are, however, other ways of understanding this teaching. For a discussion of the passage, see Joseph A. Fitzmyer 1985, 964–65.

6. Jones 1985.

7. Smedes 1984.

8. Excerpted from psychotherapy-practice electronic discussion list, June-July 1997. Quotes, in order, are from Paula Saltz, Ronald Nardi, Robert Schachter, Lori Ellison, Ronald Nardi, and Robert Ritzema.

9. Bauer, Duffy, Fountain, Halling, Holzer, Jones, Leifer, and Rowe 1992, 149–60; Halling 1994, 107–13.

10. See Schimmel, *Job,* 1987, 239–49.

11. Polen 1994, 100–101.

12. Brenner 1980.

13. Levenson 1988.

14. YHWH is a transliteration of the four Hebrew letters of the name of the God of Israel in the Hebrew Bible. It is sometimes written as Yahweh and is usually translated as "Lord."

15. To provide a trite but personal example of this, my daughter spent a year

traveling and volunteering in Africa, where she acquired a deep appreciation and affection for the warm and caring African people and cultures she encountered. Subsequently she spent several months traveling in India and repeatedly wrote home about her disappointment with the Indians she encountered because, compared to the Africans, they were colder, less caring, and less respectful of women. Somewhat later, however, she wrote, "India is starting to speak to me. I have stopped expecting to find Africa here, have *forgiven* (emphasis added) its people for not being warm and kind like my African friends. . . . India . . . speaks in harsh colors." What she means by having *forgiven its people* is that she realized that her naïve, or unfair, expectation that Indians should be like Africans, is what was causing her resentment, and that now that she no longer has such an expectation, her anger or resentment has dissipated.

16. Smedes 1984.

17. Exline, Yalie, and Lobel 1999.

18. See, e.g., Pargament 1997.

CHAPTER 6: THE ESSENCE OF REPENTANCE

1. Sanders suggests that in Jesus' day "by ordinary Jewish standards offences against fellow humans required restitution as well as repentance. . . . [Jesus] may have offered . . . inclusion in the kingdom not only *while they were still sinners* but also without requiring repentance as normally understood, and therefore he could have been accused of being a friend of people who indefinitely *remained* sinners." *Jesus and Judaism*, 206, and his discussion on 206–8 of what made Jesus' teaching so controversial.

2. Some biblical laws and narratives were morally problematic for devout Jews and Christians throughout the centuries. Because they venerated the Bible, they often felt the need to interpret it so that it conformed to the views that they believed reflected the divine will. In this story, for instance, Jewish commentators maintained that Uriah had divorced Bathsheba before leaving for the front, and so he hadn't commited adultery. Moreover, they said that Uriah had disobeyed David's orders and was therefore, according to the law of the time, guilty of a capital crime. So, in having Uriah assigned to the front line in order that he be killed, David wasn't committing murder. These forced intrepretations are motivated by the desire to have the biblical David conform to the David of the rabbinic imagination, who was a leader of great piety, probity, and Torah scholarship who could not have conceivably committed adultery or murder. Moreover, according to rabbinic law, a man who commits adultery is not permitted to marry the woman with whom he commited adultery, whereas in the biblical account, David takes Bathsheba as a wife and she becomes the mother of his heir, King Solomon.

3. Many psalms are ascribed by the editor of the Psalter to figures who experienced situations similar to those reflected in the psalm, even though it is doubtful that the ascribed author was the real author.

4. David mourns his dead child and then resumes his relationship with Bath-sheba. This is far from full repentance as it is defined in later biblical books, since David retains the fruits of his sin—the beautiful Bathsheba—and makes no reported reparation to Uriah's family. However, since the story and the psalm are both about sin, admission of guilt, and a plea for divine mercy and forgiveness, they are linked by the Psalter's editor. Note that for Nathan, David's crimes of adultery and murder are a scorning of the Lord, and not only injuries to Uriah and Bathsheba. Bathsheba is not condemned for her part in the episode. Perhaps she was pressured or coerced into sexual union with David, being understandably afraid of resisting the advances of the king. Do we we have here a biblical instance of sexual harrassment by a powerful man, escalating to adultery?

5. The doctrine of original sin, while including the notion of a human propensity to sin, is often understood to mean that at birth we are already tainted or corrupted by sin. This is why infants who are not baptized are, according to some Christian theologians, consigned to Hell when they die. They died in a state of sin, even though they never personally committed any sin. Similarly, for some Christian theologians, non-Christians are destined for eternal damnation because, given their lack of faith in and conversion to Christ, their original sin has not been removed. Judaism did not accept the doctrine of original sin.

6. The Lord doesn't explicitly tell Jonah to tell the Ninevites to repent. He tells Jonah to warn them of the Lord's intent to destroy them for their wickedness. However, the sense of the text is that the Lord wants to warn them in order that they might repent, which they do, in response to which, the Lord does not destroy Ni-nevah or the Ninevites.

7. A ritual bath that purifies one from defilement in biblical and rabbinic law becomes, in the imagination of the rabbis, a powerful metaphor for repentance. Rabbi Akiva says that God is the ritual bath into which sinners of Israel can immerse themselves as they repent on Yom Kippur or, for that matter, at any time. Just as the bath cleanses and purifies, so too does repentance remove the spiritual defilements of sin. However, if one immerses oneself in a ritual bath (*mikveh*) in order to be purified of the defilement acquired by contact with, for example, a *sheretz* (a dead rodent that defiles), while grasping onto the rodent corpse as he immerses himself in the *mikveh*, there can be no purification. So too with a sinner who, even as he repents, clings to his sin, whether in mind or in deed. Surely immersion or declarations of repentance are to no avail when the source of defilement or sin remains attached to the sinner. And are not he who would be purified and he who would be forgiven hypocrites when they refuse to abandon that which is the source of their impurity, be it ritual or spiritual?

8. Buber 1957.

9. The concept of the "self" is paradoxical in the context of thinking about repentance. To be truly penitent, one must acknowledge that he who I am today is continuous with he who I was when I sinned—last week, last year, or decades ago. Only by acknowledging the continuity between my past, my present, and my future can I regret my past, feel contrite about it, try to remedy to the extent possible its

continuous effects on the present, and hope for future purification and reconciliation. On the other hand, when we repent, we request that we be judged not only or primarily by what we were, but by who we are now, and that we now believe that we would no longer commit such a wrong. We want our victim or society to see us as discontinuous with the self of our past. Only then can we hope for mercy, forgiveness, and reconciliation. The paradox of true repentance is the assuming of responsibility for the past while hoping to be freed of that past to start anew.

10. Salaf-Us-Salih, Palazzi website.

11. Bergin 1995.

12. Kook 1978, 48–49.

13. However, in secular subcultures with ideological passion, such as secular Zionism in Eastern Europe and Palestine in the early twentieth century, or communism in Russia at the time of the revolution and for a while thereafter, there were people who experienced similar emotional and behavioral upheavals. Some of them turned away from bourgeois materialism and self-interest and toward concern for others, be they the persecuted Jewish people or the exploited masses, giving up values, careers, and opportunities for economic self-advancement to serve the cause to which they had been converted and the new life vision and mission to which they had now turned. Many of these "converts" sustained for many years their commitments to the visions and life missions to which their transformations had been directed, and were often willing to sacrifice so much—even their lives—for the truths that were "revealed" to them. Some even tried to change those traits of character that they felt were incompatible with their ideology. If you were a true socialist or communist, you had to eradicate the trait of personal self-interest for the sake of the common good.

14. Such self-reports cannot always be taken at face value. People tend to recall and interpret their past experiences in light of their present beliefs and needs. Religious converts tend to censor from their memories that which would make suspect the strict spiritual authenticity of the religious experiences they now cherish and the beliefs to which they are committed. Moreover, converts and "returnees" focus on the positive consequences of their experiences, overlooking negative ones (for example, the transformation from being an intellectually humble and tolerant doubter into a hubristic religious fanatic). Be that as it may, there is no doubt that although reports of permanent, fundamental personality and behavioral change in the accounts of many converts need to be taken with grains of salt, intense and significant changes that have many morally positive consequences do occur. Among the most famous of these conversion experiences are those of St. Paul and of St. Augustine.

15. William James 1902 (1978), 259–60.

16. Frankel 1998.

17. For example, the eighteenth-century Jewish mystic Rabbi Moses Haim Luzzatto, in his *Path of the Just,* and the seventeenth-century Anglican bishop Jeremy Taylor, in his *Holy Living,* as well as Shakespeare and Freud throughout their works.

18. It is possible that this story reflects a biblical theology that had not yet developed the idea that repentance totally forgives sins against God. See Milgrom 1990, 392–98.

19. Lazare 1995, 40.

20. Hartman 1995, 20.

21. See Exline and Baumeister 2000.

22. Etzioni 1997. 15–16.

23. See Schimmel 1988, 18–28; Schimmel 1997a; Schimmel 1997b, 24–37.

CHAPTER 7: REPENTANCE & RECONCILIATION

1. Babylonian Talmud, Bava Kama 94b.

2. Maimonides, Mishneh Torah, Book of Torts, Laws of Robbery and Returning Lost Objects, Chapter 1:13.

3. The fact that he confessed to a crime that no one knew he had committed, with the concomitant cost of social approbation, might provide some evidence of his sincerity.

4. Babylonian Talmud, Sanhedrin 25a.

5. This probably serves a moral educative function. In Aristotelian and Maimonidean ethical theory, vices are corrected by practicing virtue beyond the "mean."

6. Interestingly, Rabbi Asher rules that if the community is willing to allow him to resume his role as leader of the prayer services, they can do so, but only for their own congregation, not as blanket approval for him to serve as such anywhere else. The distinction between punishments for ritual slaughterer and cantor might be made because a dishonest ritual slaughterer can cause others to eat nonkosher meat, whereas a dishonest cantor won't prevent the congregation from praying properly. Or perhaps people can survive without eating meat but they cannot survive spiritually without prayer, and maybe this man was the only person in the town who knew how to properly conduct a worship service. Another possible explanation might be that if the congregation felt that the ostensibly repentant sinner were spiritually worthy enough to lead them in services, they had the right to make that judgment for themselves, since piety and the level of spiritual experience of prayer is subjective, unlike the objective status of meat as kosher or nonkosher.

This section has been adapted from material summarized by Dr. Nahum Rakover, 1970, in his series on Jewish Law, issued by the Israeli Ministry of Justice. I have added several of my own interpretations to the material he cites and analyzes.

7. There are also some advocates of repentance-oriented prison education who are explicit about their religious, usually Christian, motives. They operate programs of prison ministry within the guidelines of freedom of religion and the right to religious affiliation and behavior, which extends to prisoners, who can voluntarily participate in religious services and study in prison.

8. I cite Colson as an example of a criminal who was transformed by his prison experience not only to improve himself morally but to try to help others to improve themselves as well. I am not endorsing his particular theological approach to the

rehabilitation of criminals, since his fundamentalist theology is offensive to many non-Christians.

9. Moreover, a criminal who sincerely repents will want to be fully aware of his victim's pain. Even though he cannot alleviate it, he will bear a burden of guilt for many years. Often, paradoxically, he will want to feel that guilt because he believes that he deserves punishment, which can be effected by extremely unpleasant guilt. If the guilt doesn't satisfy the sinner's need for punishment or if, conversely, it is too painful a punishment for him, the penitent might seek external punishment, or even inflict upon himself mortifications of body or soul. Thus, paradoxically, the penitent's search for punishment can be fed by guilt or can alleviate it. Whatever the particular dynamic, the guilt that the repentant criminal experiences and the punishments he may take upon himself may suffice, so that society needn't add to them by refusing to accept him back into the community.

10. Etzioni and Carney (editors) 1997, 5.

11. Murphy 1997, 143–70.

12. Cohn 1993, 82–83.

13. Incarceration, in its own way, does impose penances on its inmates. True, inmates aren't expected to fast, and married inmates are entitled to periodic conjugal visits, but they are still severely restricted in their freedom to satisfy their gustatory and sexual appetites. Particularly oppressive is the lack of a sexual outlet for inmates who have no female partners, which results in situational homosexual behavior and in male-on-male rape in many prisons.

14. Baumeister 1997, chapter 5, challenges this view, claiming that most criminals have too high a self-esteem.

15. Wuthnow 1997, 82.

16. Ibid.

17. Duff 1986.

18. In his analysis of the social functions of apology and reconciliation, Nicholas Tavuchis (1991) points out that when someone has injured another by violating a social norm, and this event has become public knowledge, the community as well as the individual has been victimized. Were I to physically injure someone in a criminal assault, I would be flouting the rules of membership in my community. It would be as if I were declaring for all to hear that I do not feel bound by the social contract. In such a case, I would have to apologize in public, or at least in a manner that my apology would become public knowledge; a private apology to the victim would not suffice. The private apology, as sincere as it might be, would only address my desire for forgiveness from the victim and, if relevant, reconciliation with him or her. However, it would not address the harm I did to society at large by ignoring its strictures against assault and thereby weakening its authority. Moreover, my transgression would have, to a certain degree, removed me from the community, since my membership in it depends upon my accepting its rules. What I would have to do, then, in order to rectify the situation and regain the right of membership, would be to apologize in a manner that demonstrated my awareness of how my transgression had adversely affected my relationship with the community, and of its right to exclude

me from it. This would be accomplished when I publicly expressed my sorrow and regret for what I did, and declared that I would henceforth accept the community's norms as binding upon me.

19. Murphy himself, we have seen, defends retributive punishment on philosophical grounds, albeit with a critique of the social injustices of our society and of the inappropriate way in which our society often implements retributive punishment.

20. Excerpted from the mission statement of a restorative justice working group cosponsored by the Center for Restorative Justice of Suffolk University and the Boston Theological Institute, August 30, 1999.

21. This phenomenon has become more prevalent since the Oslo accords, in which Israel and the Palestine Liberation Organization recognized the political legitimacy of each other and undertook to negotiate a peaceful settlement of their conflict. Prior to the Oslo accords, most Israeli Jews and most Palestinians who engaged in such meetings would have been considered disloyal to their respective peoples for having met with the enemy. One hopes that these dialogues will continue, notwithstanding the de facto breakdown of the Oslo accords in 2000–2002. Indeed, the intensification of the conflict and the escalation of the level of violence makes dialogues for peace and reconciliation all the more necessary.

22. Franken Tahal, Israeli father of a son who was kidnapped and killed by members of the Palestinian Hamas organization, cited in Sennott (1999).

23. I think it is morally wrong to weigh equally all violence in a conflict, and not to make distinctions, for example, between deliberately killing an infant or targeting civilians anywhere, whether on a bus or in a market, a mosque, or a synagogue, and military action against terrorists or in self-defense. Yet some of the parents of the Parents Circle, like some political leaders on both sides of the conflict, seem to feel that long-term peace overrides the claims of justice, which would normally include punishment for unjust violence.

24. Online Journal of Peace and Conflict Resolution, 1998.

25. See Shriver 1995, 71; Muller-Fahrenholz, 1996, 53–55.

26. Greenberg 1997.

27. Gopin 2000.

28. Some Palestinian Arabs and some Israelis Jews are not religious, and appeals to repentance or forgiveness on theological grounds will not always speak to them. However, religious values and concepts often do influence nonreligious people and value systems, unconsciously or indirectly. Many secular Jews identify with Judaism's emphasis on acceptance of personal responsibility for one's wrongdoing and the upholding of justice in social life. I would venture that a similar process would be reflected among nondevout or secular Arabs socialized in an Islamic milieu and nominally Muslim.

29. *The Code of Maimonides*, chapter 2: 9, 10.

30. See, e.g., Goldziher 1967, 219–28. I am grateful to Adam Seligman for bringing this and other writings on the concept of *hilm* to my attention.

31. Palazzi, Abdul Hadi. Cultural Institute of the Italian Islamic Community. Website address: http://shell.spqr.net/islam/.

32. See Gopin 2000, especially chapters 2 and 4. Particularly important and enlightening discussions of the relevance of apology, repentance, and forgiveness in group and national conflict are Frost 1991; Tavuchis 1991; Shriver 1995; Minow 1998; and Muller-Fahrenholz 1997.

33. The idea that a sin against one can be a sin against many and that a sin committed by one is considered to have been committed by many is more explicit and apparent in communitarian societies than in our individualistic one. Religious communities, for example, maintained that there is a mutuality of responsibility between the individual and his community. No man is an island. What I do affects how the community will fulfill its role, and the community in turn will assist me in living my life in accordance with our shared vision of how a life should be led. This is why, for example, public apology and expressions of remorse by public figures in response to crimes perpetrated by individuals plays a much more important role in Japanese culture and psychology than in the United States. Japanese society sees itself as one extended family so that, at a certain level, all are responsible for all. A similar notion existed in Jewish communities, which accepted the talmudic dictum that "all of the people of Israel are responsible for one another." The responsibility was twofold. Members of the community of Israel must always be concerned about one another's welfare, and must provide material and emotional support when needed. But the responsibility extended to the moral and religious sphere as well. It was, at least in principle, everyone's duty to do what they could to assist or guarantee that everyone else would live up to the standards of Judaism. Therefore, when you saw someone do something wrong, you were supposed to chastise him and help redirect him. This collective responsibility means that when I sin, others in my community may be indirectly guilty as well if they had the power or influence, whether as a parent, a friend, a teacher, or a communal leader, to have prevented me from sinning. Given this intimate bond of mutual responsibility, which causes my moral or spiritual failure to reflect upon others as well as upon myself, it is necessary for me, as part of my apology and repentance, to let it be known to all that I have now redeemed the community from its "guilt" by accepting the values it upholds.

The following biblical ritual of atonement reflects the idea of indirect responsibility for crime.

If, in the land that the Lord your God is giving you to possess, a body is found lying in open country, and it is not known who struck the person down, then your elders and your judges shall come out to measure the distances to the towns that are near the body. The elders of the town nearest the body shall take a heifer . . . and shall break the heifer's neck there in the wadi [valley]. . . . All the elders of that town . . . shall wash their hands over the heifer . . . and they shall declare: "Our hands did not shed this blood, nor were we witnesses to it. Absolve, O Lord, your people Israel, whom you redeemed; do not let the guilt of innocent blood remain in the midst of your people Israel." Then they will be absolved of blood-guilt. So you shall purge the guilt of innocent blood from your midst, because you must do what is right in the sight of the Lord. (Deut. 21:1–9)

When an innocent person has been killed and his murderer not apprehended and punished, the community and its leaders are in some way responsible. Their guilt is, of course, not the guilt of the murderer himself, who cannot expiate himself and avoid punishment (if apprehended) by any ritual or sacrifice, as they can. The very fact, though, that they have to perform this public ritual, not of confessing, but of denying guilt and expiating whatever measure of it they might bear indicates that they are responsible to some degree for the crimes of the individual citizens of the town over which they preside. Unlike the Japanese "elders," the elders of Israel do not apologize to the victim's family or clan. Yet they must publicly acknowledge that, given their influence and authority, they need to be absolved of the guilt incurred by the shedding of innocent blood and the inability to implement justice. The Talmud is puzzled by the requirement that the elders declare "our hands did not shed this blood." Who would imagine that elders of Israel might have shed innocent blood?! they ask. The verse, say the rabbis, is not to be understood as referring to direct, actual shedding of the victim's blood. Perhaps, however, people will say that the elders did not establish the conditions that could have prevented the bloodshed in the first place, such as providing the wayfarer who was murdered with protection and safe roads, or with ample provisions so that he would not have had to expose himself to the dangers of travel. Such a failure would have made them an accessory to the crime, and it is this suspicion that they address in their disclaimer. Perhaps, I might add, the rabbis have in mind the measures that communal leaders need to implement in order to prevent sin and crime, that focus not only on victims, but on potential offenders as well, such as providing them with the proper education and socialization in moral values. Note how the ritual of absolution requires the participation of or refers to the elders of the nation, the elders of the nearest town, and the entire community of Israel. Perhaps those of us who do not worry about the moral state of the communities in which we live and who do not become involved in improving them incur some guilt when offenses occur. We all bear some responsibility, to the extent that we could have done but did not do our share. The powerful idea of collective responsibility for the individual's crime should temper somewhat the self-righteousness and intense indignation that we often feel about some criminals.

34. Dorff 1992, 193–218.

35. Shriver 1995.

36. In the Hebrew Bible people live on beyond their own death, primarily through their children. Therefore the harsh punishments that serious offenses against God or man deserve, include children as their object. From a psychological point of view, the belief that punishment for offenses can cause great suffering or death to your children can act as a powerful deterrent.

37. Dulles 1998, 38.

38. On the history of the anti-Semitism of the Catholic Church, see Carroll (2001) and Kertzer (2001).

39. I don't know of many theologians or moral philosophers who would argue that the United States today should return the entire country to Native Americans, even if the United States were to acknowledge an historic guilt of having stolen most of the land from their ancestors.

40. Kertzer 1997.

41. Steinfels 2000, A14.

42. Shriver 1995.

43. One can question whether Shriver pays sufficient attention to the racist and violent strands within the African American population, but there can be no doubt that these strands represent the views and attitudes of a minority.

44. Shriver 1995, 216.

EPILOGUE

1. South African Council of Churches, 1995, 24. Cited by de Gruchy, Cochrane, and Martin, p. 3, in Cochrane, de Gruchy and Martin 1999.

2. Niehaus 1999.

3. Biko 2000.

4. Grunebaum-Ralph and Stier 1999, 151–52.

5. Serman 2001.

6. The establishment of democracy has not removed intergroup tension and conflict in South Africa. An ominous development is the increasing radicalization of the Muslim population in Capetown, with the spread of Islamic fundamentalism in what had heretofore been a Muslim community that lived on friendly terms with other South African faith communities. This radicalization has also affected government policy, as for example, in its support of the vicious anti-Israel and anti-Jewish diatribes of many Muslims, which dominated the discourse at the failed United Nations conference on racism in Durban. The conference, which should have addressed the evils of racism in so many countries around the world was, in effect, "hijacked" by Arab extremists and their supporters only a few weeks before the Al Qaeda terrorist attack on the United States. While I was in Capetown, 20,000 Muslims marched in the city center with posters and proclamations calling for the destruction of Israel, and supporting organizations such as Hezbollah, Islamic Jihad, and Hamas, which are on the United States' list of terrorist groups. It is sad that the ANC-led South African government, which has so commendably preached and tried to promote racial harmony and to fight racism has allowed itself to succumb to the hatreds of Islamic extremism, and in the process to harm its own national interests. How it justifies this support, which conflicts with its message of nonviolence and tolerance, is unclear to me.

7. Some useful books on the TRC and on reconciliation in South Africa are Boraine (2000); Christie (2000); James and Van De Vijver (2000); Rotberg and Thompson (2000); Villa-Vicencio and Verwoerd (2000); Cochrane, de Gruchy, and Martin (1999).

Amery, Jean. "Resentments." In *At the Mind's Limits: Contemplations by a Survivor on Auschwitz and Its Realities*. Bloomington: Indiana University Press, 1980, 62–81.

Aquinas, St. Thomas. *Summa Theologiae*. Blackfriars: McGraw-Hill, 1964.

Arnold, Johann Christoph. *Seventy Times Seven: The Power of Forgiveness*. Farmington, Pa.: Plough Publishing House, 1997.

Babylonian Talmud. London: Soncino Press, 1935–1952.

Baloian, Bruce. *Anger in the Old Testament*. American University Studies Series VII, Theology and Religion, 99 (1992).

Bauer, L., J. Duffy, E. Fountain, S. Halling, M. Holzer, E. Jones, M. Leifer, and J. Rowe. "Exploring Self-forgiveness." *Journal of Religion and Health* 31, no. 2 (1992): 149–60.

Baumeister, Roy E., Julie Juola Exline, and Kristin L. Sommer. "The Victim Role, Grudge Theory, and Two Dimensions of Forgiveness." In *Dimensions of Forgiveness: Psychological Research and Theological Perspectives*, edited by Everett L. Worthington Jr. Philadelphia: Templeton Foundation Press, 1998, 79–104.

Baumeister, Roy E. *Evil: Inside Human Violence and Cruelty*. New York: W. H. Freeman, 1997.

Bergin, Allen E. "Psychology and Repentance." In *1994–1995 BYU Devotional and Fireside Speeches*. Salt Lake City: Brigham Young University, 1995, 27–34.

Bernstein, Alan E. *The Formation of Hell: Death and Retribution in the Ancient and Early Christian Worlds*. Ithaca, N.Y.: Cornell University Press, 1993.

Bible. New Revised Standard Version (NRSV). New York: Oxford University Press, 1991.

Birnbaum, Philip. *Daily Prayer Book*. New York: Hebrew Publishing Company, 1949.

Boraine, Alex. *A Country Unmasked: Inside South Africa's Truth and Reconciliation Commission*. Capetown: Oxford University Press, 2000.

Boteach, Shmuley. "A Time to Hate." *Moment Magazine*, October 2000, 42–43.

Brenner, Reeve Robert. *The Faith and Doubt of Holocaust Survivors*. New York: Jason Aronson, 1997.

Buber, Martin. "Guilt and Guilt Feelings." *Psychiatry* 20, no. 2 (1957): 114–29.

Butler, Bishop Joseph. "Upon Resentment and Upon Forgiveness of Injuries." In *The Works of Joseph Butler, D.C.L.* Vol. 2, *Sermons*, edited by W. E. Gladstone. Oxford: Clarendon Press, 1897, 115–41.

Carroll, James. *Constantine's Sword: The Church and the Jews—A History*. Boston: Houghton Mifflin, 2001.

Christensen, A., N. S. Jacobson, and J. C. Babcock, "Integrative Behavioral Couples Therapy." In *Clinical Handbook of Couples Therapy*, edited by N. S. Jacobson and A. S. Gurman. New York: Guilford, 1995, 31–64.

Christie, Kenneth. *The South African Truth Commission*. New York: St. Martin's Press, 2000.

Cochrane, James, John de Gruchy, and Stephen Martin, eds. *Facing the Truth: South African Faith Communities and the Truth and Reconciliation Commission*. Capetown: David Phillips; Athens: Ohio University Press, 1999.

Cohn, Haim H. "Judicial Cognizance of Guilt-consciousness." *Israel Law Review* 27, no. 102 (1993): 59–83.

Cordovero, Moses. *The Palm Tree of Deborah*. Translated from the Hebrew with an introduction and notes by Louis Jacobs. London: Valentine, Mitchell, 1960.

De Gruchy, John, James Cochrane, and Stephen Martin. "Faith, Struggle, and Reconciliation." In *Facing the Truth: South African Faith Communities and the Truth and Reconciliation Commission*, edited by James Cochrane, John de Gruchy, and Stephen Martin. Capetown: David Phillips; Athens: Ohio University Press, 1999, 1–11.

Delumeau, Jean. *Sin and Fear: The Emergence of a Western Guilt Culture, 13th–18th Centuries*. Translated by Eric Nicholson. New York: St. Martin's Press, 1990.

Dershowitz, Alan. *Just Revenge*. New York: Warner Books, 1999.

Dorff, Elliot N. "Individual and Communal Forgiveness." In *Autonomy and Judaism: The Individual and the Community in Jewish Philosophical Thought*, edited by Daniel H. Frank. New York: State University of New York Press, 1992, 193–218.

Duff, R. Antony. *Trials and Punishments*. Cambridge: Cambridge University Press, 1986.

Dulles, Avery. "Should the Church Repent?" *First Things*, December 1998, 36–41.

Enright, Robert D., D. Eastin, S. Golden, I. Sarinopoulos, and S. Freedman. "Interpersonal Forgiveness within the Helping Professions: An Attempt to Resolve Differences of Opinion." *Counseling and Values* 36 (1992): 84–103.

Enright, Robert D., and Catherine T. Coyle. "Researching the Process Model of Forgiveness within Psychological Interventions." In *Dimensions of Forgiveness*, edited by E. L. Worthington Jr. Philadelphia: Templeton Foundation Press, 1998, 139–61.

Enright, Robert D., and The Human Development Study Group. "Counseling within the Forgiveness Triad: On Forgiving, Receiving Forgiveness, and Self-forgiveness." *Counseling and Values*, January 1996, 40, 107–26.

Etzioni, Amitai and David Carney, eds. *Repentance: A Comparative Perspective*. Lanham, Md.: Rowman & Littlefield, 1997.

Exline, Julie Juola, and Roy F. Baumeister. "Expressing Forgiveness and Repentance: Benefits and Barriers." In *Forgiveness: Theory, Research, and Practice*, edited by Michael E. McCullough, Kenneth I. Pargament, and Carl E. Thoresen. New York: Guilford, 2000, 133–55.

Exline, Julie Juola, Ann Marie Yalie, and Marci Lobel. "When God Disappoints: Difficulty Forgiving God and Its Role in Negative Emotion." *Journal of Health Psychology* 4, no. 3 (1999): 365–79.

Fishbane, Michael. *Biblical Interpretation in Ancient Israel*. Oxford: Clarendon Press, 1985.

Fitzmyer, Joseph A. *The Gospel According to Luke*. Vol. 2. Anchor Bible, Vol. 28 A. New York: Doubleday, 1985.

Frankel, Estelle. "Repentance, Psychotherapy, and Healing through a Jewish Lens." *American Behavioral Scientist*, March 1998, 41 (6).

Frost, Brian. *The Politics of Peace*. London: Darton, Longman and Todd, 1991.

Genesis Rabbah. Midrash Bereshit Rabba. Edited by J. Theodor and C. Albeck. Berlin: 1903–1929.

Goldhizer, Ignaz. "What Is Meant by 'Al-Jahaliya.'" In *Muslim Studies*, edited by S. M. Stern. Vol. 1. London: George Allen & Unwin Ltd., 1967, 219–28.

Gopin, Marc. *Between Eden and Armageddon: The Future of World Religions, Violence, and Peacemaking*. New York: Oxford University Press, 2000.

Gottman, J. M. "A Theory of Marital Dissolution and Stability." *Journal of Family Psychology* 7 (1993a): 57–75.

———. "The Roles of Conflict Engagement, Escalation, or Avoidance in Marital Interaction: A Longitudinal View of Five Types of Couples." *Journal of Consulting and Clinical Psychology* 61 (1993b): 6–15.

Gottman, M., and L. J. Krokoff. "Marital Interaction and Marital Satisfaction: A Longitudinal View." *Journal of Consulting and Clinical Psychology* 57 (1989): 47–52.

Greenberg, Joel. *New York Times*, March 17, 1997, A6.

Halling, Steen. "Embracing Human Fallibility: On Forgiving Oneself and Forgiving Others." *Journal of Religion and Health* 33 (1994): 107–13.

Hartman, David. *Reflections on the Theme of Teshuvah (Renewal) as Found in the Bible, the Talmud, Maimonides, and Soloveitchik*. Jerusalem: Shalom Hartman Institute, 1995.

Heschel, Abraham J. *The Prophets*. New York: Harper & Row, 1962.

Himmelfarb, Martha. *Tours of Hell: An Apocalyptic Form in Jewish and Christian Literature*. Philadelphia: University of Pennsylvania Press, 1983.

Ignatius of Loyola. *The Spiritual Exercises of St. Ignatius*. New York: Doubleday, 1964.

Jacobson, Neil S., and Alan S. Gurman, eds. *Clinical Handbook of Couple Therapy*. New York: Guilford Press, 1995, 31–64.

Jacoby, Susan. *Wild Justice: The Evolution of Revenge*. New York: Harper & Row, 1983.

James, William. *The Varieties of Religious Experience.* Garden City, N.Y.: Image Books, 1978 (1902).

James, Wilmot, and Linda Van De Vijver. *After the TRC: Reflections on Truth and Reconciliation in South Africa.* Athens: Ohio University Press; Capetown: David Philips, 2000.

Jones, L. Gregory. *Embodying Forgiveness: A Theological Analysis.* Grand Rapids: Eerdmans, 1995.

Jordan, Michael J. "In Albania, A Return to 'Eye for Eye.' " *Christian Science Monitor International Edition,* August 7, 1997.

"Mid-East Dialog Groups: Building a Grass-Roots Force for Peace (View Points PEACE Dialog Forum." *Journal of Peace and Conflict Resolution 1.3 (Online),* May 15, 1998.

Kant, Immanuel. *The Metaphysics of Morals I, The Metaphysical Elements of Justice.* Translated after John Ladd. Indianapolis: Bobbs Merrill, 1965.

Kertzer, David I. *The Kidnapping of Edgardo Mortara.* New York: Knopf, 1997.

———. *The Popes against the Jews: The Vatican's Role in the Rise of Modern Anti-Semitism.* New York: Knopf, 2001.

Kolnai, Aurel. "Forgiveness." In *Ethics, Value and Reality: Selected Papers of Aurel Kolnai.* Indianapolis: Hackett, 1978, 211–24.

Kook, Abraham Isaac. *The Lights of Penitence.* Translated by Ben Zion Bokser. New York: Paulist Press, 1978.

Lang, Berel. "Forgiveness." *American Philosophical Quarterly* 31, no. 2 (1994): 105–17.

Lazare, Aaron. "Go ahead, say you're sorry." *Psychology Today.* January-February 1995, 40–43, 76–78.

Le Goff, Jacques. *The Birth of Purgatory.* Translated by Arthur Goldhammer. Chicago: University of Chicago Press, 1984.

Levenson, Jon. *Creation and the Persistence of Evil: The Jewish Drama of Divine Omnipotence.* San Francisco: Harper & Row, 1988.

Levinas, Emmanuel. "Toward the Other." In *Nine Talmudic Readings.* Bloomington: Indiana University Press, 1990, 12–29.

Lomax, Eric. *The Railway Man: A True Story of War, Remembrance, and Forgiveness.* New York: Ballantine, 1995.

Luzzatto, Moses Hayyim. *The Path of the Just.* Translated by Shraga Silverstein. New York: Feldheim, 1966.

Mackie, J. L. "Morality and the Retributive Emotions." *Criminal Justice Ethics,* Winter-Spring 1982, 3–10.

Maimonides, Moses. *The Code of Maimonides (Mishneh Torah),* Book of Torts, Laws of Robbery and Returning Lost Objects, Chapter 1:13. Translated by Hyman Klein. New Haven: Yale Judaica Press, 1954.

Marino, Gordon D. "The Epidemic of Forgiveness." *Commonweal* 122, no. 6 (March 24, 1995): 9–11.

McCullough, Michael E. "Marital Forgiveness: Theoretical Foundations and an Approach to Prevention." *Marriage and Family: A Christian Journal* 1 (1997): 81–96.

———. "Promoting Forgiveness: An Empathy-Based Model for Psychoeducation." Unpublished manual. National Institute for Health Care Research, 1996.

McCullough, Michael E., and E. L. Worthington Jr. "Encouraging Clients to Forgive People Who Have Hurt Them: Review, Critique, and Research Prospectus." *Journal of Psychology and Theology* 22 (1994): 3–20.

McCullough, Michael E., Steven J. Sandage, and Everett L. Worthington Jr. "Charles Williams on Interpersonal Forgiveness: Theology and Therapy." *Journal of Psychology and Christianity* 14 (1995): 355–64.

McCullough, Michael E., E. L. Worthington Jr., and K. C. Rachal. "Interpersonal Forgiveness in Close Relationships." *Journal of Personality and Social Psychology* 75 (1997): 321–26.

McKane, William. *Proverbs: A New Approach*. Philadelphia: Westminster Press, 1990.

Mekilta de Rabbi Ishmael. Translated by Jacob Z. Lauterbach. Philadelphia: Jewish Publication Society, 1933.

Midrash Tanhuma. "Vayera." Edited by Solomon Buber. Vilna, 1885.

Milgrom, Jacob. *Jewish Publication Torah Commentary. Numbers*. Excursus 32 and 33. Philadelphia: Jewish Publication Society, 1990, 392–98.

Minow, Martha. *Between Vengeance and Forgiveness: Facing History after Genocide and Mass Violence*. Boston: Beacon Press, 1998.

The Mishnah: A New Translation. Translated by Jacob Neusner. New Haven: Yale University Press, 1988.

Muller-Fahrenholz, Geiko. *The Art of Forgiveness: Theological Reflections on Healing and Reconciliation*. Geneva: World Council of Churches, 1997.

Murphy, Jeffrie G. "Hatred: A Qualified Defense." In *Forgiveness and Mercy*, edited by Jeffrie G. Murphy and Jean Hampton. Cambridge: Cambridge University Press, 1988.

———. "Repentance, Punishment and Mercy." In *Repentance: A Comparative Perspective*, edited by Amitai Etzioni and David Carney. Lanham, Md.: Rowman & Littlefield, 1997, 143–70.

———. "Getting Even: The Role of the Victim." In *Retribution Reconsidered: New Essays in the Philosophy of Law*. Boston: Kluwer, 1992, 61–85.

Murphy, Jeffrie G., and Jean Hampton. *Forgiveness and Mercy*. Cambridge: Cambridge University Press, 1988.

Niehaus, Carl. "Reconciliation in South Africa: Is Religion Relevant?" In *Facing the Truth: South African Faith Communities and the Truth and Reconciliation Commission*, edited by James Cochrane, John de Gruchy, and Stephen Martin. Capetown: David Phillips; Athens: Ohio University Press, 1999, 81–90.

North, Joanna. "Wrongdoing and Forgiveness." *Philosophy* 62 (1987): 499–508.

Palazzi, Abdul Hadi. Cultural Institute of the Italian Islamic Community. http://shell.spqr.net/islam/.

Pargament, Kenneth. *The Psychology of Religion and Coping: Theory, Research, Practice*. New York: Guilford, 1997.

Pinker, Steven. *How the Mind Works*. New York: Norton, 1997.

Polen, Nehemia. *The Holy Fire: The Teachings of Rabbi Kalonymus Kalman Shapira, the Rebbe of the Warsaw Ghetto*. Northvale, N.J.: Jason Aronson, 1994.

Prager, Dennis. "The Sin of Forgiveness." *Wall Street Journal*, December 15, 1991.

Psychotherapy-practice electronic discussion list, June-July, 1997.

Rakover, Nahum. *The Status of a Criminal Who Has Served His Sentence.* Jerusalem: Israeli Ministry of Justice, 1970. In Hebrew.

Reimer, David J. "The Apocrypha and Biblical Theology: The Case of Interpersonal Forgiveness." In *After the Exile: Essays in Honor of Rex Mason,* edited by John Barton and David J. Reimer. Macon, Ga.: Mercer University Press, 1996, 259–82.

Restorative Justice Working Group Mission Statement. Co-sponsored by the Center for Restorative Justice of Suffolk University and the Boston Theological Institute, August 30, 1999.

Roberts, Robert C. "Forgivingness." *American Philosophical Quarterly* 32, no. 4 (1995): 289.

Rotberg, Robert I., and Dennis Thompson, eds. *Truth v. Justice: The Morality of Truth Commissions.* Princeton: Princeton University Press, 2000.

Salaf-Us-Salih. www.geocities.com/Athens/Academy/7368/repent_sins2.htm#guide.

Sanders, E. P. *Jesus and Judaism.* Philadelphia: Fortress Press, 1985.

———. *Judaism: Practice and Belief 63 BCE–66CE.* Philadelphia: Trinity Press International, 1992.

The Sayings of the Desert Fathers. Edited by Benedicta Ward. Kalamazoo: Cistercian Publications, 1975.

Schimmel, Solomon. "Anger and Its Control in Graeco-Roman and Modern Psychology." *Psychiatry: Journal for the Study of Interpersonal Processes* 42, no. 4 (1979): 320–37.

———. "Joseph and His Brothers: A Paradigm for Repentance." *Judaism* 37, no. 1 (1988): 18–28.

———. "Free-will and Determinism in Jewish Law and Theology: A Psychological Analysis." In *Jewish Education and Jewish Statesmanship: Albert Elazar Memorial Book,* edited by Daniel Elazar. Jerusalem: Jerusalem Center for Public Affairs, 1996, 65–84.

———. "Job and the Psychology of Suffering and Doubt." *Journal of Psychology and Judaism* 11, no. 4 (1997(a)): 239–49.

———. "Some Educational Uses of Classical Jewish Texts in Exploring Emotion, Conflict and Character." *Religious Education* 92, no. 1 (1997(b)): 24–37.

———. *The Seven Deadly Sins: Jewish, Christian, and Classical Reflections on Human Psychology.* New York: Oxford University Press, 1997. First published by the Free Press in 1992.

Sennott, Charles M. "Faith and Forgiveness." *Boston Globe Magazine,* April 4, 1999, 12, 22–30.

Shriver, Donald, Jr. *An Ethic for Enemies: Forgiveness in Politics.* New York: Oxford University Press, 1995.

Skinner, B. F. *Walden Two.* New York: Macmillan, 1948.

Smedes, Lewis B. *Forgive and Forget: Healing the Hurts We Don't Deserve.* New York: Harper & Row, 1984.

South African Council of Churches. *The Truth Will Set You Free.* Johannesburg: SACC, 1995.

Steinfels, Peter. "Beliefs." *New York Times*, March 18, 2000, A14.

Sternberg, Robert. *The Triangle of Love*. New York: Basic, 1988.

The Tanakh (The Hebrew Bible). A New Translation of the Holy Scriptures. Philadelphia: The Jewish Publication Society of America, 1985.

Tangney, June, Ronda Fee, Candace Reinsmith, Angela L. Boone, and Norman Lee. "Assessing Individual Differences in the Propensity to Forgive." Paper presented at the 1999 American Psychological Association Meeting, Boston.

Tavuchis, Nicholas. *Mea Culpa: A Sociology of Apology and Reconciliation*. Stanford, Calif.: Stanford University Press, 1991.

Taylor, Jeremy. *The Rule and Exercises of Holy Living*. London: Bell and Daldy, 1857.

"Testament of Gad 6:3, 6–7." In H. C. Kee, "Testaments of the Twelve Patriarchs." In *Old Testament Pseudepigrapha*, vol. 1, *Apocalyptic Literature and Testaments*, edited by J. H. Charlesworth. London: Darton Longman & Todd and Doubleday, 1983, 775–828.

Tolstoy, Leo. *War and Peace*. New York: Penguin, 1982.

The Tosefta: Zeraim, Moed, Nashim, Nezikin. Edited by Saul Lieberman. New York: (JTSA) Jewish Theological Seminary of America, 1955–1988.

Villa-Vicencio, Charles, and Wilhelm Verwoerd. *Looking Back Reaching Forward: Reflections on the Truth and Reconciliation Commission of South Africa*. Capetown: University of Capetown Press; London: Zed, 2000.

Walker, Nigel. *Why Punish? Theories of Punishment Reassessed*. Oxford: Oxford University Press, 1991.

Walls, Jerry L. *Hell: The Logic of Damnation*. Notre Dame, Ind.: University of Notre Dame Press, 1992.

Wiesenthal, Simon, with a Symposium. *The Sunflower*. New York: Schocken, 1976.

———. *The Sunflower: On the Possibilities and Limits of Forgiveness*. Rev. and exp. ed. New York: Schocken, 1997.

Worthington, Everett Jr. "An Empathy-Humility-Commitment Model of Forgiveness Applied within Family Dyads." *Journal of Family Therapy* 20 (1998): 59–76.

———. "Trek into a Territory of Forgiveness: A Review of Robert D. Enright and Joanna North, eds., *Exploring Forgiveness*." *Contemporary Psychology* 44 (1999(a)): 325–27.

———. "The Forgiveness Teacher's Toughest Test" or "Pyramid of Forgiveness." *Spirituality and Health* (1999(b)): 30–31.

———. "Forgiveness, the Stain-Remover after Trauma." *Christian Counseling Today*, 1999.

Wuthnow, Robert. "Repentance in Criminal Procedure: The Ritual Affirmation of Community." In *Repentance: A Comparative Perspective*, edited by Amitai Etzioni and David E. Carney. Lanham, Md.: Rowman & Littlefield, 1997, 171–86.

INDEX OF NAMES